D1155908

FLOORS, STAIRS & CARPETS

Other Publications:

AMERICAN COUNTRY

VOYAGE THROUGH THE UNIVERSE

THE THIRD REICH

THE TIME-LIFE GARDENER'S GUIDE

MYSTERIES OF THE UNKNOWN

TIME FRAME

FIX IT YOURSELF

FITNESS, HEALTH & NUTRITION

SUCCESSFUL PARENTING

HEALTHY HOME COOKING

UNDERSTANDING COMPUTERS

LIBRARY OF NATIONS

THE ENCHANTED WORLD

THE KODAK LIBRARY OF CREATIVE PHOTOGRAPHY

GREAT MEALS IN MINUTES

THE CIVIL WAR

PLANET EARTH

COLLECTOR'S LIBRARY OF THE CIVIL WAR

THE EPIC OF FLIGHT

THE GOOD COOK

WORLD WAR II

HOME REPAIR AND IMPROVEMENT

THE OLD WEST

FLOORS, STAIRS & CARPETS

TIME-LIFE BOOKS
ALEXANDRIA, VIRGINIA

Fix It Yourself was produced by
ST. REMY PRESS

MANAGING EDITOR	Kenneth Winchester
MANAGING ART DIRECTOR	Pierre Léveillé

Staff for *Floors, Stairs & Carpets*

Series Editor	Brian Parsons
Series Assistant Editor	Kent J. Farrell
Editor	Marc Cassini
Series Art Director	Diane Denoncourt
Art Director	Philippe Arnoldi
Research Editor	Donald Harman
Designer	Luc Germain
Contributing Editor	Elizabeth Cameron
Contributing Writers	Edward Earle, Patrick Godon, Geri-Lynn Kushneryk, Randy Lake, Jo Serrentino
Contributing Illustrators	Gérard Mariscalchi, Jacques Proulx
Cover	Robert Monté
Index	Christine M. Jacobs
Administrator	Denise Rainville
Accounting Manager	Natalie Watanabe
Production Manager	Michelle Turbide
Systems Coordinator	Jean-Luc Roy
Studio Director	Maryo Proulx

Time-Life Books Inc. is a wholly owned subsidiary of
THE TIME INC. BOOK COMPANY

President and Chief Executive Officer	Kelso F. Sutton
President, Time Inc. Books Direct	Christopher T. Linen

TIME-LIFE BOOKS INC.

EDITOR	George Constable
Executive Editor	Ellen Phillips
Director of Design	Louis Klein
Director of Editorial Resources	Phyllis K. Wise
Editorial Board	Russell B. Adams Jr., Dale M. Brown, Roberta Conlan, Thomas H. Flaherty, Lee Hassig, Jim Hicks, Donia Ann Steele, Rosalind Stubenberg
Director of Photography and Research	John Conrad Weiser
PRESIDENT	John M. Fahey Jr.
Senior Vice Presidents	Robert M. DeSena, James L. Mercer, Paul R. Stewart, Curtis G. Viebranz, Joseph J. Ward
Vice Presidents	Stephen L. Bair, Stephen L. Goldstein, Juanita T. James, Andrew P. Kaplan, Susan J. Maruyama, Robert H. Smith
Supervisor of Quality Control	James King
Publisher	Joseph J. Ward

Editorial Operations

Copy Chief	Diane Ullius
Production	Celia Beattie
Library	Louise D. Forstall
Correspondents	Elisabeth Kraemer-Singh (Bonn); Christina Lieberman (New York); Maria Vincenza Aloisi (Paris); Ann Natanson (Rome).

THE CONSULTANTS

Consulting editor **David L. Harrison** served as an editor for several Time-Life Books do-it-yourself series, including *Home Repair and Improvement, The Encyclopedia of Gardening* and *The Art of Sewing.*

Richard Day, a do-it-yourself writer for nearly a quarter of a century, is a founder of the National Association of Home and Workshop Writers and is the author of several home repair books.

Jay Hedden, a former editor of Popular Mechanics and Workbench magazines, has written several books on home repair.

Library of Congress Cataloging-in-Publication Data
Filoors, stairs & carpets.
 p. cm. – (Fix it yourself)
Includes index.
ISBN 0-8094-6236-2.
ISBN 0-8094-6237-0 (lib. bdg.)
1. Floors--Maintenance and repair--Amateurs' manuals.
2. Staircases--Maintenance and repair--Amateurs' manuals.
3. Carpets--Maintenance and repair--Amateurs' manuals.
 I. Time-Life Books. II. Title: Floors, stairs and carpets. III. Series.
TH2528.F58   1990
690'.16—dc20   89-29009
                                         CIP

For information about any Time-Life book, please write:
Reader Information
Time-Life Customer Service
P.O. Box C-32068
Richmond, Virginia
23261-2068

© 1990 Time-Life Books Inc. All rights reserved.
No part of this book may be reproduced in any form or by any electronic or mechanical means, including information storage and retrieval devices or systems, without prior written permission from the publisher, except that brief passages may be quoted for reviews.
First printing. Printed in U.S.A.
Published simultaneously in Canada.
School and library distribution by Silver Burdett Company, Morristown, New Jersey.

TIME-LIFE is a trademark of Time Incorporated U.S.A.

CONTENTS

HOW TO USE THIS BOOK

Floors, Stairs & Carpets is divided into three sections. The Emergency Guide on pages 8 to 13 provides information that can be indispensable, even lifesaving, in the event of a household emergency. Take the time to study this section *before* you need the important advice it contains.

The Repairs section—the heart of the book—is a comprehensive approach to troubleshooting and repairing floors, stairs and carpets. Shown below are four sample pages from the chapter on rigid flooring, with captions describing the various features of the book and how they work.

For example, if a section of your ceramic tiles is cracked, the Troubleshooting Guide on page 51 will suggest possible causes and direct you to page 57 for detailed, step-by-step instructions on how to replace the section.

Each job has been rated by degree of difficulty and by the average time it will take for a do-it-yourselfer to complete. Keep in mind that this rating is only a suggestion. Before deciding whether you should attempt a repair, first read all the instructions carefully. Then, be guided by your own confidence, and the tools and time available to you. For complex or time-consuming

---

Introductory text
Describes the construction of floors, stairs and carpets, their most common problems and basic repair approaches.

Troubleshooting Guide
To use this chart, locate the symptom that most closely resembles your floor, stair or carpet problem in column 1, review the possible causes in column 2, then follow the recommended procedures in column 3. Simple fixes may be explained on the chart; in most cases you will be directed to an illustrated, step-by-step repair sequence.

RIGID FLOORING

RIGID FLOORING

Rigid flooring of ceramic or marble tiles is available in a wide variety of styles, shapes, sizes and colors—an attractive flooring option designed to withstand the harshest rigors of daily life. Easy to maintain, rigid flooring is a popular choice for the most heavily-trafficked areas of the home: the bathrooms, the kitchen and the entrance foyers. The construction of typical rigid flooring is illustrated below; shown are standard ceramic tiles and common marble tiles. Onto a subfloor of two layers of plywood or one layer of plywood and a mortar bed, the tiles are bonded with an adhesive. Ceramic tiles are spaced about 3/16 inch apart, the joints between them filled with grout; marble tiles are usually butted together, their joints also grouted.

Consult the Troubleshooting Guide *(page 51)* to diagnose and repair the rigid flooring of your home. With regular maintenance of your ceramic *(page 52)* or marble *(page 53)* tile floor, its life can be virtually endless. If necessary, consult a tile dealer to identify your type of rigid flooring and any special cleaning or care it may require; a glazed type of tile usually can be distinguished by its glass-like surface, whether its finish is mat or shiny. Grout can loosen and crack with age; check the joints between ceramic tiles periodically and replace any damaged grout *(page 54)*. Reseal the entire joint along the edge of a bathtub or other plumbing fixture with caulk *(page 54)* rather than try to patch any damage to it.

No rigid flooring is ever completely impervious to damage. A dropped heavy object or other accidental blow can chip or crack a tile or a section of tiles. Fortunately, with rigid flooring of ceramic tiles, replacing a tile *(page 56)* or even a section of tiles *(page 57)* is usually easy—of greatest difficulty can be the finding of the identical replacement tile or tiles. If you have not saved any original tiles of the flooring, purchase contrasting tiles of the same size to use as accents; or, replace the tile floor *(page 58)*. Repairs to rigid flooring of marble tiles can be complicated and are best left to a marble-tile-flooring professional. For widespread damage to any rigid flooring, suspect a problem with the floor understructure *(page 62)*.

The materials necessary for repairs to rigid flooring are readily available at a building supply center; for the greatest selection of tiles, consult a tile dealer. For certain types of work on rigid flooring, special tools are required. A grout saw or scriber is needed to remove the grout from a joint; a grout float is useful for applying new grout to the joints of a section of tiles. For fitting a tile at an obstruction *(page 59)*, a glass cutter or a tile cutter is necessary to trim straight edges; tile nippers or a rod saw to trim irregular edges. Use a notched trowel with adhesive: the unnotched edges for applying it; the notched edges for combing it. Before starting any repair, refer to Tools & Techniques *(page 122)* and the Emergency Guide *(page 8)*.

Cove tile
Can be installed on wall at edge of flooring; curved shape provides transition between surfaces perpendicular to each other.

Caulk
Seals joint subjected to expansion and contraction or vulnerable to moisture such as between flooring and bathtub; use silicone or acrylic-latex type for repairs.

Ceramic tile
Common types for indoor flooring include mosaic, wall, quarry and paver; can be glazed or non-glazed. Easy to clean, maintain and repair.

Adhesive
Bonds tiles to subfloor; use type with latex additive for repairs.

Grout
Fills joints between ceramic tiles; Portland cement-based and available in a variety of colors.

Subfloor
Supports rigid flooring. Typically a layer of exterior-grade 4-by-8 panels of plywood 5/8 inch thick; a layer of interior-grade 4-by-8 panels of plywood 1/2 inch thick and spaced 1/4 inch apart nailed cross-grained to it or a mortar bed set onto it.

Marble tile
Easy to clean and maintain; repairs best left to marble tile flooring professional.

50

TROUBLESHOOTING GUIDE

SYMPTOM	POSSIBLE CAUSE	PROCEDURE
CERAMIC TILE		
Flooring surface dirty or dull	Everyday wear and tear	Maintain tile flooring (p. 52) □○
Caulk stained or discolored	Everyday wear and tear; accidental spill; black spots of mildew due to high humidity	Maintain tile flooring (p. 52) □○; wipe up spills immediately and ventilate room to reduce humidity
	Caulk damaged	Replace caulk (p. 54) □○
Caulk loose or cracked	Shrinking or shifting of caulk with age	Replace caulk (p. 54) □○
Grout stained or discolored	Everyday wear and tear; accidental spill; black spots of mildew due to high humidity	Maintain tile flooring (p. 52) □○; wipe up spills immediately and ventilate room to reduce humidity
	Grout damaged	Replace grout (p. 54) ▤○▲
Grout loose or cracked	Shrinking or shifting of grout with age	Replace grout (p. 54) ▤○▲
Tile or tiles stained or discolored	Everyday wear and tear; accidental spill; black spots of mildew due to high humidity	Maintain tile flooring (p. 52) □○; wipe up spills immediately and ventilate room to reduce humidity
	Tile or tiles damaged; glaze worn off	Replace tile (p. 56) ▤○▲, section of tiles (p. 57) ▤○▲ or tile floor (p. 58) ■○▲
Tile or tiles loose, chipped, cracked, sunken or heaved	Accidental blow; house settlement with age	Replace grout (p. 54) ▤○▲; replace tile (p. 56) ▤○▲, section of tiles (p. 57) ▤○▲ or tile floor (p. 58) ■○▲
	Floor understructure faulty	Troubleshoot floor understructure (p. 62)
MARBLE TILE		
Flooring surface dirty or dull	Everyday wear and tear	Maintain tile flooring (p. 53) □○
Caulk stained or discolored	Everyday wear and tear; accidental spill; black spots of mildew due to high humidity	Maintain tile flooring (p. 53) □○; wipe up spills immediately and ventilate room to reduce humidity
	Caulk damaged	Replace caulk (p. 54) □○
Caulk loose or cracked	Shrinking or shifting of caulk with age	Replace caulk (p. 54) □○
Tile or tiles stained or discolored	Everyday wear and tear; accidental spill; black spots of mildew due to high humidity	Maintain tile flooring (p. 53) □○; wipe up spills immediately and ventilate room to reduce humidity
	Tile or tiles damaged	Call marble tile flooring professional
Tile or tiles loose, chipped, cracked, sunken or heaved	Accidental blow; house settlement with age	Call marble tile flooring professional
	Floor understructure faulty	Troubleshoot floor understructure (p. 62)

DEGREE OF DIFFICULTY: □ Easy ▤ Moderate ■ Complex
ESTIMATED TIME: ○ Less than 1 hour ◑ 1 to 3 hours ● Over 3 hours
▲ Special tool required

51

Anatomy diagrams
Locate and describe the various components of a floor, stair or carpet.

Variations
Differences in floor, stair and carpet construction are described throughout the book, particularly if a repair procedure varies from one type or situation to another.

Degree of difficulty and time
Rate the complexity of each repair and how much time the job should take for a homeowner with average do-it-yourself skills.

Special tool required
Some repairs call for a specialized tool; in this example, a grout saw is required to remove old grout.

repairs such as replacing an entire ceramic tile floor, you may wish to call for professional help. You will still have saved time and money by diagnosing the problem yourself.

Most of the repairs in *Floors, Stairs & Carpets* can be made with standard household tools and equipment. Any special tool required is indicated in the Troubleshooting Guide. Basic tools—and the proper way to use them—along with information on fasteners, abrasives and finishes is presented in the Tools & Techniques section starting on page 122. If you are a novice at home repair, read this chapter in preparation for a job.

Repairing a floor, staircase or carpet can be simple and worry-free if you work logically and systematically, and follow all safety tips and precautions. Always use the proper tool for the job—and use it correctly. Wear the recommended safety gear for the job: safety goggles when there is a risk of eye injury; work gloves with sharp or rough materials; rubber gloves with chemicals; respiratory protection against dust or hazardous vapors. Concentrate on the job and take periodic breaks to inspect your work; do not rush or take short cuts. Keep children and pets safe from harm out of the work area.

Name of repair
You will be referred by the Troubleshooting Guide to the first page of a specific repair job.

Step-by-step procedures
Follow the numbered repair sequence carefully. Depending on the result of each step, you may be directed to a later step or to another part of the book to complete the repair.

Lead-ins
Bold lead-ins summarize each step or highlight the key action pictured in the illustration.

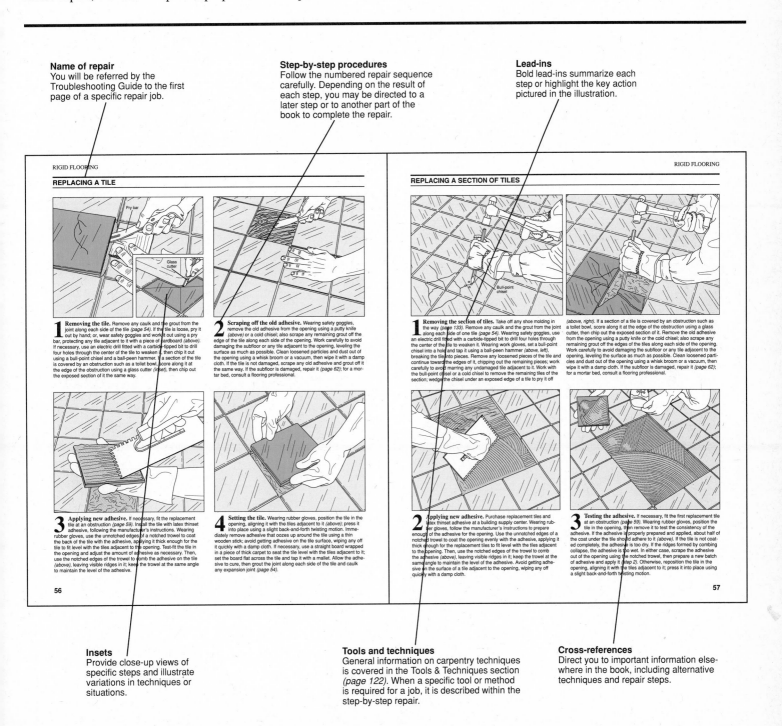

Insets
Provide close-up views of specific steps and illustrate variations in techniques or situations.

Tools and techniques
General information on carpentry techniques is covered in the Tools & Techniques section (page 122). When a specific tool or method is required for a job, it is described within the step-by-step repair.

Cross-references
Direct you to important information elsewhere in the book, including alternative techniques and repair steps.

EMERGENCY GUIDE

Preventing problems in floor, stair and carpet repair. Most accidents arise from carelessness: the improper use of tools and the mishandling of hazardous materials. Accidents, however, can befall even the most careful worker. Sharp tools can cut skin. Wood can cause splinters. Many solvents, adhesives and finishing products contain chemicals that can burn the skin or emit toxic fumes, causing dizziness, faintness or nausea. The list of safety tips at right covers basic guidelines for the repair of any floor, staircase or carpet.

Prepare yourself to handle emergencies before they occur by reading the Troubleshooting Guide on page 9; it places emergency procedures at your fingertips, providing quick-action steps to take and referring you to pages 10 to 13 for detailed instructions. Also review Tools & Techniques *(page 122)*; it provides valuable information on repair procedures and the safe use of tools. Store a well-stocked first-aid kit in a convenient, accessible location; in the event of a repair-related medical emergency, you will want anyone to be able to find it and administer first aid *(page 11)*. Fire is a life-threatening emergency. Deprive fire of its element of surprise by installing smoke detectors throughout your home. Have the correct fire extinguisher ready to snuff out a blaze before it gains the upper hand; learn how to use it before you need it *(page 12)*. A flood that engulfs a floor or carpet with several inches of standing water can have devastating effects on its condition unless prompt action is taken. Review the equipment and procedures used to cope with flooding *(page 10)* and be prepared to act quickly in any emergency requiring you to shut off electricity *(page 10)*.

Keep people away from any repair area and do not let anyone walk on an unsafe staircase or a weakened floor. Before gathering the tools and materials needed to undertake a permanent repair, use temporary barriers to block access to a potential hazard and secure your unsafe staircase *(page 12)* or damaged floor *(page 13)*. Keep an adequate stock of clean-up supplies on hand: clay-based cat litter and absorbent cloths for mopping up spills of chemicals. If you act quickly to clean up spills *(page 13)*, harm and damage can be prevented.

Whenever you are in doubt about your ability to handle an emergency, do not hesitate to call for help. Post the telephone numbers for the local fire department, hospital emergency room, poison control center, physician and ambulance service near the telephone. In most areas, dial 911 in the event you confront any life-threatening emergency. When you dispose of chemical containers and refuse or flooring materials that may contain asbestos *(page 36)*, call your local department of environmental protection or public health for information about the proper procedures and any special regulations in effect in your community.

SAFETY TIPS

1. Before beginning any repair in this book, read the entire repair procedure. Familiarize yourself with the specific safety information presented in each chapter.

2. Always use the proper tool for the job. Refer to Tools & Techniques *(page 122)* for instructions on the correct use and maintenance of tools. When tools are not in use, store them in a dry location well out of the reach of children.

3. Carefully read the label on the container of any cleaning or finishing product or adhesive. Follow the manufacturer's instructions to the letter, paying special attention to hazard warnings and storage recommendations.

4. Wear rubber gloves when using ammonia, bleach or other harsh cleaning solutions. **Caution:** Never mix bleach with ammonia or acids; together they produce a deadly gas.

5. Walk on a wet floor only if necessary—and always with caution.

6. Label the main circuit breaker, the main fuse block or the service disconnect breaker for your electrical system; also map the circuits of your home and label them at the service panel.

7. Keep a flashlight near the service panel in your home.

8. If your electrical system has been shut down due to flooding, have it inspected by a licensed electrician before restoring power.

9. Never work with electricity in damp conditions. To guard against electrical shock, plug a power tool only into an outlet that is grounded or protected by a ground-fault circuit interrupter (GFCI).

10. Keep water, wet towels and damp sponges away from electrical outlets, fixtures and switchplates.

11. Keep cleaning solutions, adhesives and other potentially harmful products out of the reach of children and pets. If you suspect a child or pet has ingested a harmful product, call your local poison control center or veterinarian immediately.

12. Contact a physician or poison control center immediately if a potentially harmful product is sprayed into the eyes. Flush the eyes thoroughly with water *(page 11)* if you are advised.

13. Always keep the work area well-ventilated when working with finishing products, solvents, adhesives, strong cleaners or chemical strippers—and follow any safety instructions of the manufacturer on the use of materials and supplies.

14. Never smoke when using any kind of adhesive or flammable solution. Be sure to store all flammable products away from sunlight and heat sources.

15. Always have a fire extinguisher rated ABC or BC on hand when working with flammable chemicals or power tools; know how to use it before you begin to work.

16. Install smoke detectors on each level of your home and test them regularly to ensure that they are in proper working order.

17. Post emergency telephone numbers for your local fire department, hospital emergency room, physician, poison control center and ambulance service near the telephone.

TROUBLESHOOTING GUIDE

SYMPTOM	PROCEDURE
Chemical fire: flames or smoke from finishing product, solvent or other chemical product	Call fire department immediately
	Control fire using ABC or BC fire extinguisher *(p. 12)*
	Have fire department inspect house—even if fire out
Chemical product ingested	Do not give victim anything to eat or drink or induce vomiting unless advised by professional
	Immediately call local poison control center, hospital emergency room or physician for instructions; provide information on victim's age and weight, and type and amount of poison ingested
	If professional medical treatment necessary, bring product container with you
Chemical product splashed in eye	Flush chemical from eye *(p. 11)*
Chemical product spilled on skin	Immediately brush off dry product or wipe off liquid product
	Wash skin thoroughly with soap and water
	If skin irritation develops, seek medical attention
Chemical product spilled in work area	Clean up chemical spill *(p. 13)*
Faintness, dizziness, nausea or blurred vision when working with chemical product	Treat exposure to toxic vapors *(p. 11)*
Electrical fire: flames or smoke from power tool, extension cord or outlet	Call fire department immediately
	Control fire using ABC or BC fire extinguisher *(p. 12)*
	Shut off electricity *(p. 10)*
	Have fire department inspect house—even if fire out
Electrical burn	Seek medical attention immediately; **Caution:** Never apply ointment to a burn
Power tool, extension cord or outlet sparks, shocks or emits burning odor	Do not touch power tool, extension cord or outlet
	Shut off electricity *(p. 10)*
	If electricity cannot be shut off immediately, protect hand with thick dry towel or heavy rubber glove and unplug power tool or extension cord from outlet
Cut or scratch	Stop bleeding and treat wound *(p. 11)*
	If wound caused by rusty or dirty object, seek medical attention for tetanus treatment
Bruise	Apply ice pack to reduce swelling
	If pain does not diminish or swelling persists, seek medical attention
Splinter	Pull out splinter *(p. 11)*
Object embedded in or under skin	Do not attempt to remove object; seek medical attention immediately
Foreign particle in eye	Remove particle with moistened end of clean cloth or tissue
	Do not rub eye or attempt to remove particle on pupil or embedded in eye
	If particle cannot be removed, cover eye with sterile gauze and seek medical attention immediately
Head injury	Check whether victim is breathing and has pulse; if not, have someone call for medical help and begin artificial resuscitation or cardiopulmonary resuscitation (CPR) if you are qualified
	If victim loses consciousness—even for only one second—seek medical attention
Finish flooring or carpeting flooded	Remove standing water using submersible pump or wet-dry vacuum *(p. 10)*
Staircase unsafe	Temporarily secure staircase *(p. 12)*
Floor unsafe	Temporarily reinforce floor *(p. 13)*

COPING WITH A FLOOD

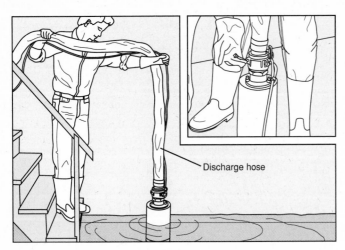

Using a submersible pump. For 2 inches or less of standing water, use a wet-dry vacuum *(step right)* or a mop and bucket. For up to 18 inches of standing water, rent a submersible pump at a tool rental agency; use a discharge hose long enough to reach an outdoor storm drain. Wearing rubber boots and rubber gloves, push the discharge hose onto the discharge pipe and close the clamp *(inset)*, then lower the pump into the water until it sits level on the floor *(above)*. Position the discharge hose at the storm drain, then plug the pump into a GFCI-protected outlet and turn it on. Turn off the pump when it no longer sucks up water.

Using a wet-dry vacuum. Remove more than 2 inches of standing water with a submersible pump *(step left)*; otherwise, use a wet-dry vacuum or a mop and bucket. Wear rubber boots and rubber gloves while operating the vacuum. Push the intake hose onto the intake fitting, then plug the vacuum into a GFCI-protected outlet and turn it on, keeping the power cord off the wet floor. Work the head of the vacuum back and forth across the floor *(above)* until the water is removed. When the tank is full, turn off and unplug the vacuum to empty it. Use one or more dehumidifiers to remove any remaining moisture.

SHUTTING OFF ELECTRICITY

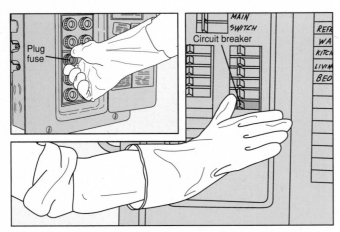

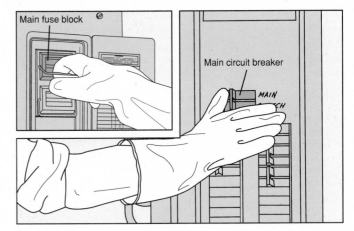

Shutting off a circuit. If the floor around the service panel is damp, stand on a dry board or wear dry rubber boots. Wear heavy rubber gloves, work only with one hand and avoid touching anything metal. Locate the circuit breaker or fuse at the service panel controlling the circuit; if the circuits are not labeled, shut off the system *(step right)*. Flip the circuit breaker toggle switch to OFF *(above)*; it may spring back to an intermediate position. At a fuse panel, grasp the plug fuse only by its insulated rim and unscrew it *(inset)*.

Shutting off the system. If the floor around the service panel is damp, stand on a dry board or wear dry rubber boots. Wear heavy rubber gloves, work only with one hand and avoid touching anything metal. Use the thumb of one hand *(above)* or a broom handle to flip off the main circuit breaker—a linked, double circuit breaker. Or, remove each main fuse block by gripping its metal handle and pulling it straight out *(inset)*; there may be more than one. If the service panel has a shutoff lever instead, switch it to OFF.

PROVIDING MINOR FIRST AID

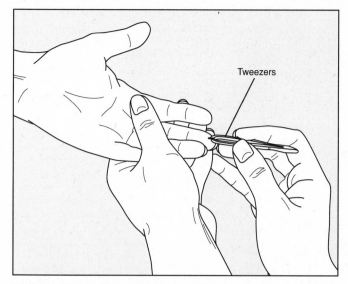

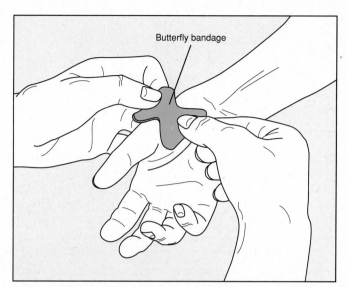

Pulling out a splinter. Wash the skin around the splinter using soap and water. A metal splinter may require treatment for tetanus; seek medical help. Otherwise, sterilize a needle and tweezers over a match flame or in alcohol. Ease out the splinter from under the skin using the needle, then pull the splinter out with the tweezers *(above)*. Wash the wound again with soap and water. If the splinter cannot be removed or becomes infected, seek medical attention.

Treating a cut or scratch. Wrap the wound in a clean cloth and apply direct pressure with your hand to stop any bleeding; keep the limb elevated. If the cloth becomes blood-soaked, place another clean cloth over it. If the wound is minor, wash it with soap and water, then apply a sterile bandage to it. For a narrow, shallow wound, draw its edges together and place a butterfly bandage on it *(above)*. If bleeding persists or the wound is deep or gaping, seek medical attention.

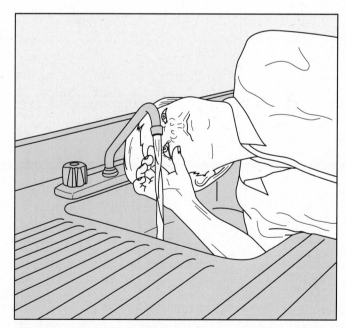

Treating exposure to toxic vapors. Exposure to toxic vapors can cause headache, dizziness, faintness, fatigue or nausea; at the first sign of any symptom, leave the work area and get fresh air. Loosen any tight clothing, especially around the waist, neck and chest; remove any clothing splashed by a chemical. If you feel faint, sit with your head lowered between your knees *(above)*. Have someone ventilate the work area and close all chemical containers. If any symptom persists, seek medical attention.

Flushing chemicals from the eye. Immediately wash out any chemical splashed into the eye. Holding the eyelids of the injured eye apart with your fingers, flush the injured eye for 15 minutes under a gentle flow of cool water from a faucet *(above)* or pitcher; tilt the head to one side to prevent the chemical from being washed into the uninjured eye. Cover the injured eye with a sterile gauze dressing and seek medical attention immediately.

CONTROLLING A FIRE

Using a fire extinguisher. Have someone call the fire department immediately. If flame or smoke comes from the walls or ceilings or the fire is large or not contained, evacuate the house and call the fire department from a neighbor's home. To control a small, contained chemical or electrical fire, use a dry-chemical fire extinguisher rated ABC or BC. **Caution:** Do not use water on a chemical or electrical fire. Pull the lock pin out of the fire extinguisher handle. Keeping the fire extinguisher upright, lift it up and aim the nozzle at the base of the fire, positioning yourself 6 to 10 feet away with your back to an accessible exit. Squeeze the two levers of the handle together and spray in a quick side-to-side motion (*left*). Keep spraying until the fire is completely extinguished. Watch carefully for flashback, or rekindling, and be prepared to spray again. If the flames spread, or the fire extinguisher empties before the fire is extinguished, evacuate the house immediately.

Class ABC or BC fire extinguisher

TEMPORARILY SECURING A STAIRCASE

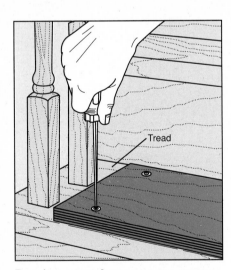

Tread

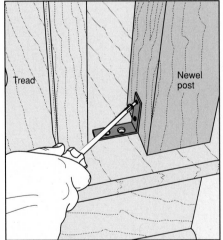

Tread

Newel post

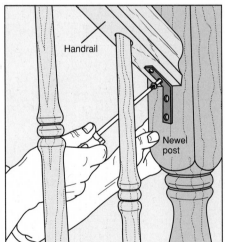

Handrail

Newel post

Bracing a tread. Cut a section of 1/2-inch plywood large enough to cover the tread. Position the plywood on the tread and use an electric drill to bore a hole for countersinking a 1-inch No. 8 wood screw at each corner through it into the tread. Drive a screw into each hole (*above*). To reduce any tripping hazard, use a rasp to bevel the front edge of the plywood at a 45-degree angle. Make a permanent repair as soon as possible (*page 78*).

Bracing a handrail. Provide temporary support to a newel post or a handrail with a metal angle bracket. To secure a newel post, position the bracket at a 90-degree angle between it and a tread or a riser. Mark the position of the screw holes in the bracket with a pencil, then use an electric drill to bore a pilot hole for a 1 1/2-inch No. 8 wood screw at each marked point. Drive in each screw with a screwdriver (*above, left*). To secure a handrail to a newel post, use two pairs of pliers to bend the bracket to fit the angle between the newel post and the handrail, if necessary. Position the bracket on the newel post and the handrail to mark the screw holes, then bore holes and drive in screws (*above, right*). Make a permanent repair as soon as possible (*page 78*).

TEMPORARILY REINFORCING A FLOOR

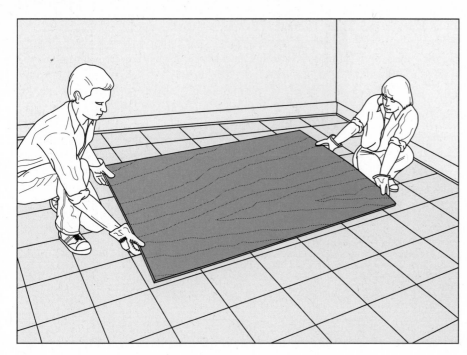

Bracing a floor section. Temporarily strengthen a floor section using a 3/4-inch sheet of plywood at least twice its length and width; if necessary, double up sheets of the plywood for added strength. Work with a helper to set the plywood down, centering it on the floor section *(left)*. To keep the plywood from moving, wedge it in place by driving nails part way into the floor section along each edge of it. If the floor section is severely weakened or too large to be covered by a single sheet of plywood, set up barricades to completely block access to it. Make a permanent repair as soon as possible.

CLEANING UP A CHEMICAL SPILL

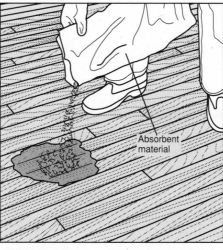

Absorbent material

Cleaning up and disposing of spilled chemicals. Immediately open windows and doors to the outdoors, extinguish all sources of heat or flame and turn off equipment operating nearby. **Caution:** Check the label of the spilled product; if it is marked EXTREMELY FLAMMABLE and you have spilled more than 1 quart, or if it is marked with POISON vapor or ventilation warnings and you have spilled more than 1 gallon, leave the spill site and call the fire department. Otherwise, clean up the spill quickly wearing rubber boots, heavy rubber gloves and safety goggles; if the label of the spilled product is marked with POISON vapor or ventilation warnings, also wear a respirator. For a small spill, wipe it up with cloths or paper towels *(above, left)*. For a large spill, spread an absorbent material such as clay-based cat litter on it *(above, center)*. When the spill is soaked up, scoop up the absorbent material with an old spatula *(above, right)* or whisk broom and dustpan. Wipe up any remaining residue using a clean cloth dampened with a solvent recommended on the product label. Place chemical-soaked waste materials in a metal container double-lined with heavy-duty plastic garbage bags. Call your local department of environmental protection or public health for recommended disposal procedures.

WOOD FLOORING

Wood flooring has an appeal that is nearly universal; its warmth and durability evoke the craftsmanship and tradition of an earlier age, yet it lends itself well to the interior design of contemporary homes. Properly-installed and well-maintained wood flooring can last as long as the house it graces. Wood flooring systems have proliferated since the 1960s; the two most common types today are shown: a strip wood floor *(below)* and a parquet tile floor *(page 15)*. All wood flooring is laid in rows on the subfloor and fastened with nails or adhesive; its edges are fitted with shoe moldings at walls and thresholds at doors. Usually the surface of wood flooring is coated with finish; there may be a wood stain under it and a buffing wax on it.

Undertake repairs to your wood flooring as soon as a problem is apparent, both to maintain the beauty and life of it and to prevent damage to the floor understructure. Clean the floor regularly to keep it shining and to protect the finish *(page 18)*. If the flooring is waxed, rewax it *(page 20)* as soon as you notice any wear or wax buildup. If the finish itself becomes scratched or thin, spot-refinish the small area *(page 19)* or put a touch-up coat of finish on the entire floor *(page 20)*; ensure that you properly identify the existing finish *(page 140)* to match it. If the finish has become so worn that the wood surface under it is showing signs of wear and discoloration, sand off the old finish *(page 22)*, then refinish the floor.

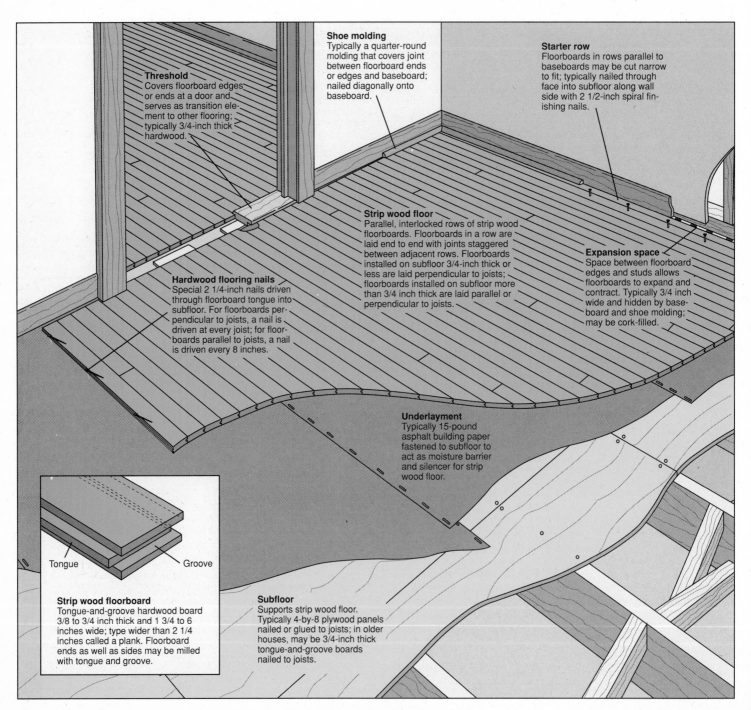

Threshold
Covers floorboard edges or ends at a door and serves as transition element to other flooring; typically 3/4-inch thick hardwood.

Shoe molding
Typically a quarter-round molding that covers joint between floorboard ends or edges and baseboard; nailed diagonally onto baseboard.

Starter row
Floorboards in rows parallel to baseboards may be cut narrow to fit; typically nailed through face into subfloor along wall side with 2 1/2-inch spiral finishing nails.

Hardwood flooring nails
Special 2 1/4-inch nails driven through floorboard tongue into subfloor. For floorboards perpendicular to joists, a nail is driven at every joist; for floorboards parallel to joists, a nail is driven every 8 inches.

Strip wood floor
Parallel, interlocked rows of strip wood floorboards. Floorboards in a row are laid end to end with joints staggered between adjacent rows. Floorboards installed on subfloor 3/4-inch thick or less are laid perpendicular to joists; floorboards installed on subfloor more than 3/4 inch thick are laid parallel or perpendicular to joists.

Expansion space
Space between floorboard edges and studs allows floorboards to expand and contract. Typically 3/4 inch wide and hidden by baseboard and shoe molding; may be cork-filled.

Underlayment
Typically 15-pound asphalt building paper fastened to subfloor to act as moisture barrier and silencer for strip wood floor.

Tongue — Groove

Strip wood floorboard
Tongue-and-groove hardwood board 3/8 to 3/4 inch thick and 1 3/4 to 6 inches wide; type wider than 2 1/4 inches called a plank. Floorboard ends as well as sides may be milled with tongue and groove.

Subfloor
Supports strip wood floor. Typically 4-by-8 plywood panels nailed or glued to joists; in older houses, may be 3/4-inch thick tongue-and-groove boards nailed to joists.

Physical damage to your floorboards or tiles can be easily repaired. Cracks and holes can be patched *(page 19)* and splintered edges reglued *(page 24)*. If the floorboards or tiles are badly damaged, you can replace them one at a time or in sections; if damage is extensive, consider replacing your strip wood floor *(page 30)* or parquet tile floor *(page 35)*. Before you begin any structural repair on wood flooring, make sure you know its features. Remove a shoe molding or a threshold to determine the floorboard thickness and the joint type of a strip wood floor; on a parquet tile floor, look for the tile size and joint type, and determine if the tiles are solid wood or laminated as well as if they are self-adhesive or require adhesive.

The materials and supplies necessary for wood flooring repairs are readily available at a lumber yard or building supply center. Most small repairs to wood flooring can be made with standard household carpentry tools. Refer to Tools & Techniques *(page 122)* before starting a job for directions on using many of the tools required. For a major repair such as refinishing or replacing the entire floor, you will need to use special tools: a drum sander, a floor edger, a commercial floor polisher or a strip floor nailer—all obtainable at a tool rental center. Ask the tool rental agent for a demonstration before you bring home the tool; carefully follow the tool manufacturer's operating instructions and safety tips when using it.

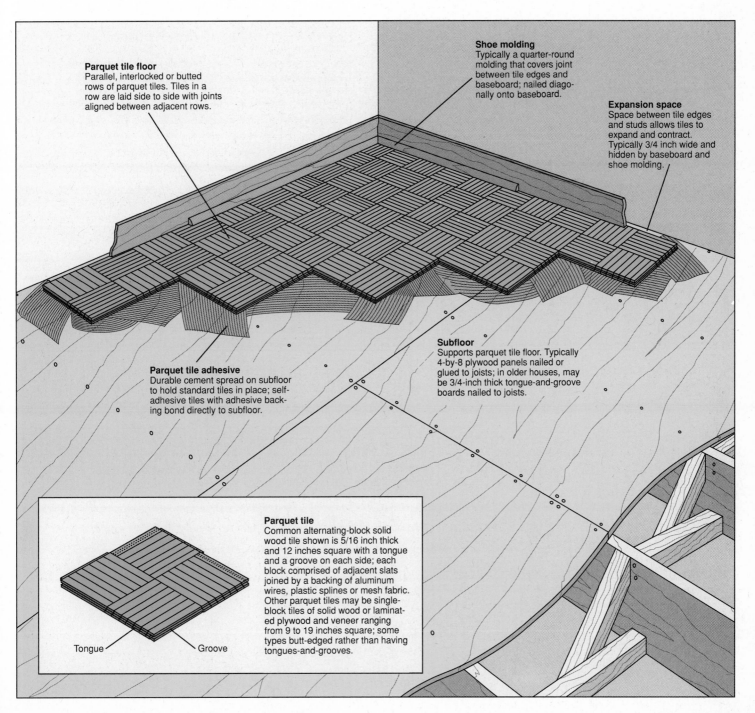

Parquet tile floor
Parallel, interlocked or butted rows of parquet tiles. Tiles in a row are laid side to side with joints aligned between adjacent rows.

Shoe molding
Typically a quarter-round molding that covers joint between tile edges and baseboard; nailed diagonally onto baseboard.

Expansion space
Space between tile edges and studs allows tiles to expand and contract. Typically 3/4 inch wide and hidden by baseboard and shoe molding.

Parquet tile adhesive
Durable cement spread on subfloor to hold standard tiles in place; self-adhesive tiles with adhesive backing bond directly to subfloor.

Subfloor
Supports parquet tile floor. Typically 4-by-8 plywood panels nailed or glued to joists; in older houses, may be 3/4-inch thick tongue-and-groove boards nailed to joists.

Parquet tile
Common alternating-block solid wood tile shown is 5/16 inch thick and 12 inches square with a tongue and a groove on each side; each block comprised of adjacent slats joined by a backing of aluminum wires, plastic splines or mesh fabric. Other parquet tiles may be single-block tiles of solid wood or laminated plywood and veneer ranging from 9 to 19 inches square; some types butt-edged rather than having tongues-and-grooves.

Tongue — Groove

15

TROUBLESHOOTING GUIDE

SYMPTOM	POSSIBLE CAUSE	PROCEDURE
STRIP WOOD FLOORING		
Flooring surface dirty or dull	Everyday wear and tear	Clean strip wood flooring (p. 18) □○
	Wax worn; wax build-up	Rewax strip wood flooring (p. 20) □○
Flooring surface stained or discolored	Everyday wear and tear	Clean strip wood flooring (p. 18) □○
	Wax worn; wax build-up	Rewax strip wood flooring (p. 20) □○
	Finish scuffed; accidental spill or burn	Repair finish damage (p. 18) ▣●; spot-refinish strip wood flooring (p. 19) ▣●
	Finish worn or damaged	Spot-refinish (p. 19) ▣● or refinish (p. 20) ▣●▲ strip wood flooring
Flooring surface cracked or gouged	Everyday wear and tear; accidental blow or impact	Repair surface damage (p. 18) ▣●; replace floorboard (p. 26) ▣●
Flooring surface slippery	Wax build-up	Rewax strip wood flooring (p. 20) □○
Flooring wax worn	Everyday wear and tear; lack of regular maintenance	Rewax strip wood flooring (p. 20) □○; maintain surface finish (p. 18) □○
Flooring finish worn or damaged	Everyday wear and tear; lack of regular maintenance	Spot-refinish (p. 19) ▣● or refinish (p. 20) ▣●▲ strip wood flooring; maintain surface finish (p. 18) □○
Floorboard edge split or splintered	Everyday wear and tear; accidental blow or impact	Repair floorboard edge (p. 24) ▣●; replace floorboard (p. 26) ▣●
Floorboard squeaks	Floorboard loose	Secure floorboard (p. 25) □○
Floorboard loose or springy	Everyday wear and tear; wood shrinkage or shifting of wood joints with age	Secure floorboard (p. 25) □○
	Floorboard damaged	Replace floorboard (p. 26) ▣●
	Floor understructure faulty	Troubleshoot floor understructure (p. 62)
Floorboard or floorboards split or cracked	Accidental blow or impact; wood shrinkage or shifting of wood joints with age	Replace floorboard (p. 26) ▣●; replace strip wood floor section (p. 28) ■● or strip wood floor (p. 30) ■●▲
	Floor understructure faulty	Troubleshoot floor understructure (p. 62)
Floorboards cupped (curling at edges) or crowned (bulging at center)	Chronic high humidity; water damage	Replace strip wood floor section (p. 28) ■● or replace strip wood floor (p. 30) ■●▲
Flooring sagging; bulged or humped	Floorboards damaged	Replace strip wood floor section (p. 28) ■● or replace strip wood floor (p. 30) ■●▲
	Floor understructure faulty	Troubleshoot floor understructure (p. 62)

DEGREE OF DIFFICULTY: □ Easy ▣ Moderate ■ Complex
ESTIMATED TIME: ○ Less than 1 hour ● 1 to 3 hours ● Over 3 hours

▲ Special tool required

SYMPTOM	POSSIBLE CAUSE	PROCEDURE
PARQUET TILE FLOORING		
Flooring surface dirty or dull	Everyday wear and tear	Clean parquet tile flooring *(p. 18)* □○
	Wax worn; wax build-up	Rewax parquet tile flooring *(p. 20)* □○
Flooring surface stained or discolored	Everyday wear and tear	Clean parquet tile flooring *(p. 18)* □○
	Wax worn; wax build-up	Rewax parquet tile flooring *(p. 20)* □○
	Finish scuffed; accidental spill or burn	Repair finish damage *(p. 18)* ▣◕; spot-refinish parquet tile flooring *(p. 19)* ▣◕
	Finish worn or damaged	Spot-refinish *(p. 19)* ▣◕ or refinish *(p. 20)* ▣●▲ parquet tile flooring
Flooring surface cracked or gouged	Everyday wear and tear; accidental blow or impact	Repair surface damage *(p. 18)* ▣◕; replace parquet tile *(p. 33)* ▣◕
Flooring surface slippery	Wax build-up	Rewax parquet tile flooring *(p. 20)* □○
Flooring wax worn	Everyday wear and tear; lack of regular maintenance	Rewax parquet tile flooring *(p. 20)* □○; maintain surface finish *(p. 18)* □○
Flooring finish worn or damaged	Everyday wear and tear; lack of regular maintenance	Spot-refinish *(p. 19)* ▣◕ or refinish *(p. 20)* ▣●▲ parquet tile flooring; maintain surface finish *(p. 18)* □○
Tile edge split or splintered	Everyday wear and tear; accidental blow or impact	Repair parquet tile edge *(p. 24)* ▣◕; replace parquet tile *(p. 33)* ▣◕
Tile squeaks	Tile loose	Secure parquet tile *(p. 32)* □○
Tile loose or springy	Everyday wear and tear; wood shrinkage or shifting of wood joints with age	Secure parquet tile *(p. 32)* □○
	Tile damaged	Replace parquet tile *(p. 33)* ▣◕
	Floor understructure faulty	Troubleshoot floor understructure *(p. 62)*
Tile or tiles split or cracked	Accidental blow or impact; wood shrinkage or shifting of wood joints with age	Replace parquet tile or tiles *(p. 33)* ▣◕; replace parquet tile floor *(p. 35)* ■●
	Floor understructure faulty	Troubleshoot floor understructure *(p. 62)*
Tiles cupped (curling at edges) or crowned (bulging at center)	Chronic high humidity; water damage	Replace parquet tiles *(p. 33)* ▣◕ or parquet tile floor *(p. 35)* ■●
Flooring sagging; bulged or humped	Tiles damaged	Replace parquet tiles *(p. 33)* ▣◕ or parquet tile floor *(p. 35)* ■●
	Floor understructure faulty	Troubleshoot floor understructure *(p. 62)*

DEGREE OF DIFFICULTY: □ **Easy** ▣ **Moderate** ■ **Complex**
ESTIMATED TIME: ○ **Less than 1 hour** ◕ **1 to 3 hours** ● **Over 3 hours**   ▲ Special tool required

MAINTAINING THE SURFACE FINISH

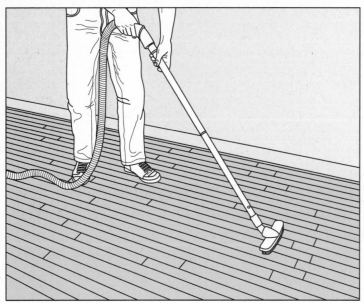

Cleaning the flooring. Vacuum the flooring regularly to keep dirt and grit from being ground into the finish. Remove any floor covering and use a soft-bristled brush attachment with the vacuum; on a strip wood floor, work along the wood grain *(above, left)*. If the flooring has a waxed finish *(page 140)*, buff the flooring after vacuuming it. Fit a household floor polisher with felt buffing pads and work from a corner of the room to the door, buffing a section of the flooring at a time until it shines. If the waxed finish lacks luster, scuffs easily or collects dirt

quickly, rewax the flooring *(page 20)*. If the flooring is unwaxed, damp-mop it on a routine basis after vacuuming. Fill a bucket with warm water; for a greasy kitchen floor, add 1 cup of vinegar per gallon of water. Never pour water directly onto the flooring; instead, soak a sponge-mop in the water, then wring it out until it is almost dry. Starting in a corner of the room and working back to the door, mop a section of the flooring at a time *(above, right)* until it is clean; change the cleaning water as it becomes dirty.

REPAIRING FINISH AND SURFACE DAMAGE

STAIN-LIFTING PROCEDURES

Stain	Procedures
White spot; food spot	Use a nylon pad dampened with water. For a stubborn stain on a waxed finish, use a nylon pad dampened with a solvent-based wood floor cleaner; otherwise, use a fine steel wool pad dampened with mineral spirits.
Burn mark	Use a nylon pad dampened with water. For a stubborn mark on a waxed finish, use a nylon pad dampened with a solvent-based wood floor cleaner; otherwise, use a fine steel wool pad dampened with mineral spirits. If cleaning does not remove the burn mark, repair the surface *(page 19)*.
Chewing gum, candle wax or tar	Lay an ice pack on the stain until the substance is brittle; then, dampen the edges of the substance with mineral spirits and use a plastic spatula to scrape it off.
Dark spot, ink, scuff mark, grease, lipstick or oil	Use a nylon pad dampened with water. For a stubborn stain on a waxed finish, use a nylon pad dampened with a solvent-based wood floor cleaner; otherwise, use a fine steel wool pad dampened with mineral spirits. If the stain has penetrated the finish into the wood, remove the finish *(page 19)* and apply a commercial wood bleach following the manufacturer's instructions; then touch up the finish *(page 19)*.

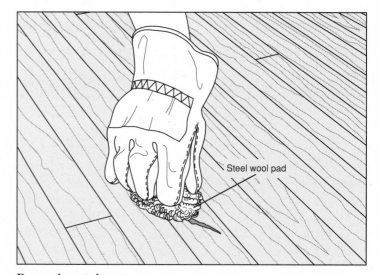

Steel wool pad

Removing stains. To remove any stain from a wood floor, first try rubbing it using a soft cloth dampened with water; if necessary, follow up with the recommended sequence of cleaning procedures at left. Identify the finish *(page 140)* and always start with the mildest cleaner recommended, gently wiping or rubbing the stain; use a stronger cleaner and scrub a stain only if necessary. To remove a stubborn stain with a nylon or steel wool pad, dampen but do not soak it with the recommended solvent. Working from the edge of the stain inward along the wood grain, gently scrub the stain *(above)*. Use a clean cloth to blot up any solvent. If necessary, spot-refinish the surface *(page 19)*.

REPAIRING FINISH AND SURFACE DAMAGE (continued)

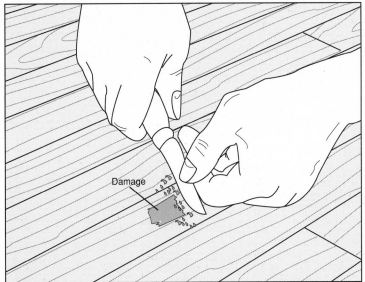

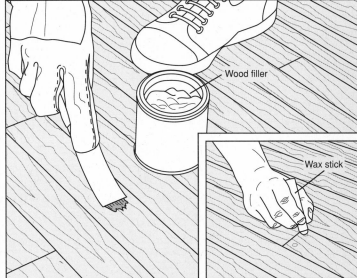

Patching cracks and gouges. Scrape off any damaged wood fibers using a sharp knife, working carefully along the wood grain *(above, left)*. Wipe the damaged surface using a soft cloth dampened with mineral spirits, then blot it dry. To patch a tiny crack, nick or hole, use a wax stick of a color that matches the wood. Rub the tip of the stick back and forth across the depression *(inset)* to fill it level with the surface. To patch a deep crack or a gouge, use a wood filler of a color that matches the wood. Following the manufacturer's instructions, wear work gloves and use a flexible putty knife to work the filler into the depression, overfilling it slightly *(above, right);* then, scrape off the excess to level it. Let the filler dry, then smooth the surface along the wood grain using fine sandpaper. Brush sanding particles off the surface and wipe it with a tack cloth, then touch up the finish *(step 2, below)*.

SPOT-REFINISHING THE FLOOR

1 Removing the damaged finish. Remove any shoe molding in the way *(page 133)*. If the surface is waxed *(page 140)*, strip off the wax *(page 20)*. For a small or superficially damaged surface, wear rubber gloves and use a fine steel wool pad moistened with mineral spirits; scrub along the wood grain until the visible damage is removed, then feather out around the scrubbed spot with light strokes. Use a clean cloth to wipe the spot dry. For a large or deeply damaged surface, use an orbital sander fitted with fine sandpaper; sand back and forth along the surface in long, smooth overlapping strokes *(above)*. Work carefully to remove only the damaged finish; avoid sanding off any penetrating stain applied to the wood to color it. Vacuum sanding particles off the surface and wipe it with a tack cloth.

2 Touching up the finish. Choose a finish to match the original *(page 140)* and follow the manufacturer's instructions to apply it. Wearing rubber gloves, use a paintbrush to apply a thin, even coat of finish on the surface, brushing along the wood grain in a smooth stroke *(above)* and feathering the edges; at the end of each stroke, lap back over the surface just coated. Repeat, making parallel overlapping strokes until the surface is coated; smooth any unevenness immediately. Allow the finish to dry, then smooth the surface with fine sandpaper and apply another coat. Continue to smooth and apply finish until the surface is uniform, feathering the edges slightly farther each time to disguise the repair. When the last coat of finish is dry, apply a coat of wax, if necessary *(page 20)*. Reinstall any shoe molding you removed.

REWAXING THE FLOOR

1 **Stripping off the old wax.** If the floor is waxed *(page 140)*, test for wax buildup by running a fingernail across it; if wax scrapes off, rewax the floor. To strip off wax, work one floor section at a time using a solvent-based wood floor cleaner. Following the manufacturer's instructions, wear rubber gloves and apply the cleaner using a stiff-bristled fiber brush, scrubbing gently along the wood grain *(above)*. Wipe the surface dry with a clean cloth.

2 **Applying new wax.** Vacuum the floor, then apply a liquid buffing wax compatible with the floor color. Coat one floor section at a time, pouring wax in a pool on the surface and spreading it with a sponge mop along the wood grain in one direction *(above)*. As the wax thins, lift the mop and reposition it, overlapping parallel strokes slightly. Continue the same way, smoothing any unevenness immediately. Let the wax dry.

3 **Polishing and buffing the wax.** To polish the floor, use a household floor polisher fitted with bristled polishing brushes. Starting at a corner and working back to a door, polish a section of the floor at a time *(above)* until the wax has a smooth and uniform luster. To buff the floor, fit the floor polisher with felt buffing pads and repeat the procedure to obtain a bright and uniform shine. Hand-buff any hard-to-reach surface with a clean, soft cloth.

REFINISHING THE FLOOR

1 **Smoothing the surface.** Clear the floor and remove the shoe moldings *(page 133)*. If the floor has a waxed finish *(page 140)*, strip the wax off it *(step 1, above)*. To remove the entire finish from the floor, first sand it *(page 22)* or strip it using a chemical stripper *(page 21)*. Otherwise, prepare the floor for a finish using a commercial floor polisher. Rent the floor polisher along with a medium sanding screen and a scrubbing pad at a tool rental agency. Load the sanding screen onto the floor polisher following the manufacturer's instructions. Wearing a dust mask, start at a corner and work in sections along and across the room with the polisher *(above)*; keep it moving to avoid gouging the wood. Vacuum sanding particles off the floor and wipe it with a tack cloth.

2 **Applying the finish.** Choose a finish *(page 140)* and follow the manufacturer's instructions to apply it; open windows and doors to the outdoors and wear a respirator. Working in stock-inged feet, use a paint pad to apply finish to one section of the floor 18 inches wide and 3 feet long at a time; load the pad and draw it lightly in one direction along the surface—along the wood grain on a strip wood floor *(above)*. When the pad starts to apply finish spottily, lift it gently to avoid creating air bubbles. Continue, overlapping parallel strokes slightly and smoothing any unevenness immediately. Allow the finish to dry, then smooth the surface using the floor polisher with the scrubbing pad *(step 1)* and apply another coat of finish; repeat as necessary. When the last coat of finish is dry, apply a coat of wax, if necessary *(step 2, above)*. Reinstall any shoe molding you removed.

STRIPPING THE FLOOR

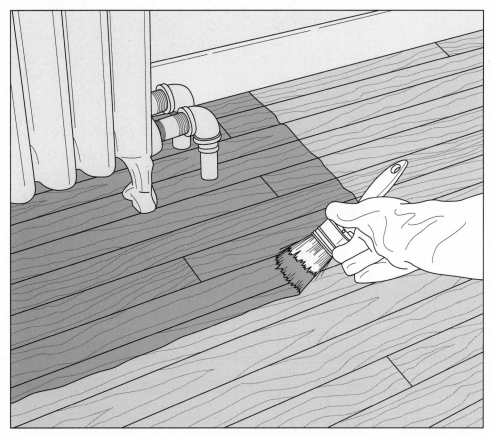

1 **Applying the stripper.** Clear the floor of obstructions; set the heads of any protruding nails. To strip the entire finish off the floor, sand it *(page 22)* or work with a chemical stripper following the manufacturer's instructions. Ventilate the work area thoroughly, opening windows and doors to the outdoors; wear rubber gloves, safety goggles, a dual-cartridge respirator rated for the stripper and a long-sleeved shirt. Working on a section 18 inches wide and 3 feet long at a time, apply the stripper with an old paintbrush *(left)*; use short, light strokes in one direction, parallel to the wood grain. Let the stripper react for the time specified by the manufacturer; do not wait longer or the stripper may harden. Then, test the stripper penetration by pressing the tip of a putty knife into the finish. If the putty knife does not penetrate to the surface under it, apply more stripper; otherwise, remove the softened finish *(step 2)*.

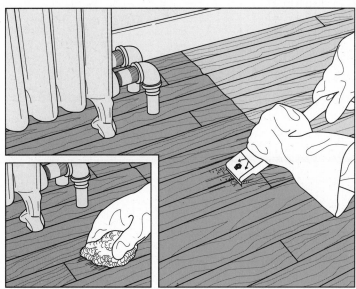

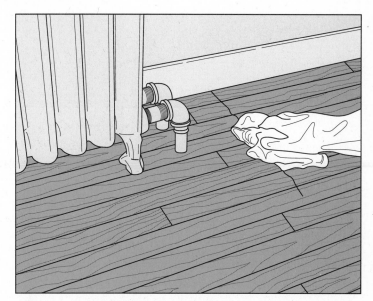

2 **Lifting the finish.** To remove the softened finish, use a paint scraper, first rounding the corners of its blade with a file. Gripping the scraper by the handle, rest its blade at the edge of the section; then, using your other hand to apply firm downward pressure, pull the scraper along the surface parallel to the wood grain, scraping off the finish in one continuous strip *(above)*. If the scraper gouges the surface, decrease your pressure. As softened finish accumulates on the blade, deposit it in a waste can. Continue lifting and disposing of softened finish until the section is stripped. To remove softened finish from joints, use a fine steel wool pad to scrub it out *(inset)*. If unstripped finish remains, apply more stripper *(step 1)*, then scrape it off. When the section is stripped, clean it *(step 3)*.

3 **Cleaning the floor.** Clean stripper residue off the surface to ensure proper adhesion of a new finish; use the solvent recommended by the stripper manufacturer. Dip a clean cloth into the solvent, dampening but not soaking it. Starting at one end of the stripped section, use a long, smooth stroke to rub on the solvent, working parallel to the wood grain *(above)*; avoid saturating the wood. Continue until the section is clean, changing to a clean cloth as necessary. To clean joints and cracks, use a stiff-bristled fiber brush dampened with the solvent to scrub them. When the section is clean, repeat the procedures to strip and clean other sections. When the entire floor is stripped and clean, safely dispose of chemical refuse; then, apply a finish to the floor *(page 20)*.

SANDING THE FLOOR

Pipe collar

1 **Preparing to sand the floor.** If the floor is not new, check that it is sandable. Remove a heating register grille, a pipe collar *(above, left)* or a door threshold, then inspect the edges of the floorboards or tiles at the edge of the opening. If the floorboards are less than 3/4 inch thick or the tiles are laminated or less than 5/8 inch thick, strip the floor using a chemical stripper *(page 21)*. Otherwise, clear the floor of obstructions; set the heads of any protruding nails. Plan the sanding job *(step 2)*, assembling the necessary tools. Ventilate the work area thoroughly, opening windows and doors to the outdoors. Close interior doors and cover wall openings with plastic sheeting *(above, right)* to minimize dust. Then, sand the floor *(step 3)*.

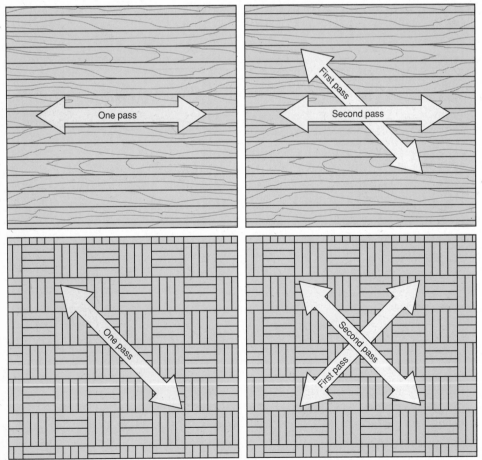

One pass

First pass
Second pass

One pass

Second pass
First pass

2 **Planning the sanding job.** Plan your sanding job according to the type of floor and its condition. To sand a floor with little or no surface damage, plan to make one pass using coarse sandpaper: for a strip wood floor, back and forth along the wood grain *(far left, top)*; for a parquet tile floor, back and forth diagonally across the tiles *(far left, bottom)*. To sand a floor with extensive surface damage, plan to make two passes: the first using very coarse sandpaper; the second using coarse sandpaper. For a strip wood floor, make the first pass back and forth diagonally across the wood grain; make the second pass back and forth along the wood grain *(near left, top)*. For a parquet tile floor, make the first pass back and forth diagonally across the tiles one way; make the second pass back and forth diagonally across the tiles the other way *(near left, bottom)*. Once you have determined the number, direction and coarseness of sandings that your floor needs, rent a drum sander and a floor edger for the job at a tool rental agency; also buy sandpaper of the necessary coarseness. To ensure you buy enough sandpaper, estimate the square footage of the floor, then ask the rental agent for advice about the amount of sandpaper needed.

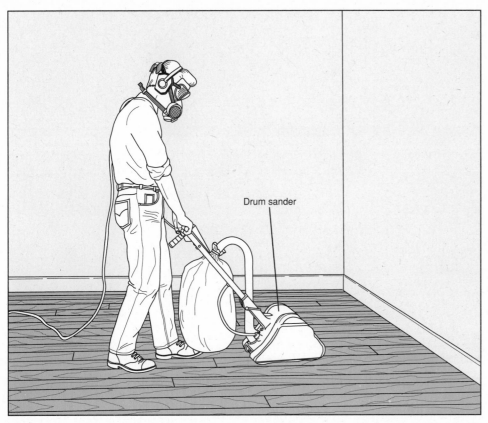

Drum sander

3 **Sanding the floor.** Load the drum sander *(page 128)* with the appropriate sandpaper *(step 2)*. Wearing heavy boots, a respirator, hearing protection and safety goggles, start at a corner to sand the floor. To sand parallel to a wall, position the sander face-on to the adjacent wall. Tilt the sander back and turn it on, then slowly lower it until the drum is on the floor—immediately moving it slowly backward to sand a continuous strip. At a point half way along the floor tilt the sander back, then lower it again and immediately move it slowly forward to sand over the same strip. As you reach the starting point, tilt the sander back and angle it sideways; then, lower it to begin sanding a parallel, overlapping strip. Continue back and forth in parallel overlapping strips *(left)* until half the floor is sanded. Then, position the sander at a corner in the other half of the room and sand the other half of the floor the same way. To sand diagonally to a wall, position the sander face-on at an angle to a corner, then use the same procedure to sand backward and forward across half the floor; then, position the sander at the corner diagonally opposite the starting corner and sand the other half of the floor. Change the sandpaper if it tears or clogs and sands poorly; empty the dust bag as it fills. When the floor is sanded, sand the edges *(step 4)*.

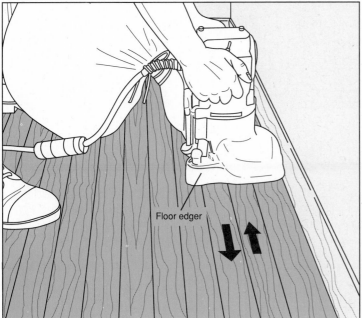

Floor edger

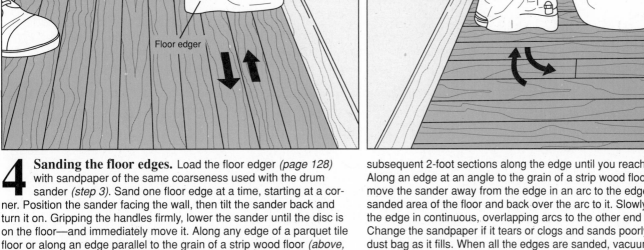

4 **Sanding the floor edges.** Load the floor edger *(page 128)* with sandpaper of the same coarseness used with the drum sander *(step 3)*. Sand one floor edge at a time, starting at a corner. Position the sander facing the wall, then tilt the sander back and turn it on. Gripping the handles firmly, lower the sander until the disc is on the floor—and immediately move it. Along any edge of a parquet tile floor or along an edge parallel to the grain of a strip wood floor *(above, left)*, move the sander sideways and back in a 2-foot strip along it, then slowly away from it in continuous and overlapping side-to-side strips to the edge of the drum-sanded area of the floor. Do the same to sand

subsequent 2-foot sections along the edge until you reach the other end. Along an edge at an angle to the grain of a strip wood floor *(above, right)*, move the sander away from the edge in an arc to the edge of the drum-sanded area of the floor and back over the arc to it. Slowly sand along the edge in continuous, overlapping arcs to the other end the same way. Change the sandpaper if it tears or clogs and sands poorly; empty the dust bag as it fills. When all the edges are sanded, vacuum sanding particles off the floor and wipe it with a tack cloth. If necessary, sand the floor again *(step 3)*. After the final sanding, touch up the sanded floor *(step 5)*.

SANDING THE FLOOR (continued)

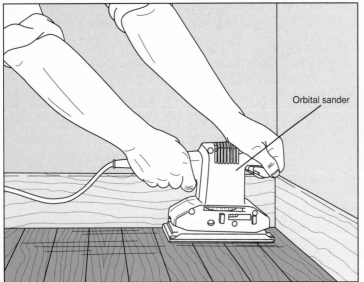

Orbital sander

Paint scraper

5 **Touching up the sanded floor.** To remove finish from areas of the floor you cannot reach with the drum sander or floor edger, use an orbital sander fitted with medium sandpaper; sand back and forth along or from side to side across the surface in long, smooth overlapping strokes *(above, left)* until the finish is removed. On any area of the floor you cannot reach with the orbital sander, use a paint scraper, first rounding the corners of its blade with a file. Gripping the scraper by the handle, rest its blade at the edge of the finish; then, using your other hand to apply firm downward pressure, pull the scraper along the surface parallel to the wood grain, scraping off the finish in one continuous strip *(above, right)*. If the scraper gouges the surface, decrease your pressure. Continue scraping off the finish in strips until you remove it all. Vacuum sanding particles off the floor and wipe it with a tack cloth. Then, smooth the surface and apply a finish to the floor *(page 20)*.

REPAIRING A FLOORBOARD OR TILE EDGE

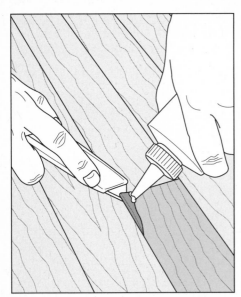

1 **Lifting and gluing a splinter.** Use the tip of a utility knife to gently lift the loose end of the splinter; if it begins to widen and break or it is dirty, remove it *(step 2)*. Otherwise, squeeze wood glue into the gap between the splinter and the wood *(above)*; gently lower and lift the splinter to work the glue into the gap. Then, press the splinter into place and wipe up any extruded glue with a damp cloth. Secure the splinter *(step 3)* until the glue cures.

2 **Removing and gluing a splinter.** Using a straightedge as a guide, score repeated cuts across the attached end of the splinter with a utility knife *(above)* to sever it from the wood. Lift out the splinter and use a toothbrush dampened with mineral spirits to clean it and the opening in the wood. Apply wood glue to the back of the splinter and the opening in the wood, then press the splinter into place. Wipe up any extruded glue with a damp cloth.

3 **Securing the splinter.** To hold in a splinter from the side of a board or tile, wedge metal washers between the splinter and the adjacent board or tile *(above)*. To hold down a splinter in the top of a board or tile, lay a small piece of waxed paper over the splinter; then, position a disposable stick on the waxed paper in line with the splinter and place a heavy weight on it. Allow the glue to cure; if necessary, spot-refinish the surface *(page 19)*.

SECURING FLOORBOARDS

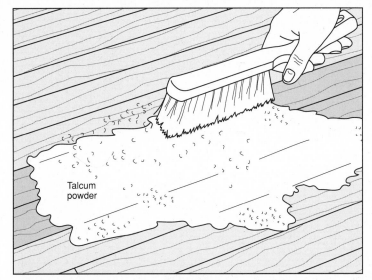

Lubricating a floorboard joint. If the joint between two floor-boards is springy, secure the floorboards *(steps below)*; if the joint only squeaks, lubricate it. Sprinkle talcum powder along the floorboards and use a whisk broom to brush the powder into the joint between them *(above)*; alternately, pour liquid buffing wax into the joint. Lay a drop-cloth on the floor to cover the floorboards, then walk back and forth on it along the joint until the squeaking stops. Remove the dropcloth and use a damp cloth to wipe the talcum powder or wax off the floorboards; let any wax residue dry, then buff it with a soft cloth. If the squeak continues, wedge the joint *(step right)*.

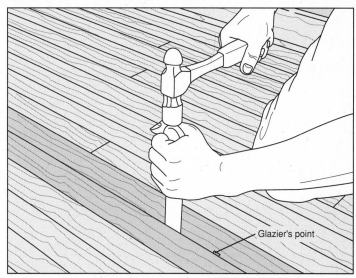

Wedging a floorboard joint. If lubricating a joint between two floorboards does not silence a squeak, try wedging the joint with glazier's points. Starting at one end, use a ball-peen hammer to drive a glazier's point into the joint every 4 inches along it; drive in the glazier's points until they are almost flush with the surface, then use an old stiff putty knife with the hammer to set the top of each glazier's point just below the surface *(above)*. Or, follow the same procedure to wedge the joint with 1-inch brads; drive in each brad until it is about 1/8 inch above the surface, then use a nail set to set its head. If the squeak continues, try securing the floorboards *(steps below)*.

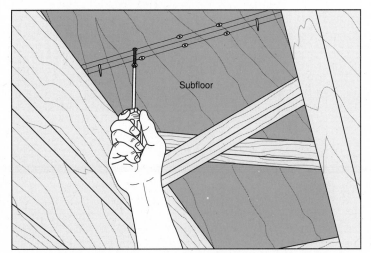

Securing floorboards from below. If there is no access to the bottom of the floor, secure the floorboards from above *(step right)*. Otherwise, work first from above with an electric drill to bore a pilot hole for a 2 1/2-inch finishing nail into the joint at each end of the springy section, then drive a nail into each hole flush with the surface. Working from below, measure the length of a protruding nail tip and subtract it from the nail length to find the floor thickness. To secure the floorboards, use No. 8 wood screws 1/2 inch shorter than the floor thickness. Mark a line between the protruding nails; then, mark a position line parallel to the line 1/2 inch from each side of it. Use the drill to bore a hole for countersinking a wood screw every 4 inches along each position line; wrap masking tape around the bit to mark the drilling depth. Drive a screw into each hole *(above)* and remove the protruding nails.

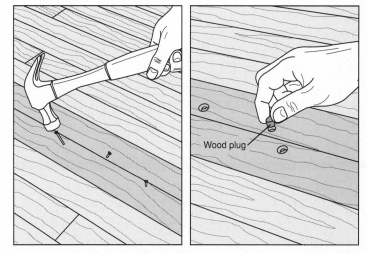

Securing floorboards from above. If there is access to the bottom of the floor, secure the floorboards from below *(step left)*. Otherwise, use an electric drill to bore a pilot hole for a 2 1/2-inch finishing nail every 3 inches along the springy joint, alternating between the floor-boards on each side of it at opposite 45-degree angles; wrap masking tape around the bit to mark the drilling depth. Drive a nail into each hole *(above, left)*, then set the nails heads using a nail set and cover them with a wax stick of a color that matches the wood. Or, bore a hole for a 2-inch No. 8 wood screw and a wood plug every 4 inches along the springy joint, alternating between the floorboards on each side of it. Drive in the screws, then fit a plug into each hole *(above, right)*, coating it and the hole with wood glue. Wipe up extruded glue with a damp cloth. Spot-refinish the surface *(page 19)*.

REPLACING A FLOORBOARD

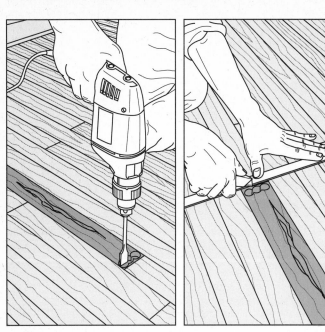

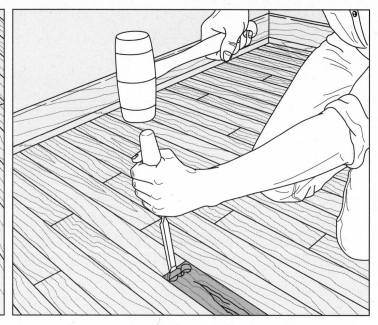

1 **Cutting the floorboard ends.** Remove any shoe molding in the way *(page 133)*. Mark cutting lines at least 12 inches apart across the floorboard, each line at least 1 inch from the end of the damaged section; if the end of the damaged section is within 16 inches of the end of the floorboard, use the end of the floorboard as the line. Wearing safety goggles, use an electric drill fitted with a 1/2-inch spade bit to bore a series of holes for a cutout across each end of the damaged section through the floorboard to the subfloor *(above, left)*. Use a

straightedge and a utility knife to score 1/8 inch deep across the floorboard at each end of the damaged section *(above, center)*. To finish the cutouts, use a wood chisel and a mallet. Make a series of cuts along each scored line, holding the chisel with its cutting edge on the line and its bevel facing the waste side, and striking the handle using the mallet *(above, right)*. Clear the waste wood out of the cutout as you go. Then, use the tip of the chisel to dig out any exposed tongue of the damaged board still lodged in the groove of an adjoining board.

2 **Removing the floorboard.** Cut a strip 1-inch wide out of the damaged floorboard and remove it in pieces. To cut the strip, use a wood chisel and a mallet to make two parallel cuts lengthwise along the center of the board from one cutout to the other cutout *(left)*. Use a pry bar to pry the strip out of the floorboard, then pry out the piece remaining on each side: the nailed tongue of one piece from the groove in the floorboard adjacent to it; the groove of the other piece off the tongue of the floorboard adjacent to it. Pry the pieces out gently to avoid damaging or lifting the adjacent floorboards. When you have removed the pieces of the damaged floorboard, inspect the exposed groove of the floorboard adjacent to the opening; if necessary, use the tip of the chisel to remove any tongue fragments lodged in it. Vacuum dust and debris out of the opening.

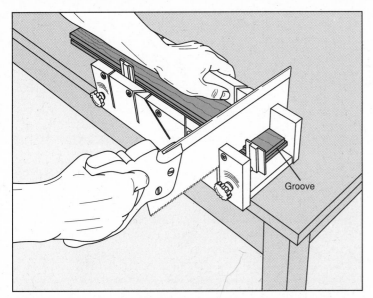

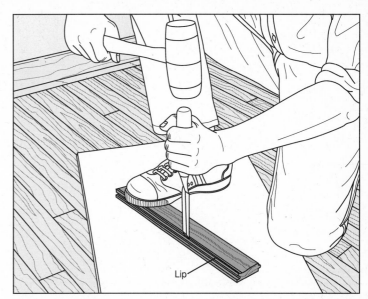

3 **Cutting a replacement floorboard.** Purchase an identical replacement floorboard at a building supply center. Measure the length of the opening in the floor, then mark the new floorboard and cut it to length using a backsaw and a miter box *(above)*; do not include any groove or tongue at the end of it. If you are installing the new board between two floorboards, trim it *(step 4)*. If you are installing the new board between a floorboard and a wall edge, cut it to width using the width of an adjacent floorboard along the wall edge as a guide, then install it *(step 5)*.

4 **Trimming the replacement floorboard.** To trim a replacement floorboard, cut the bottom lip off its groove. Lay the board face-down on a sturdy sheet of scrap wood. Use a utility knife and a straightedge to score the back of the board along the inside edge of the groove. Wearing safety goggles, start at one end of the board and make a series of shallow cuts at 1-inch intervals along the scored line using a wood chisel and a mallet *(above)*; then, reposition the chisel at the starting end of the line and make a series of deep cuts between the shallow cuts to split the lip off the board. Use a utility knife to pare off any splinters that protrude from the chiseled edge.

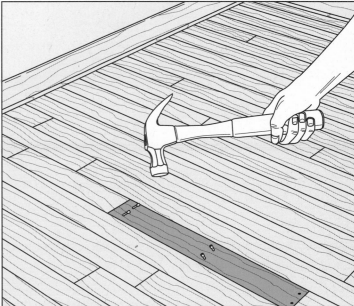

5 **Installing the replacement floorboard.** To install a replacement board in an opening between two floorboards, angle it into the opening, pushing its tongue into the exposed groove of the floorboard adjacent to the opening; then, use a a wood block and a mallet to tap it into place *(above, left)*. To install a replacement board in an opening between a floorboard and a wall edge, angle it into the opening from the wall side, pushing its tongue or groove into place; then, tap it flush with the adjacent floorboards using a wood block and a mallet. To fasten the board, nail it to the subfloor with 2 1/2-inch spiral finishing nails. Wearing safety goggles, use an electric drill to bore pilot holes for the nails at opposite 45-degree angles every 8 inches along the board 1/2 inch from each edge of it; wrap masking tape around the bit to mark the drilling depth. Drive the nails into the holes *(above, right)* and set the nail heads using a nail set; for a board at a wall edge, first wedge a wood block between it and the wall edge to keep it snug against the adjacent floorboards. Cover the nails heads with a wax stick of a color that matches the wood. Spot-refinish the surface *(page 19)*.

REPLACING A STRIP WOOD FLOOR SECTION

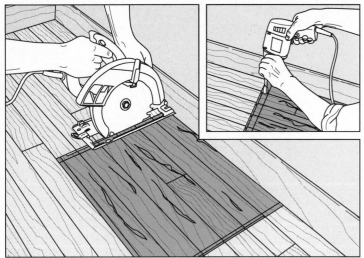

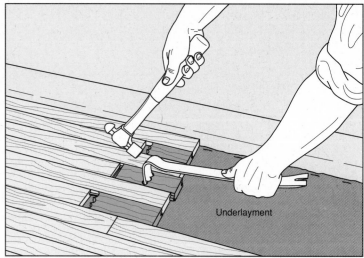

1 **Removing a section of floorboards.** Remove any shoe molding in the way *(page 133)*. Mark cutting lines at least 12 inches apart across the floorboards, each line at least 1 inch from the end of the damaged section; mark another cutting line at each end of the damaged section parallel to the first 1/2 inch farther from it. Set the blade depth of a circular saw equal to the floorboard thickness—usually 3/4 inch. Wearing safety goggles, use the circular saw to make a plunge cut *(page 131)* along each cutting line *(above, left)*. Use an electric drill fitted with a 1/2-inch spade bit to bore a series of holes for a cutout across the floorboards between each pair of cut lines *(inset)*. Finish each cutout by using a wood chisel and a mallet to clear the waste wood left between the cut lines; use the chisel tip to dig out the exposed tongue of any damaged board still lodged in the groove of an undamaged adjoining board. To remove the damaged section of

section of boards, start with the board that has its tongue fitted into an undamaged adjoining floorboard or exposed at a wall edge; remove it as you would to replace any single floorboard *(page 26)*. Working board by board across the damaged section, use a pry bar to pry out each damaged section of the other boards. Remove any ends of the boards along the opening less than 16 inches long, then stagger the ends of the remaining boards by removing a 6-inch end section of every second board. To remove an end section, use an electric drill fitted with a 1/2-inch spade bit to bore a series of holes to the subfloor across it; then, use a pry bar and a ball-peen hammer to knock it out *(above, right)*. Vacuum dust and debris out of the opening. If necessary, use a utility knife to cut out any damaged underlayment. To replace the underlayment, cut a patch of 15-pound asphalt-saturated building paper equal to the size of the damaged area and staple it in place to the subfloor.

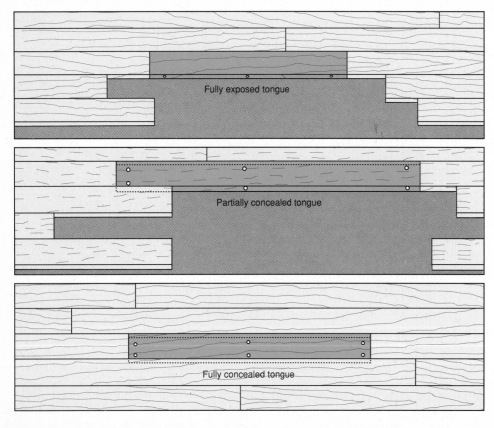

Fully exposed tongue

Partially concealed tongue

Fully concealed tongue

2 **Preparing to install a replacement section.** Purchase identical replacement floorboards at a building supply center. Inspect the opening in the floor to determine the preparations required for the replacement boards. If a replacement board will be installed with the full length of its tongue exposed *(left, top)*, cut it to length *(page 27)*. If a replacement board will be installed with part of its tongue concealed *(left, center)* or all of its tongue concealed *(left, bottom)*, cut it to length and trim it *(page 27)*. If a replacement board will be installed along a wall edge, also cut it to width, if necessary. To install the replacement boards, start with the board that can be installed with its tongue fully exposed or only partially concealed along one side of the opening.

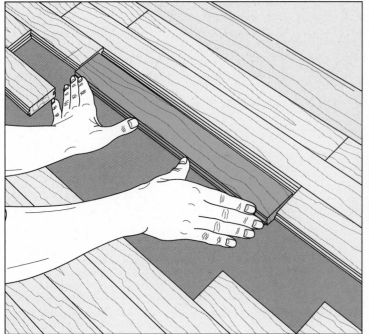

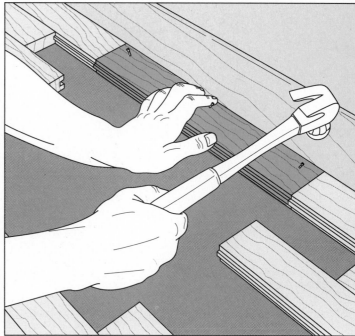

3 **Installing the first and middle boards.** To install the first board against an undamaged adjoining floorboard, fit it into the opening, pushing its groove onto the tongue of the adjoining floorboard *(above, left)*. Wearing safety goggles, use an electric drill to bore pilot holes for 2 1/4-inch hardwood flooring nails every 8 inches along the board at a 45-degree angle through its exposed tongue; start 1/2 inch from the end of it. If the tongue of the board is partially concealed, also bore pilot holes for 2 1/2-inch spiral finishing nails along it at opposite 45-degree angles through its face 1/2 inch from its groove and its concealed tongue. Drive in the nails and use a nail set to set the nail heads. To install the first board at a wall edge, fit it into the opening, lining it up with the board at each end of it; then, follow the same procedures to bore pilot holes and nail through its face 1/2 inch from the wall *(above, right)* and its exposed tongue. To install the middle boards, work board by board across the opening the same way; then, install the last board *(step 4)*.

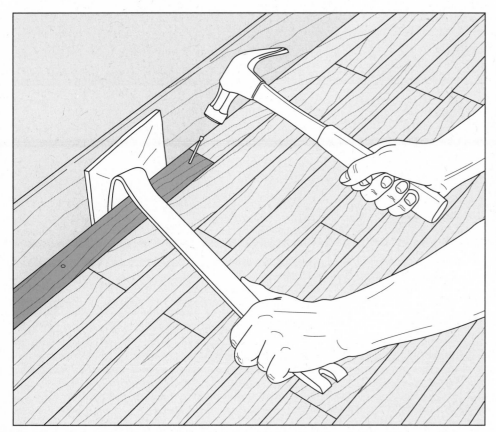

4 **Installing the last board.** To install the last replacement board in an opening between two floorboards, install it as you would a single board *(page 27)*. To install the last replacement board in an opening at a wall edge, fit it into the opening, then use a wood block and a mallet to tap it flush with the surrounding floorboards. Wearing safety goggles, use an electric drill to bore pilot holes for 2 1/2-inch spiral finishing nails at opposite 45-degree angles every 8 inches along the board 1/2 from the edge of it along the wall; start 1/2 inch from the end of it. Wedge a wood block and a pry bar between the board and the wall to hold the board in place, then drive in the nails *(left)* and use a nail set to set the nail heads. Cover the nail heads with a wax stick of a color that matches the wood. Spot-refinish the surface *(page 19)*, then reinstall any shoe molding you removed.

REPLACING A STRIP WOOD FLOOR

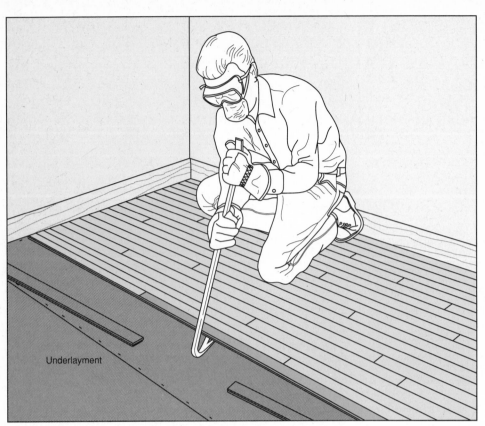

Underlayment

1 Removing the old floorboards. Clear the floor of obstructions and remove the shoe moldings from the wall edges *(page 133)*. Pry off any door threshold and remove any shims from under it; if a doorstop prevents removing a threshold, use a backsaw to cut it 6 inches above the threshold, then pry off the section. To remove the floorboards, work row by row starting with the boards that have their tongues exposed along a wall edge. Set the blade depth of a circular saw equal to the floorboard thickness—usually 3/4 inch; wearing safety goggles and a dust mask, make a plunge cut *(page 131)* along the center of the row. To remove the row, insert a pry bar into the cut at one end of it and work along the cut, prying out the board halves closest to the wall. Then, pry out the board halves adjoining the second row. Continue working board by board along each other row, fitting the pry bar under a board to pry it out *(left)*. Before you remove the last row of boards, mark a position point on the baseboard at each end of it for a starter row of replacement boards. Then, pry out the last row and remove the underlayment. Pull any protruding nail out of the subfloor and drive in a 2 1/2-inch ring nail beside the nail hole.

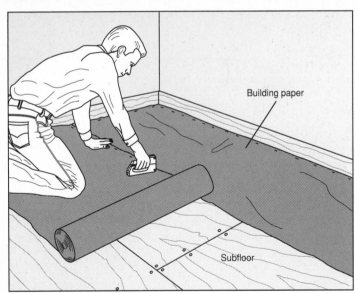

Building paper

Subfloor

2 Installing underlayment. Purchase replacement floorboards and 15-pound asphalt-saturated building paper for underlayment at a building supply center. To determine the nailing pattern for the new floorboards, use an electric drill fitted wih a 1/2-inch spade bit to bore through the subfloor, then measure its thickness. If the subfloor is more than 3/4 inch thick, nail the boards at 8-inch intervals; otherwise, also nail the boards of the starter row at joists. If necessary, mark joist locations on the baseboards at the ends of each row of subfloor nails. Lay overlapping lengths of the building paper flat on the subfloor for underlayment and staple it in place to the subfloor along each overlap *(above)* and wall edge. Mark a position line for a starter row of boards by snapping a chalk line across the floor between the position points marked on the baseboards *(step 1)*.

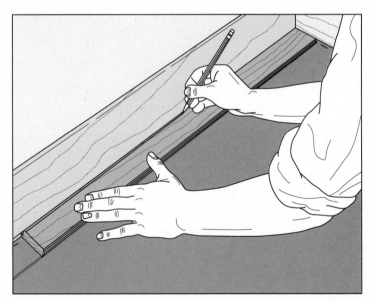

3 Installing the starter row. Lay floorboards end to end along the position line with their groove against the wall; ensure there is no joint in any doorway. If necessary, fit a board at the end of the row *(step 5)*. If a board extends under the baseboard, use the edge of it to mark a cutting line along the board *(above)*, then cut the board to width. Wearing safety goggles, use an electric drill to bore pilot holes for 2 1/2-inch spiral finishing nails at a 45-degree angle through the face of each board 1/2 inch from the wall edge; starting 1/2 inch from one end, drill every 8 inches and at each joist along the boards. Then, bore pilot holes for 2 1/4-inch hardwood flooring nails along the tongue of each board at the same interval. Drive in the nails and use a nail set to set the nail heads.

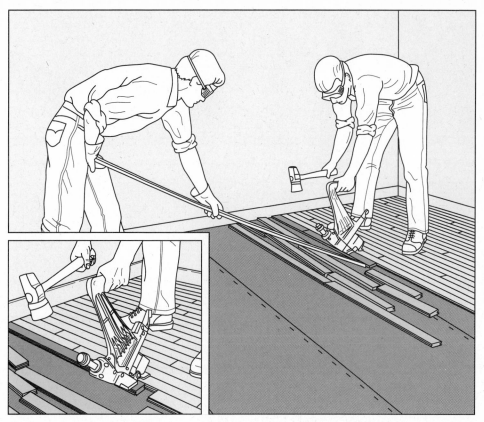

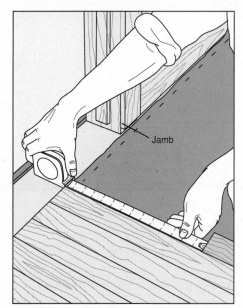

4 **Installing the floor.** Lay out and install floorboards row by row, starting with the row adjoining the starter row. Lay out a row of boards end to end with their grooves facing the tongues of the previous row; ensure there is no joint in the row less than 6 inches from a joint in the previous row. Install the boards of a row one by one, using a wood block and a mallet to tap them tightly onto the tongue of the previous row; if necessary, fit a board at the end of the row (step 5). Then, fasten each board of the row every 8 inches and 1/2 inch from each end with 2 1/4-inch hardwood flooring nails. For the first few rows, wear safety goggles and use an electric drill to bore pilot holes at a 45-degree angle through the tongue of each board; then, drive in the nails and use a nail set to set the nail heads. For the rows across the middle of the floor, use a strip floor nailer and mallet—available at a tool rental agency. Position the nailer shoe on the board tongue and strike the plunger with the mallet (inset); if necessary have a helper keep the board in position using another board (left). Fasten a few rows of boards up to the last row as you did the first few rows, then install the last row (step 6).

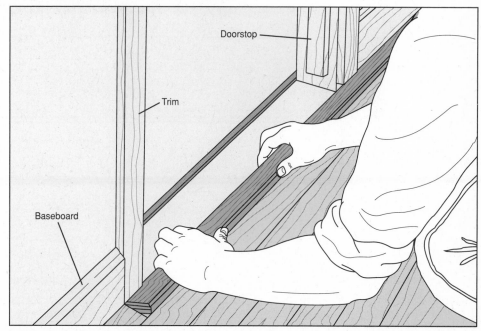

5 **Fitting a floorboard at a row end.** Measure the length of the opening at the row end. For an opening at a door threshold or trim, mark a line between the outside edges of the door jambs; then, measure between the line and the end of the last board in the row (above). For an opening at a wall, measure between the end of the last board in the row and the baseboard edge. Cut a board to length and install it as you would the others in the row (step 4).

6 **Installing the last row.** Lay out the last row of boards along the wall; ensure there is no joint at any doorway. Starting at one end of the row, fit the boards one by one. Measure the opening for a board between the previous row and the baseboard; if necessary, cut the board to width. Trim the board (page 27) and set it into the opening; at a door, angle it under the trim (above). Fasten each board of the row with 2 1/2-inch spiral finishing nails. Wearing safety goggles, use an electric drill to bore pilot holes for the nails at opposite 45-degree angles every 8 inches along the boards 1/2 inch from each edge of them. Drive in the nails and use a nail set to set the nail heads.

REPLACING A STRIP WOOD FLOOR (continued)

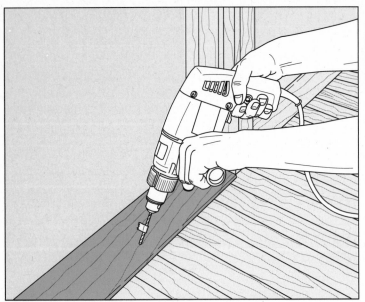

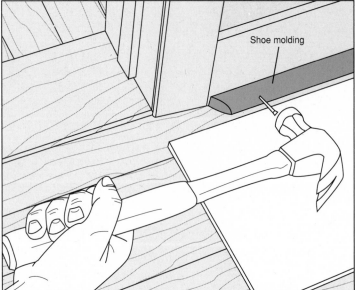

Shoe molding

7 **Finishing the floor installation.** Reinstall any threshold removed from a doorway, repositioning any shims under it. To fasten the threshold, nail it with 2 1/2-inch spiral finishing nails. Wearing safety goggles, use an electric drill to bore pilot holes for the nails at a 45-degree angle into the threshold *(above, left)*; wrap masking tape around the bit to mark the drilling depth. Drive in the nails and use a nail set to set the nail heads. If necessary, replace any section of a doorstop you cut out to remove the threshold, nailing it to the jamb

with 1-inch brads. Cover the nail heads and fill any holes in the floor, threshold and doorstop using a wax stick of a color that matches the wood. Sand the floor surface *(page 22)*, then smooth it and apply a finish *(page 20)*; if the flooring is pre-finished, clean and protect it following the manufacturer's instructions. Also sand and refinish any damaged surface of a threshold or doorstop. Reinstall or replace the shoe moldings you removed from the wall edges *(page 133)*, protecting the floor finish as you drive in nails *(above, right)*.

SECURING PARQUET TILES

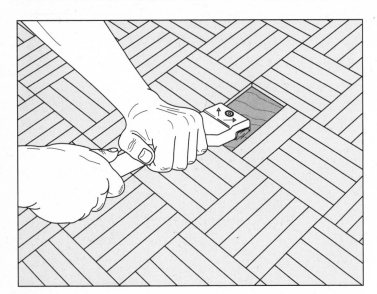

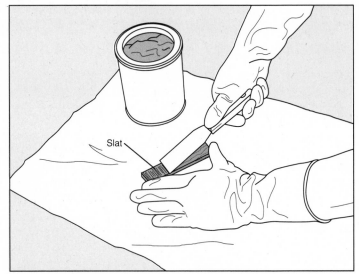

Slat

1 **Removing a tile or slat.** If a parquet tile is loose, fit the tip of a pry bar into the joint along it and try to pry it out; for a loose slat in an alternating-block parquet tile, as shown, pry out the slat. To remove an adjacent tile or slat, use a wood chisel and a mallet; fit the chisel tip bevel-side down under its exposed edge and strike the chisel handle with the mallet. If a tile is tongue-and-groove and you cannot pry it out from the tiles adjoining it, replace the tile *(page 33)*. After prying out a tile or slat, use a paint scraper to scrape old adhesive out of the opening *(above)* and off the tile.

2 **Resecuring the tile or slat.** Purchase a parquet tile adhesive recommended for the tile at a building supply center and follow the manufacturer's instructions to apply it. Wearing rubber gloves, use a putty knife to coat the back of the tile or slat *(above)* evenly with the adhesive. Fit the tile or slat into the opening, then use a wood block and a mallet to tap it into place; immediately remove any adhesive that oozes up around it using a wooden stick. Use the same procedure to resecure any other tile or slat removed. If necessary, set a weight on each tile or slat reinstalled until the adhesive cures.

REPLACING PARQUET TILES

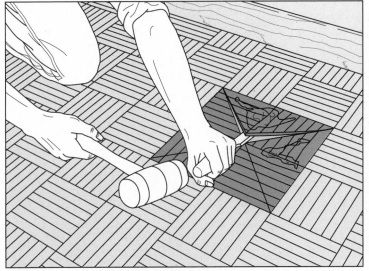

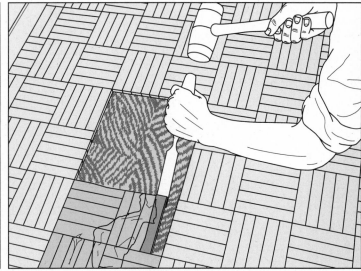

1 Removing parquet tile. Remove any shoe molding in the way *(page 133)*. Wearing safety goggles, use an electric drill fitted with a 3/4-inch spade bit to bore a series of holes through the center of the damaged section, weakening the tile or section of tiles. Or, mark cutting lines diagonally across the damaged setion between opposite corners of it, then make a plunge cut *(page 131)* along each line using a circular saw; set the blade depth equal to the tile thickness—usually 3/8 inch. Then, use a wood chisel and a mallet to chip out the damaged section. Holding the chisel bevel-side down with its tip in a hole or the

cut, strike the handle gently with the mallet to drive the tip under the damaged section *(above, left)*. Reposition the chisel and repeat, chiseling from the center in turn to the edges of the damaged section; work carefully to avoid marring any undamaged adjacent tiles. Continue the same way with the chisel and mallet, chipping out the damaged section piece by piece; if possible, chisel lengthwise under the slats *(above, right)*. Use a paint scraper to scrape adhesive out of the opening, then clean loosened particles and dust out of it using a vacuum.

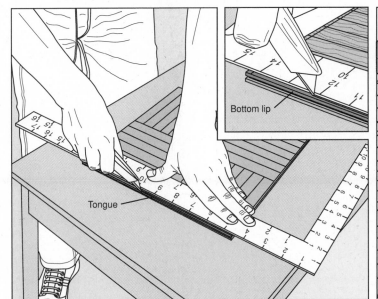

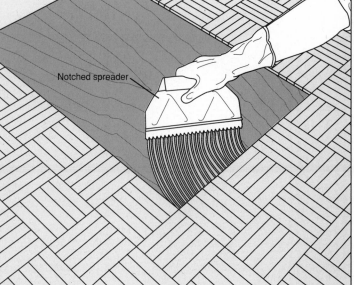

2 Preparing to install parquet tile. Purchase identical replacement tiles at a building supply center; for other than self-adhesive tiles, also a recommended tile adhesive. Lay out the replacement section of tiles in the opening, matching any pattern of the adjacent tiles. For tongue-and-groove tiles, trim as many edges off each tile as necessary to fit it snugly. To trim an edge of an alternating-block tile, remove the tongue and the bottom lip of the groove. Lay the tile face-up and score repeatedly along the tongue using a utility knife and a straightedge *(above, left)*, severing it. Then, turn the tile face-down and use the utility knife and straightedge to score along the bottom lip of the groove *(inset)*, severing it. To trim an edge of another

type of tile, trim off the tongue or the bottom lip of the groove the same way. If necessary, cut any tile to fit at a wall edge or obstruction *(step 3)*. Remove the replacement section of tiles from the opening, noting their positions. If you are using self-adhesive tiles, install them *(step 4)*. Otherwise, prepare enough of the adhesive for the opening; wear rubber gloves and follow the manufacturer's instructions. Using a notched spreader, coat the opening evenly with the adhesive *(above, right)*, leaving visible ridges in it; avoid getting adhesive on the surface of any tile adjacent to the opening, wiping it off quickly with a damp cloth. Let the adhesive set for the time specified by the manufacturer, then install the replacement section of tiles *(step 4)*.

REPLACING PARQUET TILES (continued)

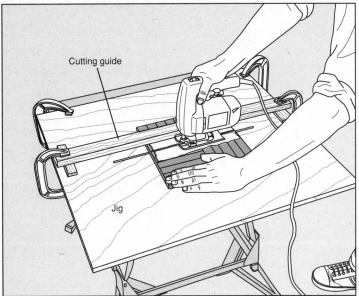

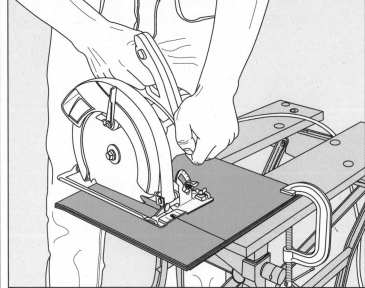

3 **Cutting parquet tile.** To cut a tile to fit at an obstruction or a wall edge, measure the opening and mark the dimensions onto the back of the tile. To cut an alternating-block tile, make a cutting jig using a section of plywood. Clamp the plywood high enough off a work surface to make a straight interior cut about 18 inches long in the center of it with a saber saw and a cutting guide. Set the tile face-down on the jig, aligning the marked line on it with the cut in the jig; place a strip of masking tape along each side of the marked line to keep the slats together as they are cut. Clamp a 1-by-2 across the tile to use as a cutting guide, then cut along the marked line with the saber saw *(above, left)*. To cut another type of tile, clamp it face-down on a work surface, the marked line on it overhanging the edge slightly. Then, cut along the marked line with a circular saw *(above, right)* or a saber saw; if necessary, use a 1-by-2 as a cutting guide.

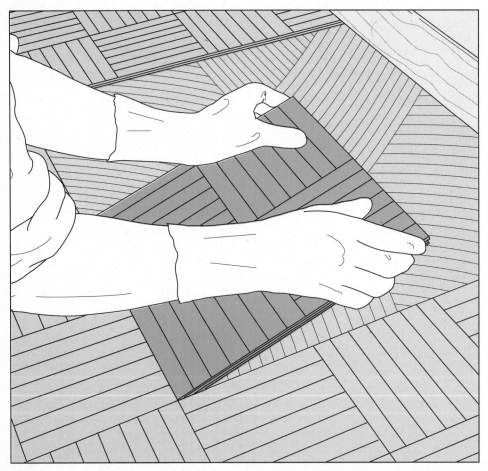

4 **Installing parquet tile.** To install the replacement section of tiles, work tile by tile from one side of the opening to the other; work toward any obstruction or wall edge. For self-adhesive tiles, peel the paper backing off each tile as you install it; for tiles installed with adhesive, wear rubber gloves. Install each untrimmed tile first, fitting any tongue and groove along an edge of it into place *(left)*, then setting it down on the adhesive and fitting it with any tongue and groove along an edge of an adjacent tile; if necessary, tap it into place with a mallet, cushioning the blows with a wood block. Avoid getting adhesive on the surface of any tile, wiping it off quickly with a damp cloth. Install each trimmed tile the same way, fitting any untrimmed edge of it into place first. If necessary, set a weight on the replacement section of tiles until the adhesive cures. Or, rent a tile roller at a tool rental agency and roll it back and forth across the replacement section of tiles; make two passes at a 90-degree angle to each other. Spot-refinish the surface *(page 19)*, then re-install any shoe molding you removed.

REPLACING A PARQUET TILE FLOOR

First chalk line

1 Preparing to install a tile floor.
Remove the shoe moldings from the wall edges *(page 133)*. Pry off any door threshold. Starting at a wall edge and working row by row across the room, remove the old tiles *(page 33)*. Purchase replacement tiles at a building supply center; for other than self-adhesive tiles, also a recommended tile adhesive. Rent a tile roller at a tool rental agency. To test-fit the tiles, snap two perpendicular chalk lines that intersect at the center of the subfloor *(page 138)*, dividing it into quadrants. Lay a tile in one quadrant at the marked corner, then lay out a row of tiles along each quadrant line between the tile and the edge of the subfloor. If the gap between the end of a row and the edge of the subfloor is less than half a tile, snap an adjusted chalk line perpendicular to the row half a tile farther from the edge of the subfloor than the first chalk line *(left)*.

Kneeling board

2 Installing a tile floor. Install the tiles of the flooring one quadrant at a time. For tiles that require adhesive, wear rubber gloves and prepare enough of the adhesive for one quadrant following the manufacturer's instructions. Using a notched spreader, work from the wall corner of the quadrant back to the center of the room to spread adhesive on the subfloor; avoid covering the chalk lines. To install the tiles, work from the center of the room back to the wall edges of the quadrant; if you are using self-adhesive tiles, peel the paper backing off each tile as you install it. Fit a tile into the angle formed by the chalk lines, carefully aligning it with the lines; then, press down firmly to bond it to the subfloor. Using the same procedure, fit a short row of a few tiles along each chalk line, working from the center tile toward the room edges. Then, using a kneeling board and working from one row to the other, fit tiles into the angle between the rows *(left, top)*. Continue, alternately extending the rows along the chalk lines, then filling the angle between the rows, until you reach the wall edges of the quadrant; if necessary, cut tiles to fit at the wall edges *(page 34)*. To seat the tiles, use the tile roller, rolling it back and forth across them *(left, bottom)*; make two passes at a 90-degree angle to each other. Use the same procedure to install the tiles in the other quadrants. Finish the floor installation as you would for a strip wood floor *(page 32)*.

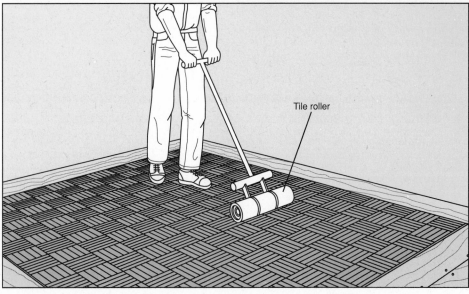

Tile roller

RESILIENT FLOORING

Durable and extremely water- and stain-resistant, resilient floor-ing is an ideal choice for high-traffic rooms of the home such as the kitchen or playroom. Two popular types of resilient flooring are shown below: tiles and sheet flooring; both types are installed on an underlayment of interior-grade plywood nailed to the sub-floor. While resilient tiles are fully adhered to the underlayment, resilient sheet flooring can be fully adhered to it, perimeter-adhered to it (held down at edges, seams and openings) or loose-laid on it (held down only by shoe moldings or wall bases). To identify sheet flooring that is fully adhered, try to gently lift it with a wet plunger. If the flooring does not lift, it is likely fully adhered. To distinguish sheet flooring that is perimeter-adhered or loose-laid, remove a shoe molding *(page 133)* or wall base *(page 40)*. If the flooring is stapled or glued at the edges, it is perimeter-adhered; otherwise, it is loose-laid.

Consult the Troubleshooting Guide *(page 37)* to diagnose and repair the resilient flooring of your home. Undertake the neces-sary repairs as soon as a problem is apparent, both to maintain the beauty and life of the flooring and to prevent any damage to the floor understructure. Clean the flooring regularly *(page 38)* to prevent dirt and grit from being ground into the surface; if rec-ommended by the flooring manufacturer, polish the flooring rou-tinely *(page 39)* to protect the surface. Minor damage to resilient tiles can be easily repaired. Loose tiles can be secured *(page 42)*; if a tile is of solid vinyl, you can patch a burn mark or gouge in the surface *(page 39)*. For other problems and with other types of tiles, you may have to replace a tile or section of tiles *(page 42)*. For resilient sheet flooring, you can repair a blister or a lifted edge *(page 45)*; if the surface is damaged, replace the sheet floor-ing section *(page 46)*.

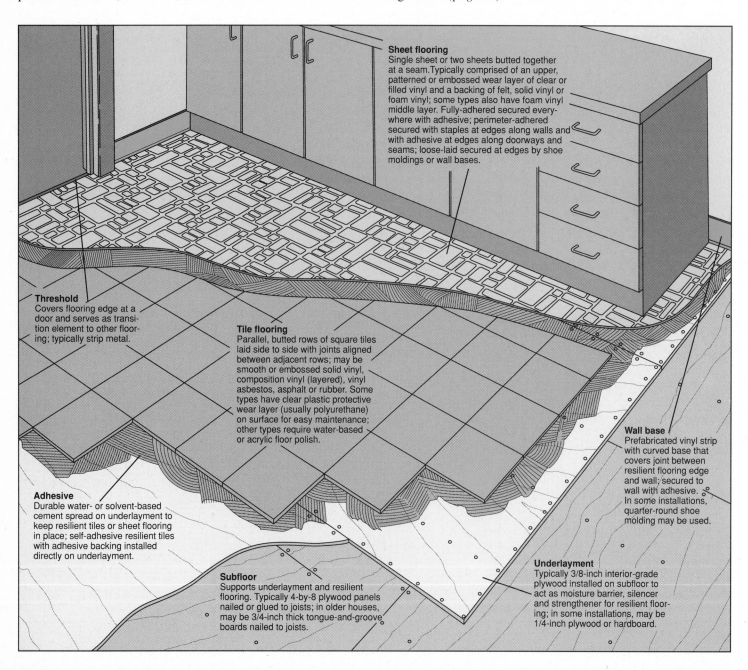

Sheet flooring
Single sheet or two sheets butted together at a seam. Typically comprised of an upper, patterned or embossed wear layer of clear or filled vinyl and a backing of felt, solid vinyl or foam vinyl; some types also have foam vinyl middle layer. Fully-adhered secured every-where with adhesive; perimeter-adhered secured with staples at edges along walls and with adhesive at edges along doorways and seams; loose-laid secured at edges by shoe moldings or wall bases.

Threshold
Covers flooring edge at a door and serves as transi-tion element to other floor-ing; typically strip metal.

Tile flooring
Parallel, butted rows of square tiles laid side to side with joints aligned between adjacent rows; may be smooth or embossed solid vinyl, composition vinyl (layered), vinyl asbestos, asphalt or rubber. Some types have clear plastic protective wear layer (usually polyurethane) on surface for easy maintenance; other types require water-based or acrylic floor polish.

Wall base
Prefabricated vinyl strip with curved base that covers joint between resilient flooring edge and wall; secured to wall with adhesive. In some installations, quarter-round shoe molding may be used.

Adhesive
Durable water- or solvent-based cement spread on underlayment to keep resilient tiles or sheet flooring in place; self-adhesive resilient tiles with adhesive backing installed directly on underlayment.

Subfloor
Supports underlayment and resilient flooring. Typically 4-by-8 plywood panels nailed or glued to joists; in older houses, may be 3/4-inch thick tongue-and-groove boards nailed to joists.

Underlayment
Typically 3/8-inch interior-grade plywood installed on subfloor to act as moisture barrier, silencer and strengthener for resilient floor-ing; in some installations, may be 1/4-inch plywood or hardboard.

If you have not saved any of the original flooring material, matching it can be a problem; you are likely to have to replace the tile floor *(page 44)* or the sheet flooring *(page 47)*. When you are removing any resilient flooring, keep in mind that the flooring and adhesive sold prior to the 1980s may contain asbestos; while harmless when installed, these materials can release hazardous fibers into the air when they are sanded or cut with power tools. Unless your resilient flooring was installed after 1986, you should assume that it may contain asbestos; protect yourself from inhaling or ingesting any fibers by removing any tile in one piece and never sanding or cutting underlayment coated with cut-back asphalt adhesive *(page 138)*; if necessary, replace the entire flooring and underlayment *(page 41)*. Consult your local department of environmental protection or public health for guidelines on the safe disposal of hazardous flooring materials.

The materials and supplies necessary for repairs to resilient flooring are readily available at a building supply center or flooring dealer. Most repairs to resilient flooring can be made with standard household tools and equipment: a utility knife, a pry bar, a hammer, a putty knife, a notched spreader, a hand roller and a heat gun. To replace an entire floor of resilient tiles or sheet flooring, you will need a tile roller—available at a tool rental agency. Consult Tools & Techniques *(page 122)* for instructions on using many of the tools required. Always wear the safety gear recommended for the job: rubber gloves when working with chemical cleaners or an adhesive; work gloves to protect your hands from cuts and scratches; and safety goggles when using a circular saw or when there is a risk of eye injury. Before starting any repair, refer to the Emergency Guide *(page 8)*; work carefully, observing all safety precautions.

TROUBLESHOOTING GUIDE continued ►

SYMPTOM	POSSIBLE CAUSE	PROCEDURE
TILES		
Flooring dirty or dull	Everyday wear and tear	Clean tile flooring (p. 38) □○
	Polish worn; polish build-up	Repolish tile flooring (p. 39) □○
Flooring surface stained or discolored	Everyday wear and tear; accidental spill; black spots of mildew due to high humidity	Clean tile flooring (p. 38) □○; wipe up spills immediately and ventilate room to reduce humidity
	Polish build-up	Repolish tile flooring (p. 39) □○
	Finish worn	Replace section of tiles (p. 42) ▣● or tile floor (p. 44) ▣●▲
Flooring surface cracked, gouged or burned	Accidental blow or impact; dropped cigarette	Repair vinyl tile surface (p. 39) □○; replace other tile (p. 42) □●
Flooring surface slippery	Polish build-up	Repolish tile flooring (p. 39) □○
Flooring surface worn	Everyday wear and tear; lack of regular maintenance	Replace section of tiles (p. 42) ▣● or tile floor (p. 44) ▣●▲; maintain tile flooring (p. 38) □○
Tile squeaks; loose, springy or lifting	Everyday wear and tear; adhesive failure or moisture damage	Secure tile (p. 42) □○ or replace tile (p. 42) □●; wipe up spills immediately and ventilate room to reduce humidity
	Underlayment damaged	Replace underlayment section (p. 40) ▣● or entire underlayment (p. 41) ■●
	Floor understructure faulty	Troubleshoot floor understructure (p. 62)
Tile or tiles split or torn	Accidental blow; house settlement with age	Replace section of tiles (p. 42) ▣● or tile floor (p. 44) ▣●▲
Flooring sagging; bulged or humped	Tiles damaged	Replace section of tiles (p. 42) ▣● or tile floor (p. 44) ▣●▲
	Underlayment damaged	Replace underlayment section (p. 40) ▣● or entire underlayment (p. 41) ■●
	Floor understructure faulty	Troubleshoot floor understructure (p. 62)
Wall base loose or damaged	Everyday wear and tear; accidental blow	Replace wall base section (p. 40) □●
SHEET FLOORING		
Flooring dirty or dull	Everyday wear and tear	Clean sheet flooring (p. 38) □○
	Polish worn; polish build-up	Repolish sheet flooring (p. 39) □○
Flooring surface stained or discolored	Everyday wear and tear; accidental spill; black spots of mildew due to high humidity	Clean sheet flooring (p. 38) □○; wipe up spills immediately and ventilate room to reduce humidity
	Polish build-up	Repolish sheet flooring (p. 39) □○
	Finish worn	Replace sheet flooring section (p. 46) ▣● or entire sheet flooring (p. 47) ▣●▲

DEGREE OF DIFFICULTY: □ Easy ▣ Moderate ■ Complex
ESTIMATED TIME: ○ Less than 1 hour ● 1 to 3 hours ● Over 3 hours   ▲ Special tool required

TROUBLESHOOTING GUIDE (continued)

SYMPTOM	POSSIBLE CAUSE	PROCEDURE
SHEET FLOORING (continued)		
Flooring surface cracked, gouged or burned	Accidental blow or impact; dropped cigarette	Replace sheet flooring section *(p. 46)* ▭◖ or entire sheet flooring *(p. 47)* ▭●▲
Flooring surface slippery	Polish build-up	Repolish sheet flooring *(p. 39)* ▢○
Flooring surface worn	Everyday wear and tear; lack of regular maintenance	Replace sheet flooring section *(p. 46)* ▭◖ or entire sheet flooring *(p. 47)* ▭●▲ ; maintain sheet flooring *(p. 38)* ▢○
Flooring squeaks; loose, springy, lifting or blistering	Everyday wear and tear; adhesive failure or moisture damage	Secure sheet flooring *(p. 45)* ▢○ or replace sheet flooring section *(p. 46)* ▭◖; wipe up spills immediately and ventilate room to reduce humidity
	Underlayment damaged	Replace underlayment section *(p. 40)* ▭◖ or entire underlayment *(p. 41)* ▮●
	Floor understructure faulty	Troubleshoot floor understructure *(p. 62)*
Flooring split or torn	Accidental blow; house settlement with age	Replace sheet flooring section *(p. 46)* ▭◖ or entire sheet flooring *(p. 47)* ▭●▲
Flooring sagging; bulged or humped	Sheet flooring damaged	Replace sheet flooring section *(p. 46)* ▭◖ or entire sheet flooring *(p. 47)* ▭●▲
	Underlayment damaged	Replace underlayment section *(p. 40)* ▭◖ or entire underlayment *(p. 41)* ▮●
	Floor understructure faulty	Troubleshoot floor understructure *(p. 62)*
Wall base loose or damaged	Everyday wear and tear; accidental blow	Replace wall base section *(p. 40)* ▢◖

DEGREE OF DIFFICULTY: ▢ **Easy** ▭ **Moderate** ▮ **Complex**
ESTIMATED TIME: ○ **Less than 1 hour** ◖ **1 to 3 hours** ● **Over 3 hours**   ▲ **Special tool required**

MAINTAINING THE FLOORING

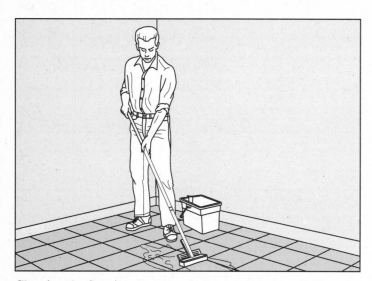

Cleaning the flooring. To remove loose dirt, vacuum the floor. To remove ground-in dirt, damp-mop the floor. Wring out a water-soaked sponge mop until it is almost dry and mop the floor a section at a time; rinse the mop as necessary. For stubborn dirt, mix a commercial floor cleaner with water following the manufacturer's instructions. Use the sponge mop to wet a floor section with the solution; wait a few minutes, then mop it up *(above)*. Repeat with water to rinse the floor a section at a time. To remove a water spot after the floor is dry, rub it with a damp sponge, then dry it with a soft cloth. If the floor is dull after cleaning, use a household floor polisher fitted with felt buffing pads to buff it until it shines; if a polished floor is dull after buffing, repolish it *(page 39)*.

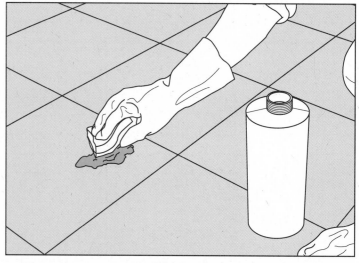

Removing a stain from the flooring. To remove a dried or gummy deposit, lay an ice pack on it until it is brittle; then, use a plastic spatula to scrape off the deposit. For an embedded stain, wear rubber gloves and use a nylon pad moistened with undiluted commercial liquid floor cleaner to gently scrub the stain *(above)*, working from the edge inward. Wipe up the residue with a damp sponge and dry the surface with a soft cloth. For a persistent stain, use a clean cloth moistened with a solution of one part household bleach and 10 parts water to vigorously rub out the stain; alternately, use a clean cloth moistened with lighter fluid. **Caution**: Lighter fluid is flammable; follow all safety precautions on the label. If you cannot remove a stain, replace the stained tile *(page 42)* or sheet flooring section *(page 46)*.

POLISHING THE FLOORING

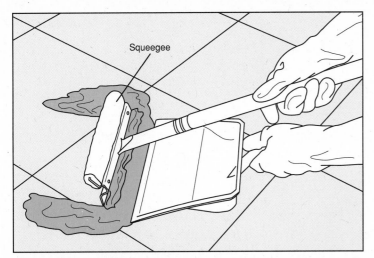

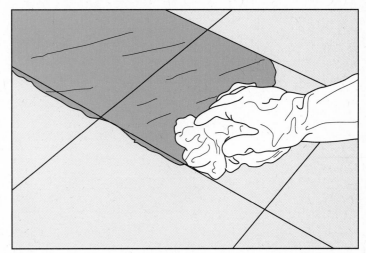

1 **Stripping off the old polish.** Clear the floor and vacuum it. To strip polish off the flooring, work a section 3 feet square at a time using a commercial floor polish remover; follow the manufacturer's instructions. Wearing rubber gloves, pour a small pool of polish remover on the section, then use a sponge mop to spread it. Wait for the polish to soften, then use a stiff-bristled fiber brush to gently scrub it off. Using a squeegee and a dust pan, scrape up the loosened residue *(above)* and dispose of it. To clean the section, wet it using a clean sponge mop soaked in water; then, wring out the mop and mop up the water. Continue section by section until the floor is stripped and clean. Let the floor dry.

2 **Applying a fresh coat of polish.** Vacuum the floor. To apply a coat of polish to the flooring, work a section 3 feet square at a time using a commercial resilient floor polish. Wet a clean cloth with the polish, then wring out any excess. Starting at the edge of a section, wipe a thin coat of polish onto the surface *(above)*; when the cloth begins to apply polish spottily, reload it and continue, smoothing out any unevenness immediately. Continue section by section until the floor is coated, then let the polish dry. For a high-gloss finish, buff the floor. Using a household floor polisher fitted with felt buffing pads, buff the floor section by section until it has a bright and uniform shine; hand-buff any hard-to-reach surface with a clean, soft cloth.

REPAIRING A VINYL TILE SURFACE

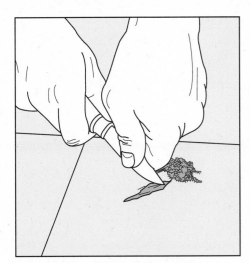

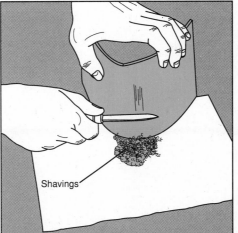

Shavings

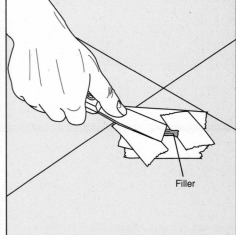

Filler

1 **Preparing to patch the surface.** Remove any discoloration from the damaged surface by scrubbing it with a nylon pad moistened with undiluted commercial liquid floor cleaner; then, dry the area with a clean cloth. If the discoloration does not scrub off, scrape it off using the sharp edge of a knife *(above);* wipe up any scrapings with a damp cloth. Fasten a strip of masking tape along each edge of the damaged surface.

2 **Patching the surface.** Prepare a filler to patch the damaged surface. Find a spare tile or buy a new tile that matches the damaged tile; if necessary, remove a tile *(page 42)* from an inconspicuous location such as a closet. Bending the tile slightly, rest it on a clean piece of cardboard; then, use the sharp edge of a knife to scrape repeatedly across the surface, removing a small quantity of fine shavings *(above, left)*. To make the filler, use a putty knife to mix clear nail polish into the shavings one drop at a time until the mixture is the consistency of thick putty. To patch the surface, use the putty knife to work the filler into the depression, overfilling it slightly *(above, right)*; then, scrape off the excess to level it. Brush a thin coat of nail polish on the wet filler. Let the patch dry, then remove the masking tape. Smooth the patch using fine steel wool, then wipe any particles off it. Brush a final coat of clear nail polish on the patch and let it dry.

REPLACING A WALL BASE SECTION

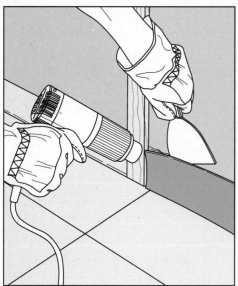

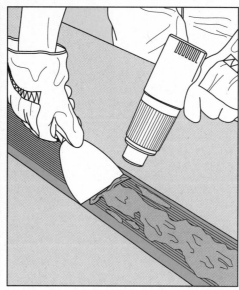

1 **Removing the wall base.** Remove the wall base one section at a time, taking off as many sections as necessary. Wearing work gloves, set a heat gun to its lowest setting. Starting at the end of a section, hold the heat gun nozzle a few inches from the surface and sweep it back and forth over a small area for 15 seconds; move the gun constantly to prevent burning the surface. Work the tip of a putty knife behind the wall base *(above, left)* separating it from the wall. Continue the same way along the wall base until you can pull off the section. Then, use the heat gun to soften any adhesive left on the wall and scrape it off with the putty knife; if the wall base is not damaged, lay it face-down on a work surface and remove the adhesive from it the same way *(above, right)*.

2 **Installing the wall base.** Purchase replacement wall base and adhesive for it at a building supply center. Install the wall base one section at a time. Wearing rubber gloves, use a notched spreader to coat the back of the wall base evenly with the adhesive, applying it to within 1/2 inch of the top edge. Press the section into place on the wall, ensuring its bottom lip rests snugly on the flooring; to bend a section around an outside corner, warm it with a heat gun. Then, run a hand roller back and forth along the section *(above)* to bond it to the wall.

REPLACING AN UNDERLAYMENT SECTION

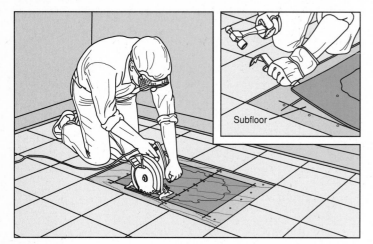

Subfloor

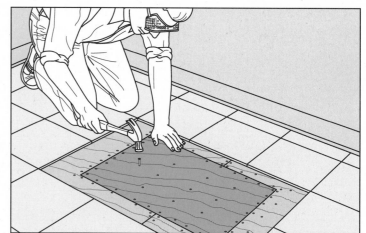

1 **Removing the section.** Remove enough tiles *(page 42)* or sheet flooring *(page 46)* to expose the damaged section of underlayment. If the adhesive on the underlayment is a cut-back asphalt type *(page 138)*, replace the entire underlayment *(page 41)*; otherwise, remove the damaged section. Mark cutting lines around the damaged section, then pull the nails out of it. Prepare to use a circular saw, setting the cutting depth equal to the underlayment thickness—typically 1/4 to 3/8 inch. Wearing safety goggles, make a plunge cut *(page 131)* at the end of one cutting line and cut to the other end of it *(above)*. Cut along the other cutting lines the same way. Use a ball-peen hammer and a pry bar to lift out the damaged section *(inset)*; replace any damaged section of subfloor under it *(page 62)*.

2 **Installing a replacement section.** Measure the length and width of the underlayment opening, then cut a plywood sheet of the same thickness as the underlayment to size for a replacement section. Fit the replacement section into the opening, then nail it to the subfloor with 1 1/4-inch ring-shank nails. Drive a nail every 3 inches along each edge of the section as well as the undamaged underlayment, then every 6 inches across the section in rows 6 inches apart *(above)*. If necessary, use an orbital sander fitted with medium sandpaper to smooth any unevenness in the surface of the section and to smooth its edges level with the surrounding underlayment. Vacuum particles off the surface, then reinstall the tiles *(page 43)* or sheet flooring section *(page 46)*.

REPLACING THE UNDERLAYMENT

Demolition bar

1 Removing the underlayment. Remove the tile floor *(page 42)* or sheet flooring *(page 47)*. Wearing work gloves, safety goggles and a dust mask, remove the underlayment panel by panel starting at the floor center. To loosen a panel, fit the flat end of a pry bar into the joint along one edge of it in line with the end of a nail row; push down on the pry bar to pry up the panel edge. Continue the same way along the edge of the panel, then in turn along the other edges of it. Prop up one corner of the panel with a wood block, then work in turn along each edge of it using a 36-inch demolition bar, prying it off the subfloor *(left)*. Working with a helper, remove the panel and pull the nails out of it. Mark an outline for a replacement panel on the subfloor using the edges of the opening as a guide. Continue the same way until all the panels are removed. If the adhesive on the panels is a cut-back asphalt type *(page 138)*, ask your local department of environmental protection or public health for recommended disposal procedures. Replace any damaged subfloor section *(page 62)*.

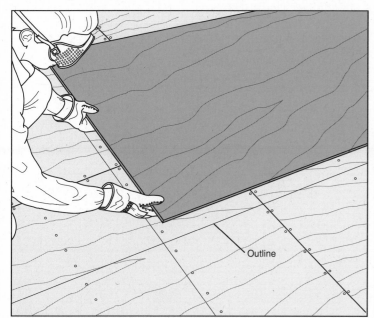

Outline

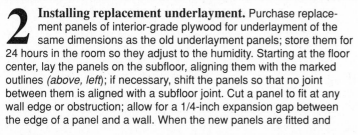

2 Installing replacement underlayment. Purchase replacement panels of interior-grade plywood for underlayment of the same dimensions as the old underlayment panels; store them for 24 hours in the room so they adjust to the humidity. Starting at the floor center, lay the panels on the subfloor, aligning them with the marked outlines *(above, left)*; if necessary, shift the panels so that no joint between them is aligned with a subfloor joint. Cut a panel to fit at any wall edge or obstruction; allow for a 1/4-inch expansion gap between the edge of a panel and a wall. When the new panels are fitted and laid in position, nail each one to the subfloor with 1 1/4-inch ring-shank nails. Drive a nail every 3 inches along each edge of the panels and every 6 inches across them in rows 6 inches apart *(above, right)*. Use a putty knife to patch any hole or crack in the surface of a panel with wood filler *(inset)*. Smooth any unevenness in the surface or at an edge of a panel using an orbital sander fitted with medium sandpaper. Vacuum particles off the surface, then reinstall the tile floor *(page 44)* or sheet flooring *(page 48)*.

SECURING TILES

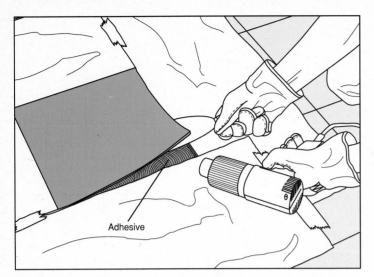

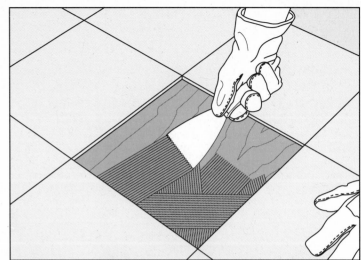

1 **Resealing the tile.** To reseal a lifted tile, use a heat gun set to its lowest heat setting to try softening and reusing the adhesive. Tape aluminum foil sheets over adjacent tiles to protect them. Wearing work gloves, lift the tile edge with a putty knife and move the heat gun back and forth to blow hot air under it *(above)*; move the gun constantly to prevent burning the tile. When the adhesive on the bottom of the tile and the surface of the underlayment is tacky, press the tile down firmly until it remains in place; cover it with a cloth and place a heavy weight on the cloth. After 30 minutes, remove the weight, the cloth and the aluminum foil. If the tile lifts again, reglue it *(step 2)*.

2 **Regluing the tile.** Tape aluminum foil sheets over adjacent tiles to protect them. Wearing work gloves, lift the tile edge with a putty knife and use a heat gun set to its lowest heat setting to blow hot air under it, softening the adhesive; continue until the tile can be pulled off. Use the heat gun to soften the adhesive on the back of the tile and the surface of the underlayment, then scrape it off with the putty knife. Wearing rubber gloves, use a notched knife to coat the opening evenly with an adhesive recommended for the tile *(above)*. Let the adhesive set for the time recommended by the manufacturer, then fit the tile into the opening and use a hand roller to press it into place.

REPLACING TILES

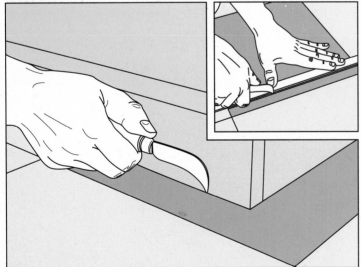

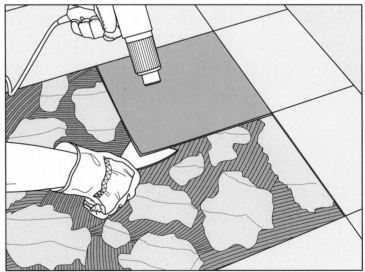

1 **Removing the tiles.** Remove any shoe molding *(page 133)* or wall base *(page 40)* and any door threshold in the way. If a damaged tile is covered by an obstruction, use a linoleum knife to cut through it along the edge of the obstruction *(above, left)*. To remove the first tile, use the linoleum knife and a straightedge to cut across it about 1 inch from an edge ot it *(inset)*. Wearing work gloves, use a heat gun set to its lowest heat setting to blow hot air into the cut along the tile; keep the gun nozzle a few inches from the surface and sweep it back and forth. When the adhesive softens, work the tip of a putty knife into the cut and pry up a section of the tile; remove the other section of the tile the same way. To remove an adjacent tile, work along the exposed edge of it using the same procedure *(above, right),* continuing to remove as many tiles as necessary. If the adhesive on the tiles is a cut-back asphalt type *(page 138)*, ask your local department of environmental protection or public health for recommended disposal procedures .

REPLACING TILES (continued)

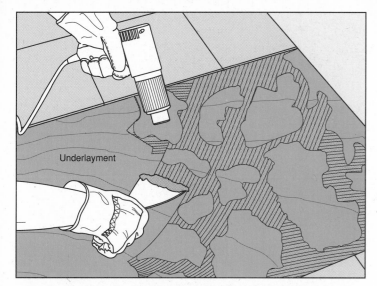

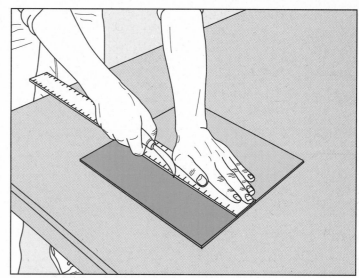

2 **Removing the old adhesive.** Using a putty knife and a heat gun set to its lowest heat setting, scrape any adhesive off the underlayment *(above)*. Vacuum particles off the underlayment and pull out any protruding nails. Replace any damaged underlayment section *(page 40)*. Purchase identical replacement tiles at a building supply center; for other than self-adhesive tiles, also a recommended tile adhesive. Lay out the replacement tiles in the opening, matching any pattern of the adjacent tiles. If necessary, cut any tile to fit at a wall edge or obstruction *(step 3)*. Remove the replacement tiles from the opening. If you are using self-adhesive tiles, install them *(step 5)*; otherwise, apply tile adhesive *(step 4)*.

3 **Cutting replacement tiles.** To cut a tile to fit at a straight-edged obstruction or a wall, measure the dimensions of the opening for it, then mark a cutting line on the back of it. Using a straightedge as a guide, score progressively deeper along the cutting line with a linoleum knife *(above)*, cutting the tile to size. To cut a tile to fit at a curved- or irregular-edged obstruction, make a cardboard template of the opening, then trace the shape of the template onto the back of the tile. Using tin snips, cut along the marked line to trim the tile to size and shape; if necessary, use a heat gun set to its lowest heat setting to slightly warm and soften the back of the tile, easing the cutting of it.

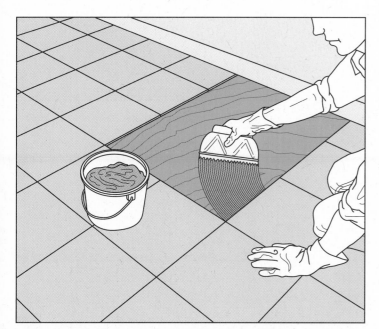

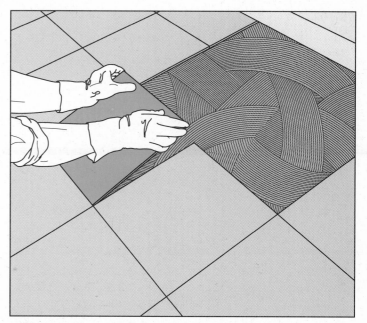

4 **Applying tile adhesive.** Wearing rubber gloves, prepare enough of the adhesive for the opening following the manufacturer's instructions. Using a notched spreader, coat the opening evenly with the adhesive *(above)*, leaving visible ridges in it; avoid getting adhesive on the surface of any tile adjacent to the opening, wiping it off quickly with a damp cloth. Let the adhesive set for the time specified by the manufacturer.

5 **Installing replacement tiles.** To install the replacement tiles, work tile by tile from one side of the opening to the other; work toward any obstruction or wall edge. For self-adhesive tiles, peel the paper backing off each tile as you install it; for tiles installed with adhesive, wear rubber gloves. Use a hand roller to press the replacement tiles down flush with the adjacent tiles. Replace any door threshold, wall base *(page 40)* or shoe molding *(page 133)* you removed. Keep traffic off the replacement tiles for 48 hours; then, if desired, polish the floor section *(page 39)*.

REPLACING A TILE FLOOR

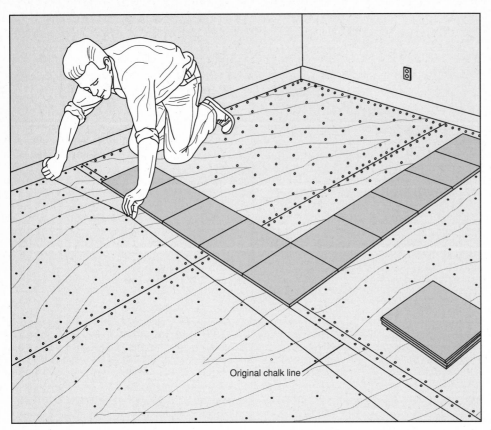

1 Preparing to install a tile floor.
Remove the shoe moldings *(page 133)* or wall bases *(page 40)* and any door threshold in the way. Starting at a wall edge and working row by row across the room, remove the old tiles *(page 42)*. If the adhesive on the underlayment is a cut-back asphalt type *(page 138)*, replace the underlayment *(page 41)*. Otherwise, use a putty knife and a heat gun set to its lowest heat setting to scrape adhesive off the underlayment, then vacuum particles off it and pull out any protruding nails; replace any damaged underlayment section *(page 40)*. Purchase replacement tiles at a building supply center; for other than self-adhesive tiles, also a recommended tile adhesive. Rent a tile roller at a tool rental agency. To test-fit the tiles, snap two perpendicular chalk lines that intersect at the center of the underlayment *(page 138)*, dividing it into quadrants. Lay a tile in one quadrant at the marked corner, then lay out a row of tiles along each quadrant line between the tile and the edge of the underlayment. If the gap between the end of a row and the edge of the underlayment is less than half a tile, snap an adjusted chalk line perpendicular to the row half a tile farther from the edge of the underlayment than the first chalk line *(left)*.

Original chalk line

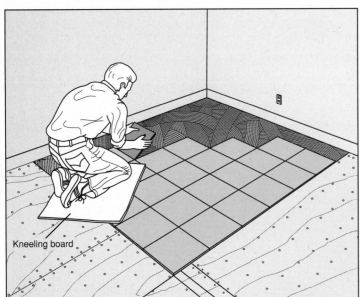

Kneeling board

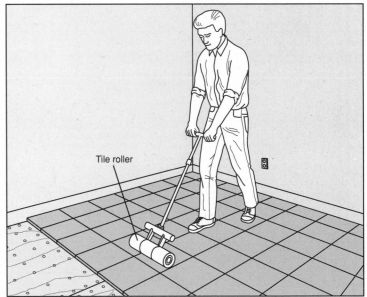

Tile roller

2 Installing a tile floor. Install the tiles of the flooring one quadrant at a time. For tiles that require adhesive, wear rubber gloves and prepare enough of the adhesive for one quadrant following the manufacturer's instructions. Using a notched spreader, work from the wall corner of the quadrant back to the center of the room to spread adhesive on the underlayment; avoid covering the chalk lines. To install the tiles, work from the center of the room back to the wall edges of the quadrant, ensuring that the tile patterns or any directional arrows on the tile backs are oriented in the same direction; if you are using self-adhesive tiles, peel the paper backing off each tile as you install it. Fit a tile into the angle formed by the chalk lines, carefully aligning it

with the lines; then, press it down firmly. Using the same procedure, lay a tile on each side of the first tile in line with the chalk lines, then fit another tile into place in the angle formed by them. Using a kneeling board, continue to extend the rows along the chalk lines and fill the angle between them *(above, left)* until you reach the walls; if necessary, cut tiles to fit at the wall edges *(page 43)*. To seat the tiles, use the tile roller, rolling it back and forth across them *(above, right)*; make two passes at a 90-degree angle to each other. Use the same procedure to install the tiles in the other quadrants, then reinstall any shoe molding *(page 133)*, wall base *(page 40)* or door threshold you removed. Keep traffic off the floor for 48 hours; then, if desired, polish it *(page 39)*.

SECURING SHEET FLOORING

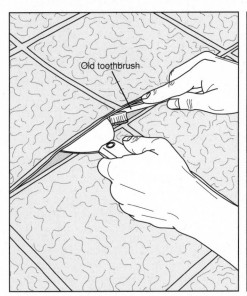

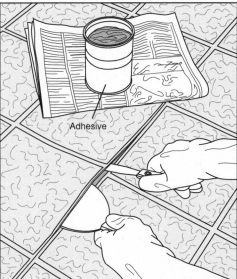

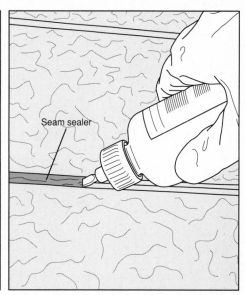

Regluing a lifted edge. If there is a gap between the sheet flooring edges along a seam, replace the sheet flooring section *(page 46)*. Otherwise, gently raise the lifted edge with a putty knife, then use an old toothbrush moistened with undiluted commercial liquid floor cleaner to scrub under it *(above, left)*; scrape old adhesive off the underlayment using an old knife. Wipe the area clean with a cloth and let it dry. Wearing rubber gloves, raise the lifted edge again and use a small putty knife to spread a thin layer of adhesive recommended for the flooring onto the underlayment *(above, center)*; work from one end of the edge to the other end of it. Let the adhesive set for the time speci-

fied by the manufacturer, then press the edge down and use a hand roller to secure it. Use a damp cloth to wipe up extruded adhesive, then cover the edge with a cloth and place a heavy weight on it. When the adhesive is dry, remove the weight and cloth, then seal the edge using a commercial seam sealer recommended for the flooring. **Caution:** Seam sealer is toxic and flammable; follow all safety precautions on the label. Working from one end of the edge to the other end of it, hold the applicator at an angle and gently squeeze it, ejecting a continuous bead of sealer *(above, right)*. Keep traffic off the edge until the sealer is dry.

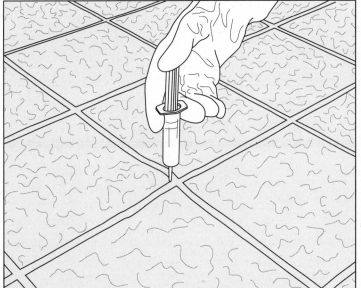

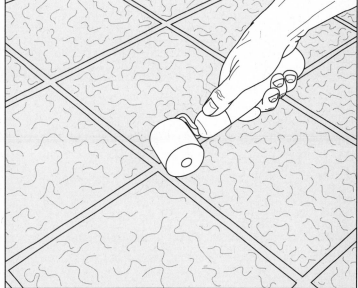

Regluing a blistered surface. To repair a sheet flooring blister 3 inches square or larger, use a straightedge and a utility knife to make a clean cut across the center of it along a pattern line. Press the flooring flat on each side of the cut; if the edges overlap, use the utility knife to trim off the overlap. Then, reglue each edge as you would a lifted edge *(step above)*. To repair a sheet flooring blister less than 3 inches square, use a syringe-style glue injector with a metal needle sold specially for sheet flooring. Wearing rubber gloves, jab the injector needle into the center of the blister, preferably at a point on a pattern line. Watching the injector scale, press gently on the plunger *(above, left)*,

injecting 1/4 ounce of glue for every square inch of blister. Remove the injector and press the blister down flat, then use a hand roller to roll back and forth across it *(above, right)*; use a damp cloth to wipe up any extruded glue. Cover the area with a cloth and place a heavy weight on it. Let the glue dry for the time specified by the manufacturer, then remove the weight and the cloth. If necessary, seal the hole made by the injector needle using a commercial seam sealer recommended for the flooring; follow the manufacturer's instructions. **Caution:** Seam sealer is toxic and flammable; follow all safety precautions on the label.

REPLACING A SHEET FLOORING SECTION

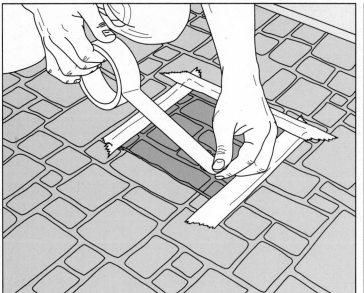

1 **Removing a sheet flooring section.** Remove any shoe molding *(page 133)*, wall base *(page 40)* or door threshold in the way. Find a matching piece of replacement sheet flooring slightly larger than the damaged section. Position the replacement piece on top of the damaged section and align its pattern lines, then tape its edges to the flooring with masking tape *(above, left)*. Simultaneously cut the replacement section to size and cut out the damaged section using a straightedge and a utility knife, following any pattern lines *(above, right)*. Lift off the replacement section and dispose of the tape and cut edges. Remove the damaged section, pulling any staples out of it. If the dam-

aged section is adhered to the underlayment, delaminate it by working the tip of the utility knife under its upper wear layer and peeling it off, exposing the backing. If the backing is intact and you suspect no damage to the underlayment, prepare a replacement section by delaminating it *(step 2)*. Otherwise, wet the backing with a solution of mild detergent and water, then use a putty knife to scrape it off the underlayment. Vacuum particles off the underlayment and pull out any protruding nails; replace any damaged underlayment section *(page 40)*. Then, install the replacement section *(step 3)*.

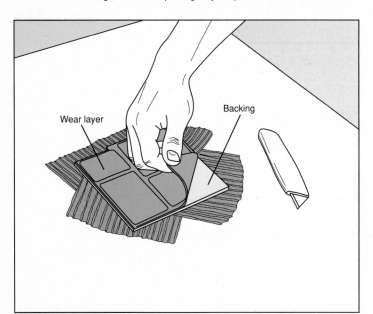

Wear layer   Backing

2 **Delaminating a replacement section.** Delaminate the replacement section if the backing of the damaged section remains adhered to and intact on the floor. Spread a layer of adhesive recommended for the flooring on a scrap of plywood and press the replacement section onto it; let the adhesive dry for the time specified by the manufacturer. To delaminate the replacement section, work the tip of a utility knife under an edge of its upper wear layer to loosen it, then peel it off the backing *(above)*. Install the wear layer as a replacement section onto the backing of the damaged section *(step 3)*.

3 **Installing the replacement section.** Wearing rubber gloves, use a notched spreader to coat the opening with an even layer of adhesive recommended for the flooring; lift up any unsecured flooring edge and use a putty knife to apply a wide band of adhesive onto the underlayment under it. Let the adhesive set, then fit the replacement section into the opening *(above)* and use a hand roller to secure it. Use a damp cloth to wipe up extruded adhesive. Keep traffic off the replacement section until the adhesive cures; seal its edges using a commercial seam sealer *(page 45)*.

REPLACING SHEET FLOORING

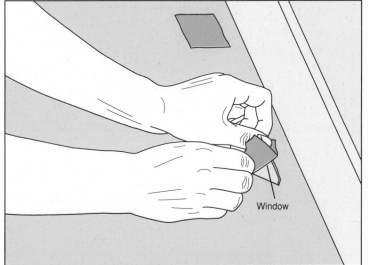

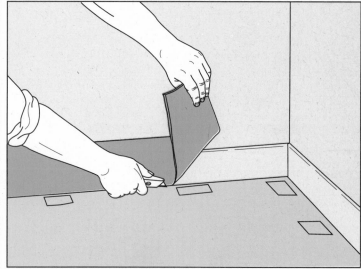

1 **Preparing to install replacement flooring.** Measure the floor dimensions and purchase enough replacement sheet flooring to cover it; if you need more than one sheet of flooring, have the edges along each seam marked. If you plan to fully adhere the flooring or if there will be a seam, also buy enough adhesive recommended for the flooring; if you plan to adhere only the flooring perimeter, buy the staples recommended for the flooring. Remove the shoe moldings *(page 133)* or wall bases *(page 40)* and any door threshold. Before removing the old flooring, make a template of it to use for cutting the replacement flooring to size. To make a template, follow the flooring manufacturer's instructions to use any pattern-making kit provided with the new flooring. Alternately, use kraft paper and masking tape. Cut a length of kraft paper 6 inches longer than the longest floor edge. Position the paper along the floor edge 1/8 inch from the wall with its ends lapped up the adjacent walls. Use a utility knife to cut windows in the paper along the floor edges; then stick masking tape over the windows *(above, left)* to secure the paper to the flooring under it. Working across the floor to the other side, continue to lay down and tape together overlapping lengths of paper to cover the entire floor; if necessary, cut a length of paper to fit around any obstruction. When the floor is covered, use the utility knife to trim off any length of paper lapped up a wall *(above, right)*. Then, carefully roll up and remove the template in one piece.

2 **Removing the old flooring.** Remove the old flooring in strips 8 inches wide, working from one side of the floor to the other side of it. If the old flooring is stapled along the edges, wear work gloves and use an old screwdriver to pry out the staples. Starting 8 inches from a wall, slit the flooring from one end to the other end of it parallel to the wall with a utility knife. If the strip is not adhered to the underlayment, lay a cardboard core across one end of it and work toward the other end of it, rolling it up onto the core. If the strip is adhered to the underlayment, delaminate it by working the tip of the utility knife under the upper wear layer and peeling it off the backing; roll up the wear layer. To remove any backing still adhered to the underlayment, wet it with a solution of mild detergent and water to soften it, then use a putty knife to scrape it off. Continue to cut and roll up *(left)* or delaminate and scrape up parallel strips until you remove all the old flooring. If any adhesive left on the underlayment is a cut-back asphalt type *(page 138)*, replace the underlayment *(page 41)*. Otherwise, use a putty knife and a heat gun set to its lowest heat setting to remove any adhesive from the underlayment. Vacuum particles off the underlayment and pull out any protruding nails; replace any damaged underlayment section *(page 40)* .

REPLACING SHEET FLOORING (continued)

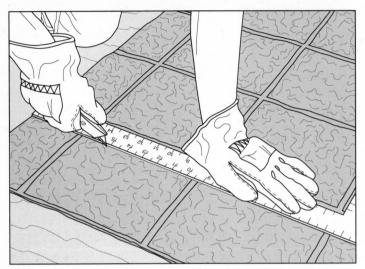

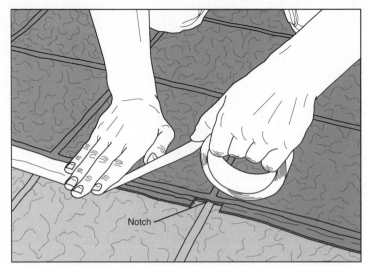

Notch

3 **Cutting replacement flooring.** Lay the replacement flooring flat in a work area. If there are two sheets, align them for a seam *(step 4)*. Otherwise, lay the template on the flooring, centering it with any pattern lines; tape it to the flooring with masking tape. Mark a cutting outline on the flooring around the template edges, then remove the template. Using a utility knife and a straightedge, cut along the outline *(above)*; keep any waste for repairs. Lay the flooring flat on the floor for installation; check the fit along the edges at walls, doors and obstructions and use the utility knife to trim off any excess. If there is no seam, adhere the flooring *(step 5)*, adhere the perimeter *(step 7)* or leave the flooring loose and finish up *(step 8)*. If there is a seam, adhere the flooring, then the seam *(steps 5 and 6)*; or, adhere the seam, then the perimeter *(steps 6 and 7)*.

4 **Aligning sheets of replacement flooring for a seam.** To align two sheets of replacement flooring for a seam, position them flat in a work area with their store-marked edges butted together. Using a utility knife and a straightedge, cut rectangular notches along the store-marked edge of one replacement sheet; make a notch 1 inch long at each pattern line perpendicular to the edge as wide as the first pattern line parallel to it. Reposition the notched replacement sheet to overlap the other replacement sheet and use the notches to align their patterns; then, tape the sheets together securely using masking tape *(above)*. Cut the seamed sheets of replacement flooring to size *(step 3)*.

5 **Adhering the flooring.** For flooring with no seam, adhere half of it at a time. Starting at one edge of the flooring along a wall, roll it back to the floor center, exposing the underlayment. Wearing rubber gloves, use a notched spreader to coat the underlayment evenly with adhesive, working from the floor edge back to the center *(far left)*. Let the adhesive set for time specified by the manufacturer. Then, roll the flooring back out over the adhesive and seat it immediately. Use the tile roller to roll back and forth over the flooring *(near left)*; make two passes at a 90-degree angle to each other. Secure the flooring edges by rolling them with a hand roller. Follow the same procedure to adhere the other half of the flooring, then finish up *(step 8)*. For flooring with a seam, work the same way, carefully rolling the flooring back toward the seam and stopping 18 inches from it. After adhering the flooring on each side of the seam; adhere the seam *(step 6)*.

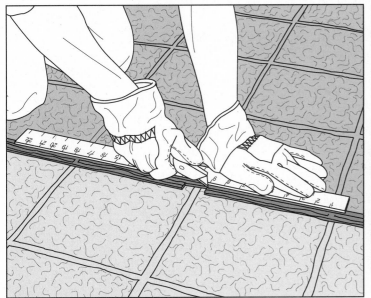

Seam line

6 **Cutting and adhering a flooring seam.** Remove the masking tape from the overlapped flooring edges along the seam. To cut the seam, use a straightedge and a utility knife to make a clean cut through the flooring sheets, following a pattern line on the notched sheet as close to the notches as possible *(above, left)*; dispose of the waste pieces. If you are adhering only the flooring perimeter, mark a seam line on the underlayment. Roll the flooring on each side of the seam back 18 inches to expose the underlayment; if the flooring is already adhered *(step 5)*, roll it back as far as possible. Wearing rubber gloves, use a notched spreader to coat the underlay-

ment evenly with adhesive; if you are adhering only the flooring perimeter, apply a band of adhesive the width recommended by the flooring manufacturer along the marked seam line *(above, right)*. Allow the adhesive to set for the time specified by the manufacturer, then roll the flooring on each side of the seam back over the adhesive and seat it immediately. For fully-adhered flooring, use a tile roller to roll back and forth over it, working toward the seam; then, finish up the job *(step 8)*. For perimeter-adhered flooring, use a hand roller to roll back and forth along the seam edges; then, adhere the perimeter *(step 7)*.

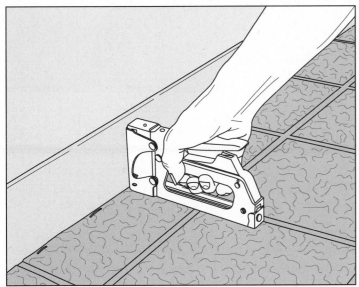

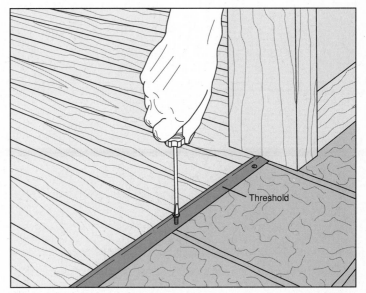

Threshold

7 **Adhering the flooring perimeter.** To adhere the flooring perimeter, first pull back the edge from any doorway or other opening. Wearing rubber gloves, use a notched spreader to apply an even coat of adhesive on the exposed underlayment along the edge of the doorway or other opening; push the edge down and use a hand roller to roll back and forth along it to secure it. Then, adhere the flooring perimeter along the walls and any obstructions using a staple gun loaded with staples of the size recommended by the flooring manufacturer; drive a staple every 3 inches through the flooring into the underlayment *(above)* as close as possible to the wall or obstruction.

8 **Finishing the flooring installation.** Keep traffic off the flooring for 24 hours after you have finished installing it. Seal any flooring seam using a commercial seam sealer recommended for the flooring, following the manufacturer's instructions. **Caution:** Seam sealer is toxic and flammable; follow all safety precautions on the label. Then, reinstall or replace any shoe molding *(page 133)* or wall base *(page 40)* you removed. Put back any threshold removed from a doorway, positioning it and screwing it through the flooring into the underlayment *(above)*. Clean the flooring *(page 38)*; then, if recommended by the flooring manufacturer, polish it *(page 39)*.

RIGID FLOORING

Rigid flooring of ceramic or marble tiles is available in a wide variety of styles, shapes, sizes and colors—an attractive flooring option designed to withstand the harshest rigors of daily living. Easy to maintain, rigid flooring is a popular choice for the most heavily-trafficked areas of the home: the bathrooms, the kitchen and the entrance foyers. The construction of typical rigid flooring is illustrated below; shown are standard ceramic tiles and common marble tiles. Onto a subfloor of two layers of plywood or one layer of plywood and a mortar bed, the tiles are bonded with an adhesive. Ceramic tiles are spaced about 3/16 inch apart, the joints between them filled with grout; marble tiles are usually butted together, their joints also grouted.

Consult the Troubleshooting Guide *(page 51)* to diagnose and repair the rigid flooring of your home. With regular maintenance of your ceramic *(page 52)* or marble *(page 53)* tile floor, its life can be virtually endless. If necessary, consult a tile dealer to identify your type of rigid flooring and any special cleaning or care it may require; a glazed type of tile usually can be distinguished by its glass-like surface, whether its finish is mat or shiny. Grout can loosen and crack with age; check the joints between ceramic tiles periodically and replace any damaged grout *(page 54)*. Reseal the entire joint along the edge of a bathtub or other plumbing fixture with caulk *(page 54)* rather than try to patch any damage to it.

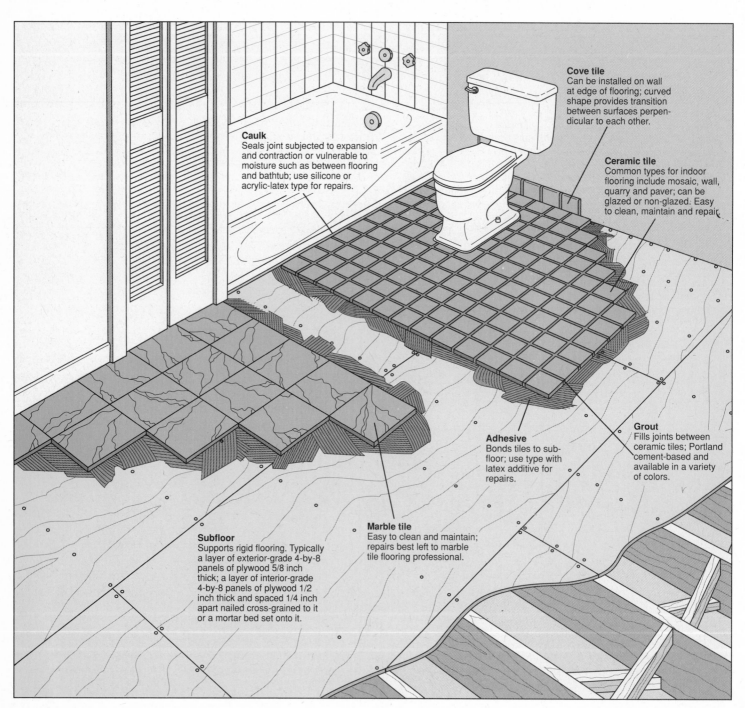

Caulk
Seals joint subjected to expansion and contraction or vulnerable to moisture such as between flooring and bathtub; use silicone or acrylic-latex type for repairs.

Cove tile
Can be installed on wall at edge of flooring; curved shape provides transition between surfaces perpendicular to each other.

Ceramic tile
Common types for indoor flooring include mosaic, wall, quarry and paver; can be glazed or non-glazed. Easy to clean, maintain and repair.

Adhesive
Bonds tiles to subfloor; use type with latex additive for repairs.

Grout
Fills joints between ceramic tiles; Portland cement-based and available in a variety of colors.

Subfloor
Supports rigid flooring. Typically a layer of exterior-grade 4-by-8 panels of plywood 5/8 inch thick; a layer of interior-grade 4-by-8 panels of plywood 1/2 inch thick and spaced 1/4 inch apart nailed cross-grained to it or a mortar bed set onto it.

Marble tile
Easy to clean and maintain; repairs best left to marble tile flooring professional.

No rigid flooring is ever completely impervious to damage. A dropped heavy object or other accidental blow can chip or crack a tile or a section of tiles. Fortunately, with rigid flooring of ceramic tiles, replacing a tile *(page 56)* or even a section of tiles *(page 57)* is usually easy—of greatest difficulty can be the finding of the identical replacement tile or tiles. If you have not saved any original tiles of the flooring, purchase contrasting tiles of the same size to use as accents; or, replace the tile floor *(page 58)*. Repairs to rigid flooring of marble tiles can be complicated and are best left to a marble-tile flooring professional. For widespread damage to any rigid flooring, suspect a problem with the floor understructure *(page 62)*.

The materials necessary for repairs to rigid flooring are readily available at a building supply center; for the greatest selection of tiles, consult a tile dealer. For certain types of work on rigid flooring, special tools are required. A grout saw or scriber is needed to remove the grout from a joint; a grout float is useful for applying new grout to the joints of a section of tiles. For fitting a tile at an obstruction *(page 59)*, a glass cutter or a tile cutter is necessary to trim straight edges; tile nippers or a rod saw to trim irregular edges. Use a notched trowel with adhesive: the unnotched edges for applying it; the notched edges for combing it. Before starting any repair, refer to Tools & Techniques *(page 122)* and the Emergency Guide *(page 8)*.

TROUBLESHOOTING GUIDE

SYMPTOM	POSSIBLE CAUSE	PROCEDURE
CERAMIC TILE		
Flooring surface dirty or dull	Everyday wear and tear	Maintain tile flooring *(p. 52)* □○
Caulk stained or discolored	Everyday wear and tear; accidental spill; black spots of mildew due to high humidity	Maintain tile flooring *(p. 52)* □○; wipe up spills immediately and ventilate room to reduce humidity
	Caulk damaged	Replace caulk *(p. 54)* □○
Caulk loose or cracked	Shrinking or shifting of caulk with age	Replace caulk *(p. 54)* □○
Grout stained or discolored	Everyday wear and tear; accidental spill; black spots of mildew due to high humidity	Maintain tile flooring *(p. 52)* □○; wipe up spills immediately and ventilate room to reduce humidity
	Grout damaged	Replace grout *(p. 54)* ◨○▲
Grout loose or cracked	Shrinking or shifting of grout with age	Replace grout *(p. 54)* ◨○▲
Tile or tiles stained or discolored	Everyday wear and tear; accidental spill; black spots of mildew due to high humidity	Maintain tile flooring *(p. 52)* □○; wipe up spills immediately and ventilate room to reduce humidity
	Tile or tiles damaged; glaze worn off	Replace tile *(p. 56)* ◨○▲ , section of tiles *(p. 57)* ◨◐▲ or tile floor *(p. 58)* ■◐▲
Tile or tiles loose, chipped, cracked, sunken or heaved	Accidental blow; house settlement with age	Replace grout *(p. 54)* ◨○▲ ; replace tile *(p. 56)* ◨○▲ , section of tiles *(p. 57)* ◨◐▲ or tile floor *(p. 58)* ■◐▲
	Floor understructure faulty	Troubleshoot floor understructure *(p. 62)*
MARBLE TILE		
Flooring surface dirty or dull	Everyday wear and tear	Maintain tile flooring *(p. 53)* □○
Caulk stained or discolored	Everyday wear and tear; accidental spill; black spots of mildew due to high humidity	Maintain tile flooring *(p. 53)* □○; wipe up spills immediately and ventilate room to reduce humidity
	Caulk damaged	Replace caulk *(p. 54)* □○
Caulk loose or cracked	Shrinking or shifting of caulk with age	Replace caulk *(p. 54)* □○
Tile or tiles stained or discolored	Everyday wear and tear; accidental spill; black spots of mildew due to high humidity	Maintain tile flooring *(p. 53)* □○; wipe up spills immediately and ventilate room to reduce humidity
	Tile or tiles damaged	Call marble tile flooring professional
Tile or tiles loose, chipped, cracked, sunken or heaved	Accidental blow; house settlement with age	Call marble tile flooring professional
	Floor understructure faulty	Troubleshoot floor understructure *(p. 62)*

DEGREE OF DIFFICULTY: □ **Easy** ◨ **Moderate** ■ **Complex**
ESTIMATED TIME: ○ **Less than 1 hour** ◐ **1 to 3 hours** ● **Over 3 hours**　　　　　▲ **Special tool required**

MAINTAINING A TILE FLOOR

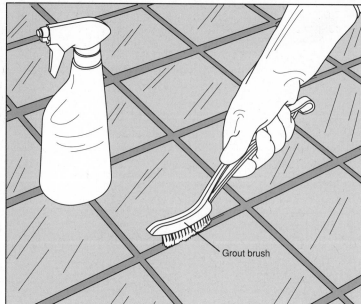

Cleaning the flooring. If the flooring is of marble tiles, clean and buff it *(page 53)*. Otherwise, clean the flooring regularly to protect the tiles and grout, preventing any discoloring or mildew; glazed tiles, in particular, are vulnerable to scratches from dirt or grit particles. Work from one end of the flooring to the other end of it on a small section at a time. Sweep the flooring with a soft-bristled broom or vacuum it using a brush attachment. Then, damp-mop the flooring using a solution of 1/2 cup mild laundry detergent per gallon of warm water *(above, left)* or a non-acidic commercial floor cleaner; an acidic cleaner can damage the grout. Remove any stain from the flooring using a commercial tile cleaner; wearing rubber gloves, follow the manufacturer's instructions to apply a small amount of the cleaner and scrub the surface with a grout brush *(above, right)* or an old toothbrush. Wipe the surface dry with a clean, soft cloth. To remove mildew, work the same way using a solution of one part 5.25 percent hypochlorite laundry bleach per two parts of warm water or a commercial mildew remover. **Caution:** Do not mix bleach with acid or ammonia. After cleaning the flooring, periodically seal it *(step below)*.

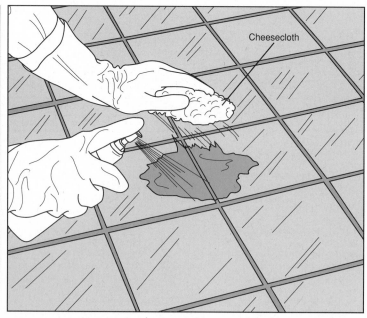

Sealing the flooring. Apply a commercial tile sealer periodically to the flooring to help protect it and ease regular maintenance. Consult a tile dealer for the tile sealer recommended for your type of flooring; if it is of glazed tiles, a tile sealer is not necessary. Clean the flooring *(step above)*, then follow the manufacturer's instructions to prepare and apply the tile sealer. Wearing rubber gloves, work from one end of the flooring to the other end of it on a small section at a time, wiping the tile sealer onto the surface with a clean, soft cloth *(above, left)* or mop; do not pour the tile sealer directly onto the flooring. Apply only a thin, uniform coat of the tile sealer and wipe off any excess; allow the flooring to dry overnight. If the flooring is of glazed or other tiles that do not require a sealer, apply a commercial grout sealer of liquid silicone to the grout. Following the manufacturer's instructions, spray the grout sealer onto the surface or apply it with a soft cloth, immediately wiping up any excess *(above, right)*; allow the flooring to dry overnight.

MAINTAINING A MARBLE TILE FLOOR

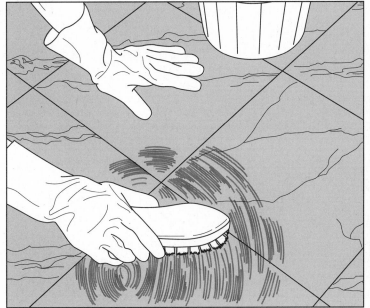

Cleaning and buffing the flooring. If the flooring is not of marble tiles, clean and seal it *(page 52)*. Otherwise, clean the flooring regularly to protect the tiles and grout, preventing any discoloring or mildew. Work from one end of the flooring to the other end of it on a small section at a time. Sweep the flooring with a soft-bristled broom or vacuum it using a brush attachment. Then, damp-mop the flooring using a mild solution of unscented dishwashing liquid and warm water. Remove any stain from the flooring using a mild, non-abrasive household cleanser or a commercial marble-tile cleaner; wearing rubber gloves, soak the surface with hot water, then follow the manufacturer's instructions to apply the cleanser or cleaner and scrub gently with a soft-bristled fiber brush *(above, left)*. Rinse the surface with clean water and wipe it dry using a soft cloth. If necessary, repeat the procedure; remove any deep stain with a poultice *(step below)*. If the flooring is dull, wipe it with a damp cloth and apply a commercial marble-tile polish. Wearing rubber gloves, follow the manufacturer's instructions to apply a thin, uniform coat of the polish using a soft cloth; allow the flooring to dry for 20 minutes, then buff it by hand with a clean, soft cloth *(above, right)* or using a floor polisher fitted with felt buffing pads.

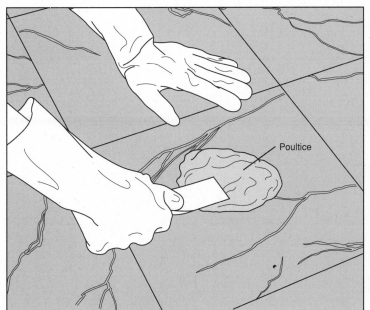

Poultice

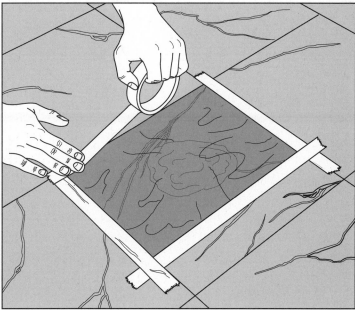

Removing a deep stain from the flooring. To remove a deep stain from the flooring, use a poultice; if the stain is oil-based, consult a marble-tile dealer for the removal method recommended. To make the poultice, wear rubber gloves and mix whiting powder or white gypsum plaster with 5.25 percent hypochlorite laundry bleach or a 6 percent solution of hydrogen peroxide into a stiff, thick paste. Apply a heavy coat of the poultice to the surface with a wooden or plastic spatula *(above, left)*, then cover it with a sheet of plastic and seal the edges using masking tape *(above, right)*. Leave the poultice in place on the surface for at least 24 hours, then take off the plastic and remove the poultice with the spatula. Rinse the surface with clean water and wipe it dry using a soft cloth. If necessary, repeat the procedure; if the stain persists, consult a marble-tile professional. Otherwise, clean and buff the flooring *(step above)*.

REPLACING CAULK

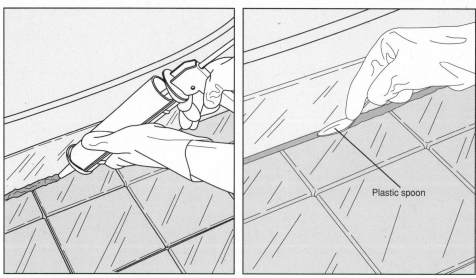

1 Removing the old caulk. If the caulk along a joint between the flooring and a fixture such as a bathtub is damaged, remove it. Cut the caulk with a utility knife *(above)* or a single-edged razor, working carefully to avoid scratching the flooring or fixture; pull it out using your fingers. Scrub the joint using a mild, non-abrasive household cleanser and an old toothbrush to clean off remaining particles; wipe it dry with a soft cloth.

2 Applying new caulk. When the joint is clean and dry, recaulk it. Wearing rubber gloves, load a tube of silicone or acrylic latex caulk into a caulking gun and cut the tip off the tube at a 45-degree angle, providing an opening for a thin bead of caulk; use a long nail or an awl to break any tube seal. Holding the gun at a 45-degree angle to the joint at one end of it, squeeze the trigger to eject a continuous bead of caulk along it *(above, left)*. Then, smooth and shape the joint by running along it with a plastic spoon *(above, right)* or a wet finger, pressing the caulk into it in a slightly concave shape. Allow the caulk to cure.

REPLACING GROUT

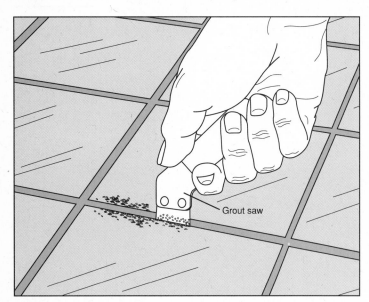

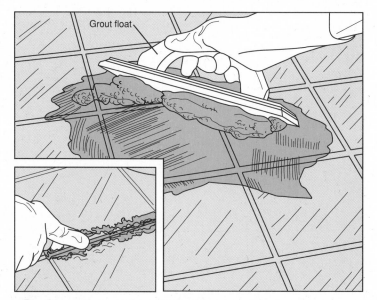

1 Removing the old grout. Wearing safety goggles and a dust mask, scrape any damaged grout out of each joint using a carbide-tipped grout saw *(above)* or scriber. Pull the blade of the saw or scriber repeatedly along the joint, raking it to a uniform depth; work carefully to avoid damaging any tile edge. Continue the same way along each joint; if you are replacing a damaged tile, remove the grout from the joint along each side of it, then try to pry it off. Clean loosened particles and dust out of each raked joint using a whisk broom or a vacuum, then wipe it with a damp cloth.

2 Spreading new grout. Purchase latex-based grout at a building supply center. Wearing rubber gloves, follow the manufacturer's instructions to prepare enough grout to fill the joints; mix the dry ingredients, then add the latex slowly until the grout is spreadable but not runny. To fill one joint at a time, press the grout into it with a finger *(inset)*, then strike it *(step 4)*. Otherwise, use a grout float to apply a small amount of grout onto the flooring. Holding the float at a 45-degree angle to the flooring, spread the grout diagonally across the tiles, forcing it into the joints *(above)*.

REPLACING GROUT (continued)

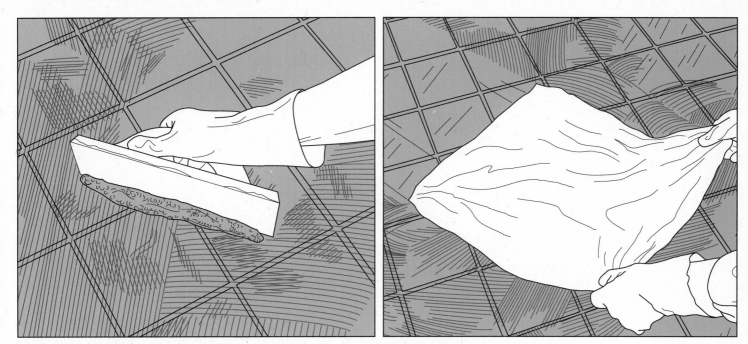

3 **Removing the excess grout.** When each joint is packed with grout, use the grout float to scrape any excess grout off the tiles. Holding the float at a 90-degree angle to the flooring, slide it diagonally across the tiles, collecting the excess grout on it *(above, left)*; work carefully to avoid digging any grout out of a joint. Wait 2 to 3 minutes for the joints to harden slightly, then wipe any remaining grout off the tiles using an old towel. Soak the towel with water and wring it out, then drag it unfolded diagonally across the tiles *(above, right)*. Continue the same way until the remaining grout is removed from the tiles, rinsing out the towel periodically.

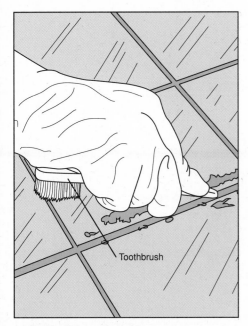

Toothbrush

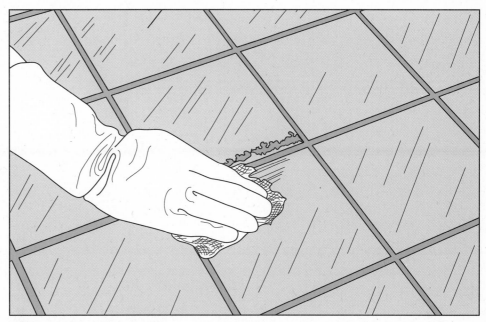

4 **Striking the joints.** If the tile edges are not beveled, clean the flooring *(step 5)*. If the tile edges are beveled, wait about 15 minutes for the grout of each joint to harden slightly. Then, strike each joint to smooth and shape it; wearing rubber gloves, run along it with the end of an old toothbrush *(above)*, pressing the grout into it in a slightly concave shape.

5 **Cleaning the flooring.** Wipe the flooring using a clean, soft cloth or sponge. Wearing rubber gloves, soak the cloth or sponge in water and wring it out until it is almost dry, then wipe diagonally across the tiles with it *(above)*; work carefully to avoid rubbing any grout out of a joint. Continue the same way until only a hazy film remains on the tiles, rinsing out the cloth or sponge periodically. Wait about 15 minutes for the flooring to dry, then work the same way using a clean, soft cloth to wipe the hazy film off the tiles. Allow the grout to harden overnight, then rub any particles off the tiles using a non-metallic kitchen scouring pad. Maintain the flooring *(page 52)*, waiting at least one week for any new grout to cure before sealing it.

REPLACING A TILE

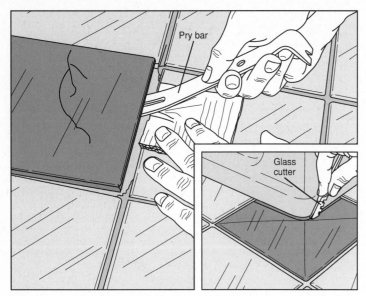

1 **Removing the tile.** Remove any caulk and the grout from the joint along each side of the tile *(page 54)*. If the tile is loose, pry it out by hand; or, wear safety goggles and work it out using a pry bar, protecting any tile adjacent to it with a piece of cardboard *(above)*. If necessary, use an electric drill fitted with a carbide-tipped bit to drill four holes through the center of the tile to weaken it, then chip it out using a bull-point chisel and a ball-peen hammer. If a section of the tile is covered by an obstruction such as a toilet bowl, score along it at the edge of the obstruction using a glass cutter *(inset)*, then chip out the exposed section of it the same way.

2 **Scraping off the old adhesive.** Wearing safety goggles, remove the old adhesive from the opening using a putty knife *(above)* or a cold chisel; also scrape any remaining grout off the edge of the tile along each side of the opening. Work carefully to avoid damaging the subfloor or any tile adjacent to the opening, leveling the surface as much as possible. Clean loosened particles and dust out of the opening using a whisk broom or a vacuum, then wipe it with a damp cloth. If the tile is not damaged, scrape any old adhesive and grout off it the same way. If the subfloor is damaged, repair it *(page 62)*; for a mortar bed, consult a flooring professional.

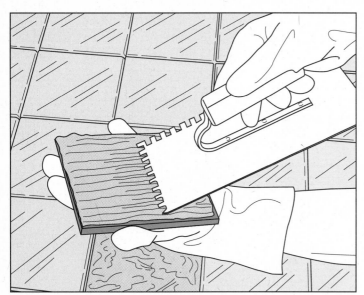

3 **Applying new adhesive.** If necessary, fit the replacement tile at an obstruction *(page 59)*. Install the tile with latex thinset adhesive, following the manufacturer's instructions. Wearing rubber gloves, use the unnotched edges of a notched trowel to coat the back of the tile with the adhesive, applying it thick enough for the tile to fit level with the tiles adjacent to the opening. Test-fit the tile in the opening and adjust the amount of adhesive as necessary. Then, use the notched edges of the trowel to comb the adhesive on the tile *(above)*, leaving visible ridges in it; keep the trowel at the same angle to maintain the level of the adhesive.

4 **Setting the tile.** Wearing rubber gloves, position the tile in the opening, aligning it with the tiles adjacent to it *(above)*; press it into place using a slight back-and-forth twisting motion. Immediately remove adhesive that oozes up around the tile using a thin wooden stick; avoid getting adhesive on the tile surface, wiping any off it quickly with a damp cloth. If necessary, use a straight board wrapped in a piece of thick carpet to seat the tile level with the tiles adjacent to it; set the board flat across the tile and tap it with a mallet. Allow the adhesive to cure, then grout the joint along each side of the tile and caulk any expansion joint *(page 54)*.

REPLACING A SECTION OF TILES

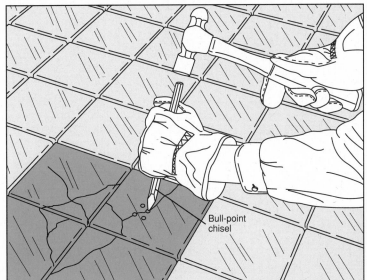

1 Removing the section of tiles. Take off any shoe molding in the way *(page 133)*. Remove any caulk and the grout from the joint along each side of one tile *(page 54)*. Wearing safety goggles, use an electric drill fitted with a carbide-tipped bit to drill four holes through the center of the tile to weaken it. Wearing work gloves, set a bull-point chisel into a hole and tap it using a ball-peen hammer *(above, left)*, breaking the tile into pieces. Remove any loosened pieces of the tile and continue toward the edges of it, chipping out the remaining pieces; work carefully to avoid marring any undamaged tile adjacent to it. Work with the bull-point chisel or a cold chisel to remove the remaining tiles of the section; wedge the chisel under an exposed edge of a tile to pry it off

(above, right). If a section of a tile is covered by an obstruction such as a toilet bowl, score along it at the edge of the obstruction using a glass cutter, then chip out the exposed section of it. Remove the old adhesive from the opening using a putty knife or the cold chisel; also scrape any remaining grout off the edges of the tiles along each side of the opening. Work carefully to avoid damaging the subfloor or any tile adjacent to the opening, leveling the surface as much as possible. Clean loosened particles and dust out of the opening using a whisk broom or a vacuum, then wipe it with a damp cloth. If the subfloor is damaged, repair it *(page 62)*; for a mortar bed, consult a flooring professional.

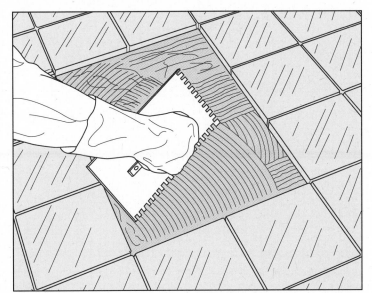

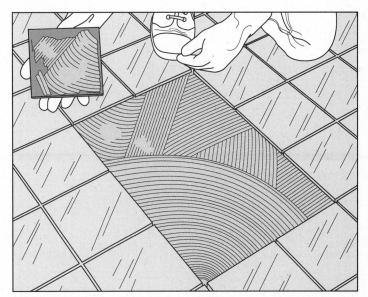

2 Applying new adhesive. Purchase replacement tiles and latex thinset adhesive at a building supply center. Wearing rubber gloves, follow the manufacturer's instructions to prepare enough of the adhesive for the opening. Use the unnotched edges of a notched trowel to coat the opening evenly with the adhesive, applying it thick enough for the replacement tiles to fit level with the tiles adjacent to the opening. Then, use the notched edges of the trowel to comb the adhesive *(above)*, leaving visible ridges in it; keep the trowel at the same angle to maintain the level of the adhesive. Avoid getting adhesive on the surface of a tile adjacent to the opening, wiping any off quickly with a damp cloth.

3 Testing the adhesive. If necessary, fit the first replacement tile at an obstruction *(page 59)*. Wearing rubber gloves, position the tile in the opening, then remove it to test the consistency of the adhesive. If the adhesive is properly prepared and applied, about half of the coat under the tile should adhere to it *(above)*. If the tile is not coated completely, the adhesive is too dry. If the ridges formed by combing collapse, the adhesive is too wet. In either case, scrape the adhesive out of the opening using the notched trowel, then prepare a new batch of adhesive and apply it *(step 2)*. Otherwise, reposition the tile in the opening, aligning it with the tiles adjacent to it; press it into place using a slight back-and-forth twisting motion.

REPLACING A SECTION OF TILES (continued)

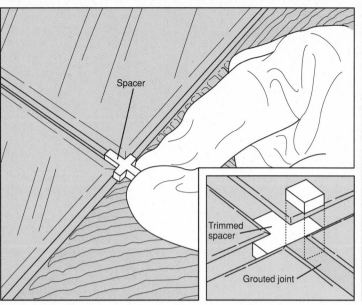

Spacer

Trimmed spacer

Grouted joint

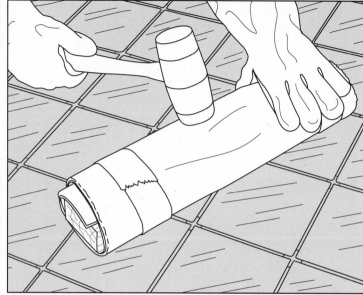

4 **Setting the tiles.** Wearing rubber gloves, immediately remove any adhesive that oozes up around the replacement tile using a thin wooden stick; avoid getting adhesive on the tile surface, wiping any off it quickly with a damp cloth. Set a tile spacer gently on the adhesive at each corner of the tile *(above, left)*; at any corner of it adjacent to a grouted joint or other obstruction, trim a tile spacer to fit *(inset)*. Continue setting the remaining tiles of the section the same way, positioning each tile in the opening and pressing it into place,

then setting tile spacers at its corners. If necessary, fit any tile at an obstruction *(page 59)*. To seat the tiles level with the tiles adjacent to them, use a straight board wrapped in a piece of thick carpet. Set the board flat across the tiles and tap it with a mallet *(above, right)*. Check that the tiles are level using a carpenter's level; if necessary, carefully pry out a tile to reset it. Allow the adhesive to cure, then pull out the tile spacers using pliers or an awl. Grout the joints of the tiles and caulk any expansion joint *(page 54)*. Put back any shoe molding you removed.

REPLACING A TILE FLOOR

First chalk line

1 **Preparing to install the flooring.** Take off any shoe molding *(page 133)*, then remove the tiles as you would for a section of tiles *(page 57)*. Clean particles and dust off the subfloor using a whisk broom or a vacuum, then damp-mop it. If the subfloor is damaged, repair it *(page 62)*; for a mortar bed, consult a flooring professional. Purchase replacement tiles and latex thinset adhesive at a building supply center. To test-fit the tiles, use a chalk line to mark two lines at a 90-degree angle to each other that intersect at the center of the subfloor *(page 138)*, dividing it into quadrants. Position a tile in one quadrant at the marked corner and align it with the lines, then place tile spacers at its corners. Working from the tile to the edge of the subfloor, lay a row of tiles along each line of the quadrant the same way; allow for a 1/4-inch joint at the edge of the subfloor. If there is a gap of less than half of a tile between the tile at the end of a row and the edge of the subfloor, mark an adjusted line for the quadrants parallel to the first line and half of a tile farther from the edge of the subfloor than it *(left)*; mark an adjusted line for each first line, if necessary. Then, work from the marked corner of the quadrants in turn to opposite edges of the subfloor to divide the quadrants into a grid, marking lines parallel to each line for the quadrants at a distance equal to four tiles and tile spacers.

REPLACING A TILE FLOOR (continued)

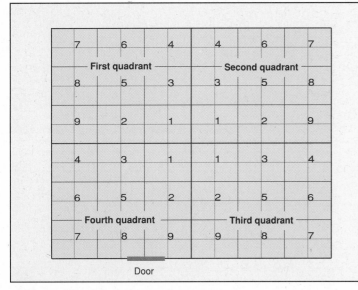

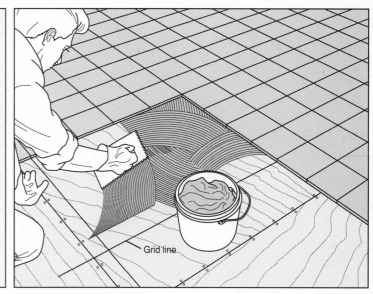

Grid line

2 **Setting the tiles.** Set the tiles of the flooring one grid and quadrant at a time, following a sequence for completing the flooring without applying your weight on any tile. Work grid by grid from the marked corner of a quadrant toward an edge of the subfloor opposite the door, then back out of the quadrant toward an edge of the subfloor near the door *(above, left)*; mirror the same grid sequence for the other quadrants. Wearing rubber gloves, follow the manufacturer's instructions to prepare enough of the adhesive for one quadrant. Use the unnotched edges of a notched trowel to coat grid 1 of the first quadrant evenly with the adhesive, then use the notched edges of the trowel

to comb it, leaving visible ridges in it. Position the first tile in the grid at the marked corner and align it with the lines, then press it into place and gently set tile spacers at its corners. Work the same way to position a tile on each side of the first tile, completing the grid as you would to set any section of tiles *(page 58)* and fitting any tile at an obstruction *(steps below)*. Use the same procedure to set the tiles in each grid of the quadrant, repeating it for the other quadrants *(above, right)*. Allow the adhesive to cure, then pull out the tile spacers using pliers or an awl. Grout the joints of the tiles and caulk any expansion joint *(page 54)*. Put back any shoe molding you removed.

FITTING A TILE AT AN OBSTRUCTION

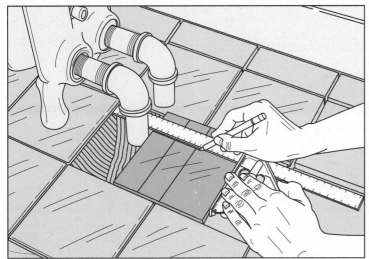

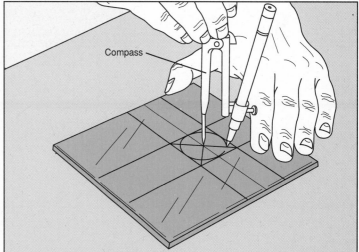

Compass

Marking around an obstruction. At a straight-edged obstruction, trim a tile with a glass cutter *(page 60)* or a tile cutter *(page 61)*. At an irregular-edged obstruction, mark a tile *(page 60)*. To fit a tile around an obstruction such as the pipe of a radiator, position an edge of it along one edge of the opening, butting it against the obstruction and aligning it with the tile under it. Using a combination square, draw a line marking each side of the obstruction across the tile at a 90-degree angle to the edge of it butted against the obstruction. Reposition the tile along an adjacent edge of the opening, butting its adjacent edge against the obstruction; align it and draw a line marking each side of the obstruction

across it the same way *(above, left)*. Locate the center point of the obstruction on the tile by drawing lines between opposite corners of the intersecting lines, then draw a line across the tile at a 90-degree angle to an edge of it through the center point. To draw the circular shape of an obstruction on the tile, use a compass set at the marked center point opened to the distance between it and a marked side of the obstruction *(above, right)*. To trim the tile, use a glass cutter or a tile cutter along the marked center line; use tile nippers or a rod saw along the marked curved line of any half circle *(page 61)*.

FITTING A TILE AT AN OBSTRUCTION (continued)

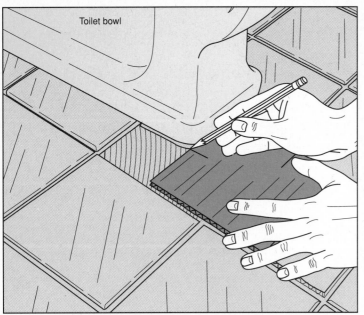

Marking along an obstruction. At a straight-edged obstruction, trim a tile with a glass cutter *(step below)* or a tile cutter *(page 61)*. To fit a tile around an obstruction, mark it *(page 59)*. At an irregular-edged obstruction such as a toilet bowl, mark a tile using a template. For the template, cut a sheet of cardboard equal to the size of a tile using a utility knife. Position an edge of the template along one edge of the opening, butting it against the obstruction and aligning it with the tile under it. Using a pencil, draw a line marking the side of the obstruction on the template. Reposition the template along the adjacent edge of the open-

ing, butting its adjacent edge against the obstruction; align it and draw a line marking the side of the obstruction on it the same way *(above, left)*. Try drawing a line marking the shape of the obstruction on the template between the two marked lines using a french curve or a compass. Trim the template to size and test-fit it; continue trimming it as necessary to fit it, allowing for a grouted joint at the obstruction. When the template fits, trace its shape onto a tile *(above, right)*. To trim the tile, use tile nippers or a rod saw *(page 61)*.

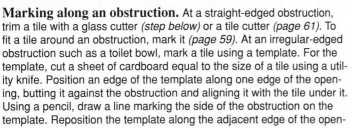

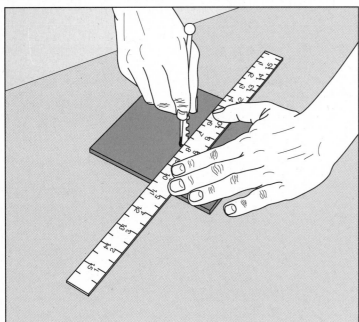

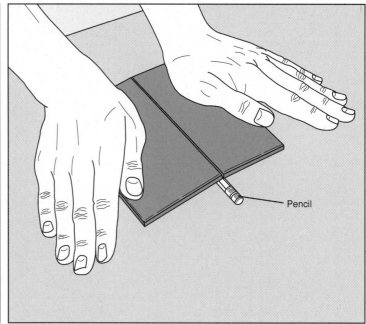

Trimming a straight edge with a glass cutter. To trim a tile along other than a marked straight line, use tile nippers or a rod saw *(page 61)*. To trim a tile along a marked straight line, use a tile cutter *(page 61)* or a glass cutter. Set the tile on a flat, even surface. Wearing safety goggles, use a metal straightedge as a guide to score firmly once across the tile along the marked line with the glass cutter *(above, left)*, leaving a visible scar; use a straightedge with a non-skid backing, especially for a glazed tile. If the scored line across the tile is close to

an edge of it, trim it along the scored line using tile nippers or a rod saw. If the scored line across the tile is close to the center of it, snap it along the scored line using a pencil. Set the pencil under the tile directly below and aligned with the scored line, then position your hands on opposite sides of the scored line at the same distance from it. Applying balanced, uniform pressure with the heels of your hands, press down on the tile to snap it cleanly along the scored line *(above, right)*.

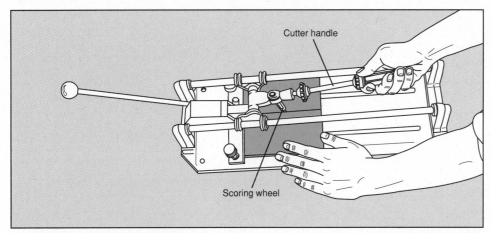

Cutter handle

Scoring wheel

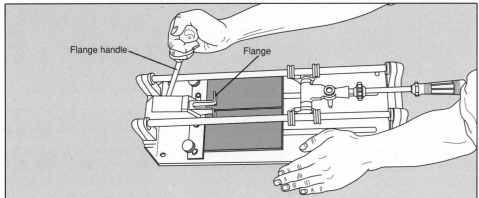

Flange handle

Flange

Trimming a straight edge with a tile cutter. To trim a tile along other than a marked straight line, use tile nippers or a rod saw *(steps below)*. To trim a tile along a marked straight line, use a glass cutter *(page 60)* or a tile cutter. Set the tile cutter on a flat, even surface with its cutter handle and its flange handle at opposite ends of it. Wearing safety goggles, position the tile in the tile cutter, the marked line on it parallel to the cutter handle and aligned with the scoring wheel. Hold the tile securely in position with one hand, then lift the cutter handle slightly and push it firmly once across the tile *(left, top)*, leaving a visible scar along the marked line with the scoring wheel. Flip up the cutter handle to raise the scoring wheel off the tile, then slide it back to its starting position. Flip up the flange handle to set the flanges against the tile and pull it across the tile *(left, bottom)*, snapping the tile cleanly along the scored line.

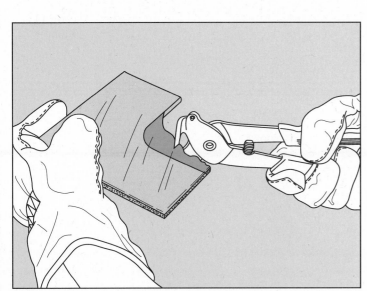

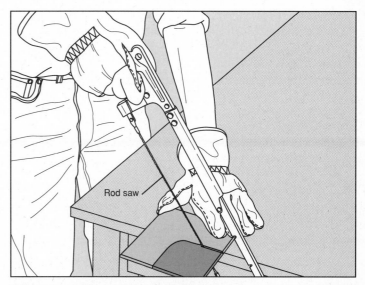

Rod saw

Trimming an irregular edge with tile nippers. To trim a tile along a marked straight line, use a glass cutter *(page 60)* or a tile cutter *(step above)*. To trim a tile along other than a marked straight line, use a rod saw *(step right)* or tile nippers. Wearing safety goggles and work gloves, hold the tile with one hand and use the tile nippers to notch an edge of its waste material. Starting at the notch, work with the tile nippers to bite off one small chip of the tile waste material at a time, continuing toward the marked line *(above)*. As you reach the marked line on the tile, stop periodically to test-fit the tile. After trimming the tile with the tile nippers, smooth any rough edge using an abrasive stone.

Trimming an irregular edge with a rod saw. To trim a tile along a marked straight line, use a glass cutter *(page 60)* or a tile cutter *(step above)*. To trim a tile along other than a marked straight line, use tile nippers *(step left)* or a rod saw. Fit the rod saw into the frame of a hacksaw as you would any other hacksaw blade, then position the tile at the edge of a flat work surface; if necessary, secure it in place with a C clamp, protecting it with a wood block. Wearing safety goggles and work gloves, cut the tile along the marked line using the rod saw *(above)*, making slow, steady upstrokes and downstrokes with the full length of the blade. After trimming the tile with the rod saw, smooth any rough edge using an abrasive stone.

FLOOR UNDERSTRUCTURE

The floor understructure is the sturdy, level platform that supports the finish flooring and carpeting, as well as the structural framing, for the story of the house on it. Often, an irritating squeak, dip or bounce in the finish flooring can be traced to an understructure fault. However, usually only the understructure for the first story of a house is accessible for inspection and repair; the understructure for any second story is in most instances concealed above the ceiling of the first story. A typical floor understructure for the first story of a house is shown at right; the specific size and spacing of the components may vary according to local building code. Sill plates set on the top of the foundation walls and post-supported girders that span the distance between the walls support joists laid on top of them. The joists, in turn, support a subfloor of panels or boards that provides a base for the finish flooring or carpeting.

Although wood is a common and durable building material, understructure components of it can weaken with age, resulting in cracks or sags; and wood is always vulnerable to rot and insect damage. If an inspection or repair of your finish flooring or carpeting does not lead to the solving of a problem, suspect a flaw in the floor understructure. To inspect the floor understructure, start by examining the section of it directly below the faulty flooring section; have a helper walk across the faulty flooring while you look for loose joints and moving components, as well as damage to the wood that might be the cause of the problem. If you find wood that is soft and spongy, pitted or crumbling, suspect rot or insect damage *(page 126)* and carefully inspect the entire floor understructure; for any rot or insect damage to a girder or for extensive damage to an understructure component, consult a building professional. In most instances, minor damage to the subfloor, a joist, a sill plate, a girder or a post can be easily repaired. To help in your diagnosis, consult the Troubleshooting Guide on pages 64 and 65.

Understructure repairs range from the simple to the complex. A minor repair such as reinforcing the subfloor at a joist *(page 65)* or between joists *(page 66)* can be performed quickly with basic cutting and fastening tools such as a hammer, a saw and a chisel; a more involved repair such as bracing a joist with scabs *(page 69)* or installing a sister joist *(page 70)* requires you to rent and install a telescoping jack. A major repair such as installing an intermediate girder *(page 72)* can take several days and calls for a number of helpers, as well as many different tools and techniques. Before starting an understructure repair, refer to Tools & Techniques *(page 122)* and the Emergency Guide *(page 8)*; then, consult your local building inspection office to ensure that the repair is made in compliance with the current building code. If you have any doubt about your ability to successfully complete a repair, do not hesitate to call a building professional. Wear the safety gear prescribed for the job: safety goggles and a safety helmet to work overhead; a dust mask to cut or drill into wood or concrete; and work gloves to handle pressure-treated wood.

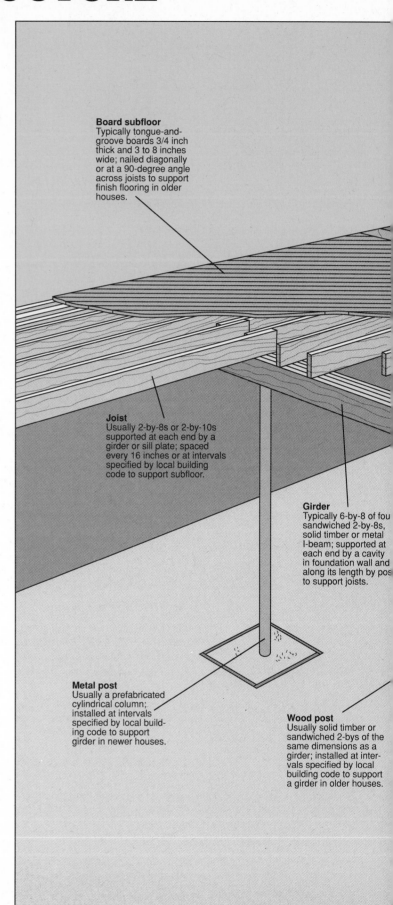

Board subfloor
Typically tongue-and-groove boards 3/4 inch thick and 3 to 8 inches wide; nailed diagonally or at a 90-degree angle across joists to support finish flooring in older houses.

Joist
Usually 2-by-8s or 2-by-10s supported at each end by a girder or sill plate; spaced every 16 inches or at intervals specified by local building code to support subfloor.

Girder
Typically 6-by-8 of four sandwiched 2-by-8s, solid timber or metal I-beam; supported at each end by a cavity in foundation wall and along its length by post to support joists.

Metal post
Usually a prefabricated cylindrical column; installed at intervals specified by local building code to support girder in newer houses.

Wood post
Usually solid timber or sandwiched 2-bys of the same dimensions as a girder; installed at intervals specified by local building code to support a girder in older houses.

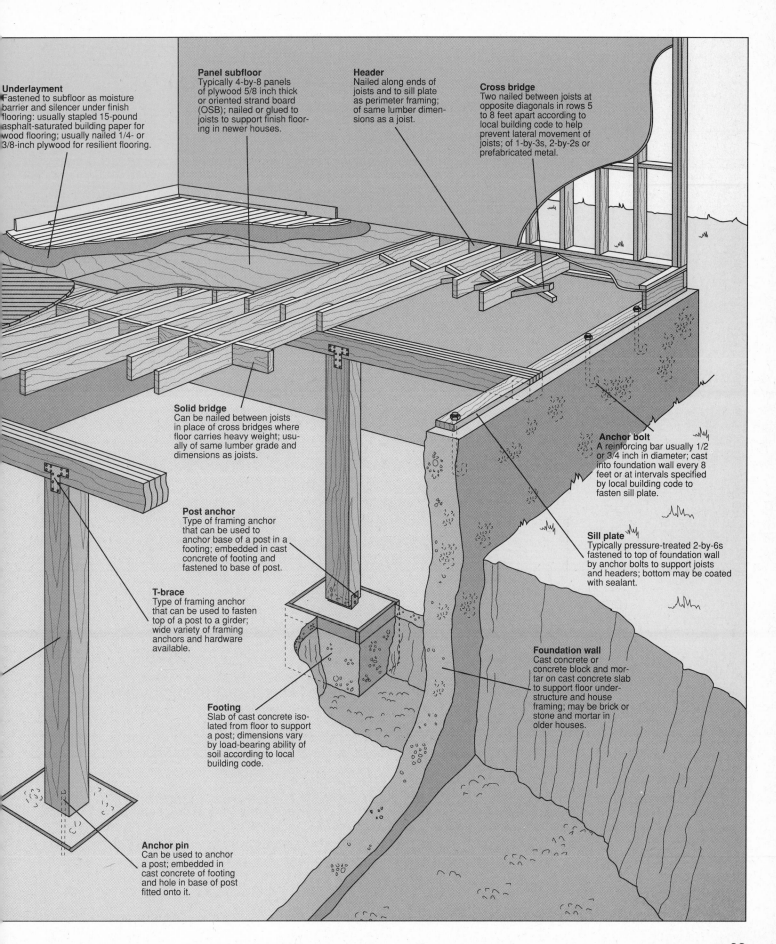

Underlayment
Fastened to subfloor as moisture barrier and silencer under finish flooring; usually stapled 15-pound asphalt-saturated building paper for wood flooring; usually nailed 1/4- or 3/8-inch plywood for resilient flooring.

Panel subfloor
Typically 4-by-8 panels of plywood 5/8 inch thick or oriented strand board (OSB); nailed or glued to joists to support finish flooring in newer houses.

Header
Nailed along ends of joists and to sill plate as perimeter framing; of same lumber dimensions as a joist.

Cross bridge
Two nailed between joists at opposite diagonals in rows 5 to 8 feet apart according to local building code to help prevent lateral movement of joists; of 1-by-3s, 2-by-2s or prefabricated metal.

Solid bridge
Can be nailed between joists in place of cross bridges where floor carries heavy weight; usually of same lumber grade and dimensions as joists.

Anchor bolt
A reinforcing bar usually 1/2 or 3/4 inch in diameter; cast into foundation wall every 8 feet or at intervals specified by local building code to fasten sill plate.

Post anchor
Type of framing anchor that can be used to anchor base of a post in a footing; embedded in cast concrete of footing and fastened to base of post.

Sill plate
Typically pressure-treated 2-by-6s fastened to top of foundation wall by anchor bolts to support joists and headers; bottom may be coated with sealant.

T-brace
Type of framing anchor that can be used to fasten top of a post to a girder; wide variety of framing anchors and hardware available.

Foundation wall
Cast concrete or concrete block and mortar on cast concrete slab to support floor understructure and house framing; may be brick or stone and mortar in older houses.

Footing
Slab of cast concrete isolated from floor to support a post; dimensions vary by load-bearing ability of soil according to local building code.

Anchor pin
Can be used to anchor a post; embedded in cast concrete of footing and hole in base of post fitted onto it.

63

TROUBLESHOOTING GUIDE

SYMPTOM	POSSIBLE CAUSE	PROCEDURE
Floor squeaks	Finish flooring faulty	Troubleshoot wood flooring (p. 14) or resilient flooring (p. 36)
	Gap between subfloor and joist; subfloor or joist movement	Reinforce subfloor at joist (p. 65) □○; reinforce subfloor between joists (p. 66) □○ or reinforce joists (p. 67) □○
Floor springy	Finish flooring faulty	Troubleshoot wood flooring (p. 14) or resilient flooring (p. 36)
	Gap between subfloor and joist; subfloor or joist movement	Reinforce subfloor at joist (p. 65) □○; reinforce subfloor between joists (p. 66) □○ or reinforce joists (p. 67) □○
	Subfloor section damaged	Replace subfloor section (p. 66) ■●
	Joist damaged	Brace joist with scabs (p. 69) □●▲ or install sister joist (p. 70) □●▲
Floor bulged or humped	Finish flooring or carpeting faulty	Troubleshoot wood flooring (p. 14), resilient flooring (p. 36), rigid flooring (p. 50) or carpet (p. 106)
	Subfloor section damaged	Replace subfloor section (p. 66) ■●
	Joist crowned (curved upward)	Brace crowned joist with scabs (p. 70) □●
Floor sags or dips at center	Gap between subfloor and joist; subfloor or joist movement	Reinforce subfloor at joist (p. 65) □○; reinforce subfloor between joists (p. 66) □○ or reinforce joists (p. 67) □○
	Subfloor section damaged	Replace subfloor section (p. 66) ■●
	Joist damaged	Brace joist with scabs (p. 69) □●▲ or install sister joist (p. 70) □●▲; for more than one joist, install intermediate girder (p. 72) ■●▲
	Girder damaged	Brace girder with scabs (p. 75) ▣●▲
	Post damaged	Replace post (p. 76) ▣●▲
Floor sags or dips near exterior wall	Gap between subfloor and joist; subfloor or joist movement	Reinforce subfloor at joist (p. 65) □○; reinforce subfloor between joists (p. 66) □○ or reinforce joists (p. 67) □○
	Subfloor section damaged	Replace subfloor section (p. 66) ■●
	Joist damaged	Brace joist with scabs (p. 69) □●▲ or install sister joist (p. 70) □●▲; for more than one joist, install intermediate girder (p. 72) ■●▲
	Header section damaged	Reinforce header section (p. 71) □○
	Sill plate section damaged	Replace sill plate section (p. 74) ▣●▲
Bridge between joists split or cracked; or wood spongy	Rot or insect damage	Check for rot and insect damage (p. 126) □○
	Wood shrinkage; house settlement	Replace bridge (p. 68) □○
Subfloor split or cracked; or wood spongy	Rot or insect damage	Check for rot and insect damage (p. 126) □○
	Wood shrinkage; house settlement	Replace subfloor section (p. 66) ■●
Subfloor sagging	Gap between subfloor and joist; subfloor or joist movement	Reinforce subfloor at joist (p. 65) □○; reinforce subfloor between joists (p. 66) □○ or reinforce joists (p. 67) □○
	Subfloor section damaged	Replace subfloor section (p. 66) ■●
	Joist supporting subfloor damaged	Brace joist with scabs (p. 69) □●▲ or install sister joist (p. 70) □●▲; for more than one joist, install intermediate girder (p. 72) ■●▲
	Header supporting subfloor damaged	Reinforce header section (p. 71) □○
	Sill plate supporting joist under subfloor damaged	Replace sill plate section (p. 74) ▣●▲
	Girder supporting joist under subfloor damaged	Brace girder with scabs (p. 75) ▣●▲
	Post supporting girder and joists under subfloor damaged	Replace post (p. 76) ▣●▲
Joist split or cracked; or wood spongy	Rot or insect damage	Check for rot and insect damage (p. 126) □○
	Wood shrinkage; house settlement	Reinforce subfloor between joists (p. 66) □○ or reinforce joists (p. 67) □○; brace crowned joist with scabs (p. 70)□●; brace sagging joist with scabs (p. 69) □●▲ or install sister joist (p. 70) □●▲; for more than one sagging joist, install intermediate girder (p. 72) ■●▲

DEGREE OF DIFFICULTY: □ **Easy** ▣ **Moderate** ■ **Complex**
ESTIMATED TIME: ○ **Less than 1 hour** ● **1 to 3 hours** ● **Over 3 hours**   ▲ **Special tool required**

TROUBLESHOOTING GUIDE

SYMPTOM	POSSIBLE CAUSE	PROCEDURE
Joist crooked, twisted, crowned (curved upward) or sagging	Joist damaged	Reinforce subfloor between joists *(p. 66)* □○ or reinforce joists *(p. 67)* □○; brace crowned joist with scabs *(p. 70)*□◖; brace sagging joist with scabs *(p. 69)* □◖▲ or install sister joist *(p. 70)* □◖▲; for more than one sagging joist, install intermediate girder *(p. 72)* ■●▲
	Sill plate supporting joist damaged	Replace sill plate section *(p. 74)* ◪●▲
	Girder supporting joist damaged	Brace girder with scabs *(p. 75)* ◪◖▲
	Post supporting girder under joist damaged	Replace post *(p. 76)* ◪●▲
Header split or cracked; or wood spongy	Rot or insect damage	Check for rot and insect damage *(p. 126)* □○
	Wood shrinkage; house settlement	Reinforce header section *(p. 71)* □○
Sill plate split or cracked; or wood spongy	Rot or insect damage	Check for rot and insect damage *(p. 126)* □○
	Wood shrinkage; house settlement	Replace sill plate section *(p. 74)* ◪●▲
Girder split or cracked; or wood spongy	Rot or insect damage	Check for rot and insect damage *(p. 126)* □○
	Wood shrinkage; house settlement	Brace girder with scabs *(p. 75)* ◪◖▲
Girder crooked, twisted or sagging	Girder damaged	Brace girder with scabs *(p. 75)* ◪◖▲
	Post supporting girder damaged	Replace post *(p. 76)* ◪●▲
Post split or cracked; or wood spongy	Rot or insect damage	Check for rot and insect damage *(p. 126)* □○
	Wood shrinkage; house settlement	Replace post *(p. 76)* ◪●▲
Post wobbly, twisted or leaning	Post damaged	Replace post *(p. 76)* ◪●▲

DEGREE OF DIFFICULTY: □ Easy ◪ Moderate ■ Complex
ESTIMATED TIME: ○ Less than 1 hour ◖ 1 to 3 hours ● Over 3 hours

▲ Special tool required

REINFORCING THE SUBFLOOR AT A JOIST

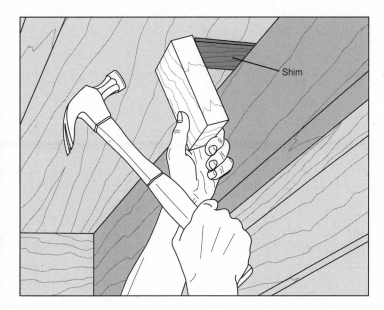

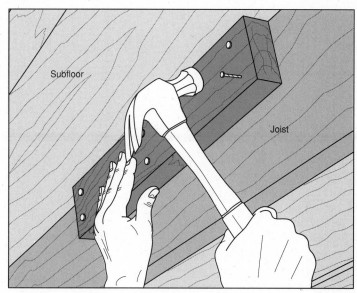

Installing a shim. Working from below the faulty floor section, locate any gap between a joist and the subfloor. For a gap that spans a long distance, install a cleat *(step right)*. For a short gap, install a wood shim to support the subfloor. Using a handsaw or a chisel, cut a wedge-shaped shim that is slightly thicker than the gap at one end and tapered to a point at the other end. Coat the top and bottom of the shim with wood glue, then insert the tapered end into the gap; holding a wood block against the thick end, use a hammer to tap the shim snugly into place *(above)*.

Installing a cleat. Working from below the faulty floor section, locate any gap between a joist and the subfloor. For a gap that spans a short distance, install a shim *(step left)*. For a long gap, install a cleat to support the subfloor. To make a cleat, use a handsaw to cut a 2-by-4 slightly longer than the gap. Wearing safety goggles and a safety helmet, position the cleat along the gap, butting the side of it against the joist and the top of it against the subfloor. To fasten the cleat, nail it to the joist with 2 1/2-inch common nails, driving a nail into the top and bottom of it every 6 inches along it *(above)*.

REINFORCING THE SUBFLOOR BETWEEN JOISTS

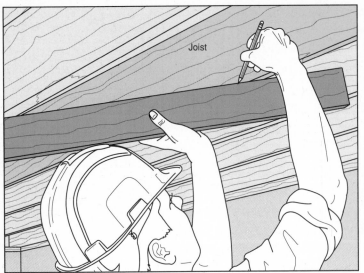

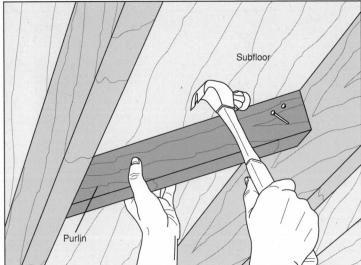

Installing a purlin. Working from below the faulty floor section, locate any sag in the subfloor between two joists. For a small sag, install a purlin across the center of it to raise the subfloor; for a large sag, install as many purlins as necessary to raise the subfloor, spacing them evenly. To make a purlin, use a 2-by-4. Wearing a safety helmet, hold the 2-by-4 at a 45-degree angle across the joist on each side of the sag, its 2-inch side butted against the bottom; then, using the inside edge of each joist as a guide, mark a cutting line across the top at each end of it *(above, left)*. Use a saw to cut the marked 2-by-4 to length. Wearing safety goggles, fit the purlin between the joists with its 2-inch side facing up, pushing it firmly against the subfloor until its top is level with the top of the joists; if you cannot push it to a level position by hand, use a jack to raise it as you would for a joist *(page 68)*. To fasten the purlin, use 2-inch box nails to toe-nail *(page 135)* it to the joists *(above, right)*, driving in two nails at each end of it.

REPLACING A SUBFLOOR SECTION

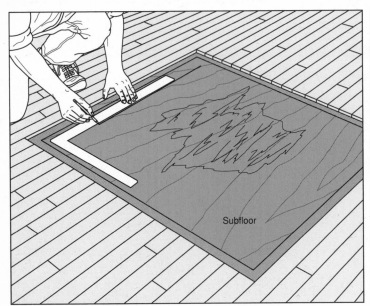

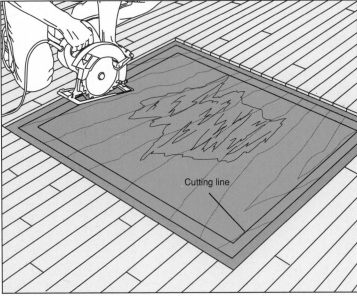

1 Removing the damaged section. Working from below the faulty floor section, check the subfloor for signs of rot or insect damage *(page 126)*; for extensive damage, consult a building professional. For minor damage, replace the subfloor section. With a helper working from above, note the location of the nearest joist beyond opposite edges of the damaged section and the adjacent edges of the damaged section between the joists. Working from above, remove enough of the carpet *(page 106)*, rigid flooring *(page 50)*, resilient flooring *(page 36)* or wood flooring *(page 14)* to expose the damaged section. Using a carpenter's square, mark cutting lines around the damaged section; mark each edge along the center of the nearest joist using the nails in the subfloor as a guide, then mark each adjacent edge between the joists *(above, left)*. Pull the nails out of the damaged section. Prepare to use a circular saw, setting the cutting depth equal to the subfloor thickness—typically 5/8 inch if it is of plywood; 3/4 inch if it is of board. Wearing safety goggles, make a plunge cut *(page 131)* at a cutting line *(above, right)*, then continue along to the end of it; reverse the saw direction and use the same procedure to cut to the other end of it. Cut along the other cutting lines the same way, then use a pry bar to lift out the damaged section.

REPLACING A SUBFLOOR SECTION (continued)

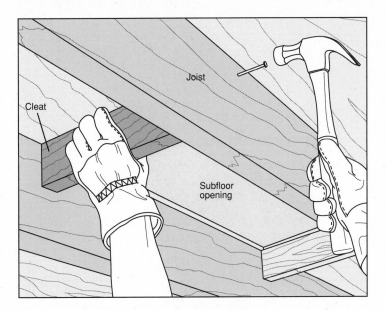

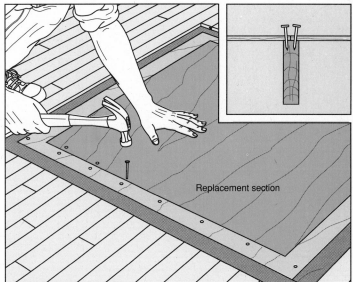

2 **Installing cleats.** Work from below to install a cleat under each cut edge of the subfloor between the joists. To make a cleat, measure the length of the cut edge between the joists; then, use a saw to cut a 2-by-4 to length. Wearing safety goggles and a safety helmet, fit the cleat between the joists with its 2-inch side facing up, pushing it firmly against the subfloor until its top is level with the top of the joists; center it along the cut edge. To fasten the cleat, nail through the joist at each end of it with 3-inch box nails, driving a nail into the top *(above)* and bottom of it; to fasten another cleat on the other side of a joist, toe-nail *(page 135)* it to the joist.

3 **Installing the replacement section.** Work from above to measure the length and width of the subfloor opening, then cut a plywood sheet of the same thickness as the subfloor to size for a replacement section. Fit the replacement section into the opening and nail it every 6 inches to the cleats and joists under it with 2 1/2-inch ring-shank nails; also nail the cut edges of the undamaged subfloor to the cleats and joists *(above)*, driving in each nail of a pair at a slight angle toward the other *(inset)*. Then, reinstall any wood flooring *(page 14)*, resilient flooring *(page 36)*, rigid flooring *(page 50)* or carpet *(page 106)* you removed.

REINFORCING A JOIST

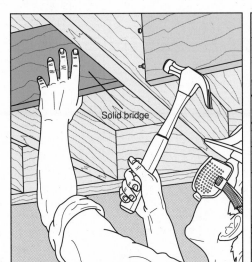

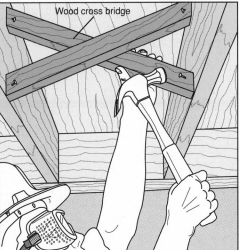

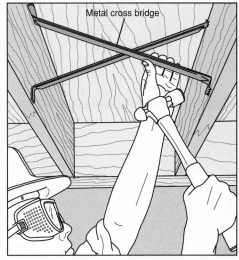

Installing bridges. Working from below the faulty floor section, check for movement of a joist. If there is no bridge between the joist and the joist on each side of it, install a solid bridge or two cross bridges every 6 to 8 feet along it to reinforce it; if a bridge is damaged, remove it *(page 68)* and install a new one. To make a solid bridge, measure the distance between the joists, then cut a piece of lumber of the same grade and dimensions as the joists to length. Wearing safety goggles and a safety helmet, position the bridge and fasten it with 3-inch common nails, driving two nails through the joist at each end of it *(above, left)*; offset it from any bridge on the other side of a joist, as shown. For cross bridges, measure the distance between the top of one joist and the bottom of the other joist. To make a wood cross bridge, cut a 2-by-2 or a 1-by-3 to length, beveling the ends; buy a metal cross bridge at a building supply center. To install a wood cross bridge, fit it between the joists and toe-nail *(page 135)* two 2 1/2-inch box nails through each end of it into the joist *(above, center)*, driving a nail into opposite sides. To install a metal cross bridge, position it between the joists and use a ball-peen hammer to pound one end of it into the top of one joist and the other end of it into the bottom of the other joist *(above, right)*.

REPLACING A BRIDGE

Wood cross bridge

Removing bridges. If a bridge fastened between joists is damaged or obstructs your repair, remove it. Wear safety goggles and a safety helmet. To remove a solid wood bridge or a wood cross bridge from between two joists, pull out its nails using a pry bar, a claw hammer or a nail puller. If necessary, use a ball-peen hammer to drive a pry bar between one end of the bridge and the joist *(left)*, then pry the end of it away from the joist. Wearing work gloves, work by hand to twist the bridge and loosen the other end of it, pulling it free of the other joist; or, use a small sledgehammer to knock it from between the joists. To remove a metal cross bridge from between two joists, use a pry bar to pry the bottom end of it out of the joist; then, wear work gloves to twist the bridge by hand and loosen the top end of it, pulling it free of the other joist. After completing your repair, reinstall any bridge you removed; replace any damaged bridge *(page 67)*.

JACKING A JOIST

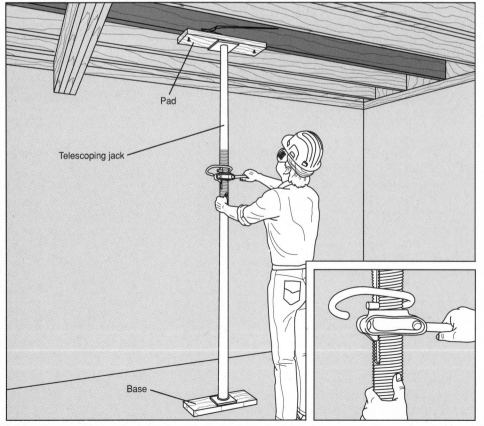

Pad

Telescoping jack

Base

Supporting or raising a joist. To support or raise a joist, rent a telescoping jack at a tool rental agency. Remove any bridges attached to the joist *(step above)*. Using 3-inch box nails, temporarily nail a 2-by-8 pad 2 feet long to the bottom of the joist at the point to be supported or raised—usually at the center of it or any damaged section of it. Then, place a 2-by-8 base 2 feet long on the floor directly below the pad. Set up the jack *(page 137)*, positioning its base plate on the 2-by-8 base. Turning the handle of the screw jack assembly counterclockwise *(inset)*, extend the jack until its top plate presses firmly against the 2-by-8 pad, supporting the joist in place. To raise the joist, continue extending the jack *(left)*; raise the joist no more than 1/8 inch per day, having a helper check nearby walls on the stories above it for cracks. If a crack develops while raising the joist, consult a building professional. If you are repairing the joist, raise it until it is level, then install a sister joist *(page 70)* or brace it with scabs *(page 69)*.

BRACING A SAGGING JOIST WITH SCABS

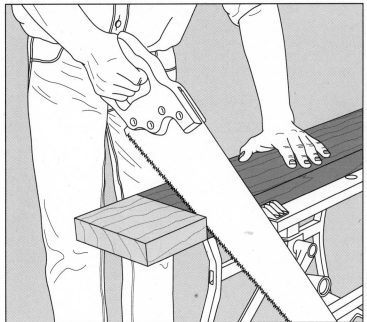

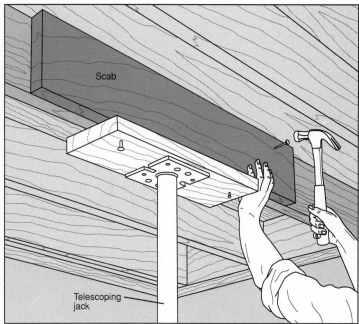

1 **Installing the first scab.** Working from below the faulty floor section, check for a sagging joist. If more than one joist sags, install an intermediate girder *(page 72)*. If a joist is damaged extensively or sags along its entire length, install a sister joist *(page 70)*. If the damage to the joist is localized and the sag is slight, reinforce the joist by installing a scab on each side of the damaged section. Remove any bridges attached to the joist, then use a telescoping jack to raise the joist until it is level *(page 68)*. To make each scab, use a saw to cut a piece of lumber of the same grade and dimensions as the joist 4 feet longer than the damaged section *(above, left)*. Wearing safety goggles and a safety helmet, position a scab against one side of the joist, centering it on the damaged section; temporarily nail it to the joist with 3-inch common nails *(above, right)*, driving in two nails at each end and the center of it.

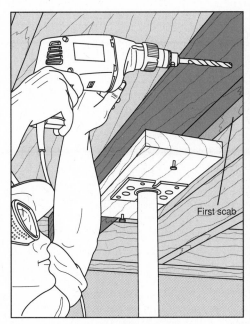

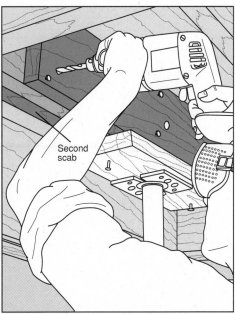

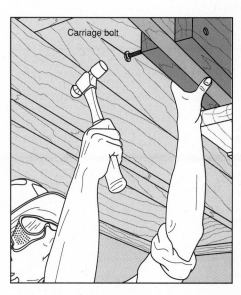

3 **Fastening the scabs.** Insert a carriage bolt through each hole in the scabs and joist, tapping it with a ball-peen hammer *(above)* until its head is flush against the scab. Fit the threaded end of each carriage bolt with a washer, then thread a nut onto it by hand; tighten each nut in turn using a wrench. Remove the telescoping jack, then reinstall any bridges you removed *(page 67)*.

2 **Installing the second scab.** Before installing the second scab, bore holes for carriage bolts through the first scab and the joist; plan to use carriage bolts that are 6 inches long. Fit an electric drill with an auger bit of the same diameter as a carriage bolt. Working on the side of the joist opposite the scab for greatest maneuvering, bore a hole every 12 to 16 inches through the joist and the scab *(above, left)*, alternating between the top and the bottom about 2 inches from any edge. Position the second scab on the side of the joist opposite the first scab and temporarily nail it to the joist; work on the side of the joist opposite it to finish boring the holes, inserting the bit in turn into each hole in the first scab and the joist *(above, right)*.

BRACING A CROWNED JOIST WITH SCABS

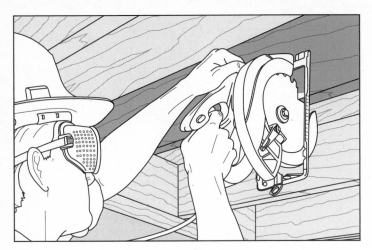

1 **Notching the joist.** Working from below the faulty floor section, check for an upward-curved or crowned joist. Remove any bridges attached to the joist *(page 68)*, then locate the point at which it peaks. Run a string along the bottom from one end to the other end of the joist, fastening each end of it with a nail; then, mark the point on the bottom of the joist at which the gap between the string and it is greatest and remove the string. Wearing safety goggles and a safety helmet, use a circular saw to notch the joist at the marked point *(above)*, cutting about 1/3 of the way across its width. Working from above, place a heavy object on the floor above the joist. Inspect the joist daily to determine when it is level—this may take a week. When the joist is level or if it begins to crack, install a scab along each side of it on the notched section *(step 2)*.

2 **Installing scabs.** To make each scab, cut a piece of lumber of the same grade and dimensions as the joist 6 feet long. Wearing safety goggles and a safety helmet, position a scab along one side of the joist, centered on the notched section; temporarily nail it with 3-inch common nails. Working on the side of the joist opposite the scab for greatest maneuvering, bore a hole for a carriage bolt every 12 to 16 inches through the scab and the joist, alternating between the top and the bottom about 2 inches from any edge. Position the second scab on the side of the joist opposite the first scab and temporarily nail it, then work on the side of the joist opposite it to finish boring the holes. Install a carriage bolt in each hole, fit it with a washer and thread a nut onto it by hand; tighten each nut in turn using a wrench *(above)*. Reinstall any bridges you removed *(page 67)*.

INSTALLING A SISTER JOIST

1 **Positioning the sister joist.** Working from below the faulty floor section, check for a sagging joist. If more than one joist sags, install an intermediate girder *(page 72)*. If the damage to a joist is localized and the sag is slight, brace the joist with scabs *(page 69)*. If the joist is damaged extensively or sags along its entire length, install a sister joist alongside it. Remove any bridges attached to the damaged joist, then use a telescoping jack to raise the damaged joist until it is level *(page 68)*. To make a sister joist, use a saw to cut a piece of lumber of the same grade and dimensions as the damaged joist equal in length to it. Wearing safety goggles and a safety helmet, work with a helper to position the sister joist alongside the damaged joist, angling it to fit one end into place between the subfloor and girder *(left)*; fit the other end into place between the subfloor and sill plate or girder the same way. Turn the sister joist upright and push it flush against the joist; if necessary, use a small sledgehammer to pound it into place. If you cannot turn the sister joist upright, remove it and use a chisel to narrow the ends, then reposition it.

INSTALLING A SISTER JOIST (continued)

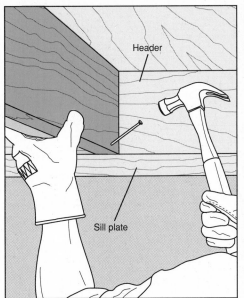

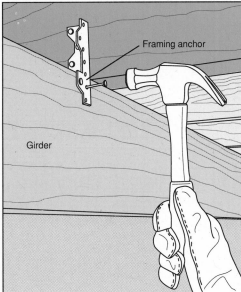

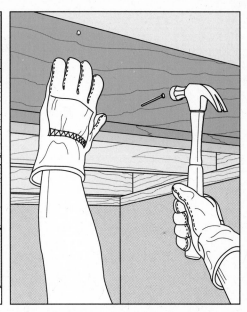

2 **Fastening the sister joist.** Fasten the sister joist at each end to the sill plate or girder on which it rests and along its length to the damaged joist. Using a 3-inch box nail, toe-nail *(page 135)* the sister joist to a sill plate *(above, left)*; also toe-nail the sister joist to the header on the sill plate. Use a framing anchor and the nails for it to fasten the sister joist to a girder; fit the framing anchor into position against the sister joist and girder, then nail it in place *(above, center)*. Fasten the sister joist to the damaged joist every 12 to 16 inches with 4-inch common nails, alternating between the top and the bottom edge *(above, right)*; clinch any protruding nail tip, bending it flush against the surface with the hammer. Remove the telescoping jack, then reinstall any bridges you removed *(page 67)*.

REINFORCING A HEADER SECTION

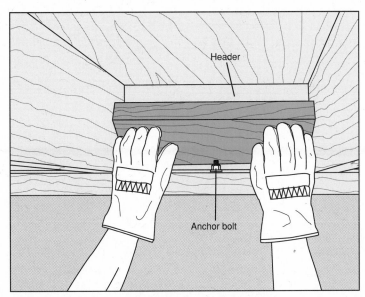

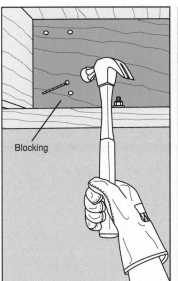

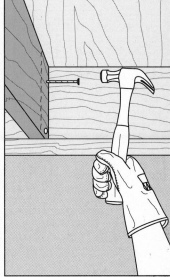

1 **Installing blocking.** Working from below the faulty floor section, check the header for signs of rot or insect damage *(page 126)*; for extensive damage, consult a building professional. For minor damage to a small section of the header, reinforce the section between two joists with blocking. To make blocking, measure the length of the header section between the joists, then wear work gloves and a dust mask to cut a piece of pressure-treated lumber of the same dimensions as the joists to length; apply wood preservative to any cut edge. Wearing safety goggles and a safety helmet, fit the blocking between the joists, angling it behind any anchor bolt in the sill plate *(above)*; then, push the blocking flush against the header section.

2 **Fastening the blocking.** Fasten the blocking to the header section behind it and to the joist at each end of it using 2 1/2-inch common nails. To fasten the blocking to the header section behind it, drive a nail through the top and the bottom of the blocking into the header section a few inches from each end of it. To fasten the blocking to the joist at each end of it, toe-nail *(page 135)* through the top and the bottom of the blocking into the side of the joist *(above, left)*; if there is access to the end of a joist on the side of it opposite the blocking, also drive a nail through the top and the bottom of the joist into the end of the blocking *(above, right)*.

INSTALLING AN INTERMEDIATE GIRDER

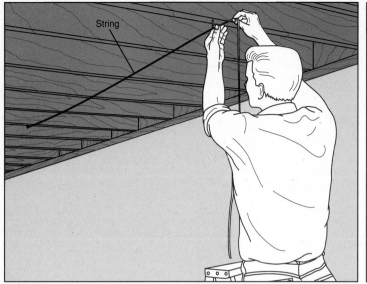

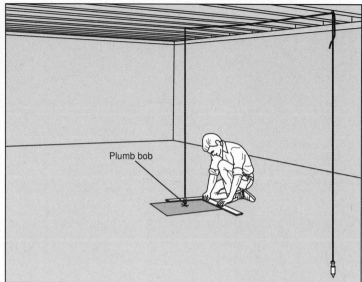

1 **Marking the intermediate girder location.** Working from below the faulty floor section, check for a sagging joist. If a joist is damaged extensively or sags along its entire length, install a sister joist *(page 70)*. If the damage to the joist is localized and the sag is slight, brace the joist with scabs *(page 69)*. If more than one joist sags, install an intermediate girder. Consult a building professional for the specific girder dimensions, post spacing and footing size recommended. Remove any bridges attached to the joists *(page 68)*, then locate the line along which the sag is greatest. Run a string across the bottom of the joists perpendicular to them every 2 feet along them; ensure the strings run at the same height by fastening each end to a level joist,

driving a 2 1/2-inch nail 1/2 inch into it and tying the string around the base of the nail head *(above, left)*. Measure the gaps between each string and the bottom of the joists; use the string along which you measure the smallest gaps to mark the location for the girder and remove the other strings. Use the nail at each end of the string marking the girder location to mark the location for a post, hanging a plumb bob from it; if the distance between the ends of the string is greater than the post spacing recommended, mark the location for each additional post needed by hanging a plumb bob from a joist at a point along the string the same way. Mark the locations for footings of the size recommended on the floor using the point below each plumb bob as a center point *(above, right)*.

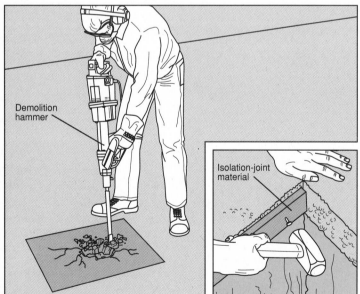

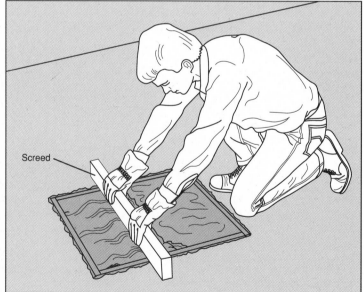

2 **Installing the footings.** Rent a demolition hammer at a tool rental agency and use it to break up the concrete at each footing location. Wearing ear protection, safety goggles, a dust mask and work gloves, chip holes 6 to 8 inches apart in the concrete within the footing marks, cracking it into pieces *(above, left)*. Use a spade to remove the concrete pieces and the gravel or soil below them, digging to the depth recommended. To prepare each hole for concrete, install 1/2-inch isolation-joint material along the floor edge on each side it; buy the isolation-joint material at a building supply center, cut it to size and

use a small sledgehammer to fasten it with masonry nails *(inset)*. Buy pre-mixed concrete and follow the manufacturer's instructions to mix it, then use a spade to fill each hole with it. Level the surface of the concrete with a 2-by-4 screed slightly longer than the width of the footing, pulling it slowly across the surface and working it from side to side to keep concrete from adhering to it *(above, right)*; to fill in any low spots, keep a small amount of concrete ahead of it. Let the concrete cure for 5 days, regularly moistening it with water to keep it from drying out.

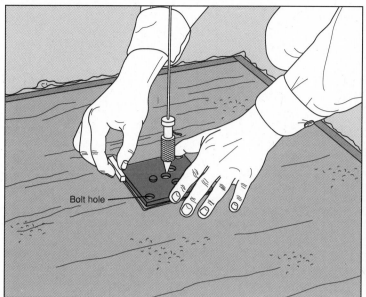

Bolt hole

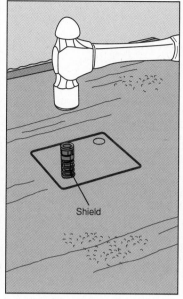

Shield

Lag bolt

3 Installing permanent jacks for posts. Use permanent metal jacks as posts to support the girder. Buy as many jacks as necessary at a building supply center, along with lag bolts and shields to fasten them to the footings; if necessary, rent a 1/2-inch hammer drill at a tool rental agency to drill holes for the shields in the footings. To position each jack on its footing, rehang the plumb bob from the point on the joist used to locate the footing center point *(step 1)*. Center the base plate of the jack on the footing under the plumb bob and mark its outline and bolt-hole positions *(above, left)*, then remove it.

Wearing safety goggles and a dust mask, use the hammer drill to drill a hole in the footing at each bolt-hole mark equal in diameter to a shield and equal in depth to its length. Tap a shield into each hole with a ball-peen hammer *(above, center)*, then reposition the base plate on the footing. Check that the base plate is level using a carpenter's level; if necessary, insert a shim under an edge to level it. Then, install the lag bolts, fitting each one in turn into a shield and driving it with a socket wrench *(above, right)* until its head is tight against the base plate. Install a jack on each base plate following the manufacturer's instructions for your model.

Intermediate girder

Top plate

4 Installing the intermediate girder. To make the intermediate girder, measure the distance between the outside edges of the top plates on the jacks installed to support the ends of it. Then, cut lumber of the same grade and dimensions as the joists to length, cutting as many pieces as necessary to make a girder of the thickness recommended. To make a girder of four 2-by-8s, as shown, use 3-inch common nails; fasten one 2-by-8 to another 2-by-8 by driving a nail every 12 to 16 inches along it, alternating between the top and the bottom edges of it, then fasten a 2-by-8 to each side of the fastened 2-by-8s the same way. To install the girder, wear safety goggles and a safety helmet and work with helpers. Extend the jacks following the manufacturer's instructions for your model until there is just enough room to fit the girder between their top plates and the bottom of the joists. Steadying the jacks, lift the girder and slide it onto the top plates, centering it squarely on them *(left)*. Then, extend the jacks until the top of the girder is flush against the bottom of the joists, supporting but not raising them. Use a carpenter's level to check that each jack is plumb; if necessary, use a small sledgehammer to tap it into position. Then, fasten each jack to the girder by driving a nail fitted with a washer through each hole in the top plate into the girder.

INSTALLING AN INTERMEDIATE GIRDER (continued)

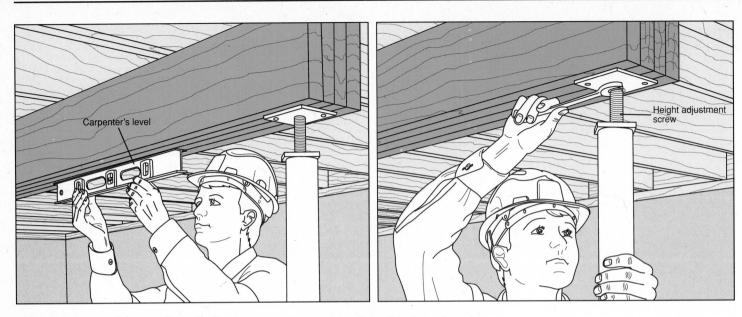

5 **Raising the intermediate girder.** To check that the intermediate girder is level, work along the bottom of it using a carpenter's level *(above, left)*; if necessary, adjust it until it is level by extending or lowering a jack, using a wrench to turn the height adjustment screw *(above, right)*. When the girder is level, extend each jack by an equal amount, raising the girder and the joists supported by it no more than 1/8 inch per day and 1/2 inch per week. Each time you extend the jacks, check that the girder is level and have a helper check nearby walls on the stories above it for cracks. If a crack develops while raising the girder, consult a building professional. Otherwise, continue extending the jacks the same way, raising the girder until the joists supported by it are level.

REPLACING A SILL PLATE SECTION

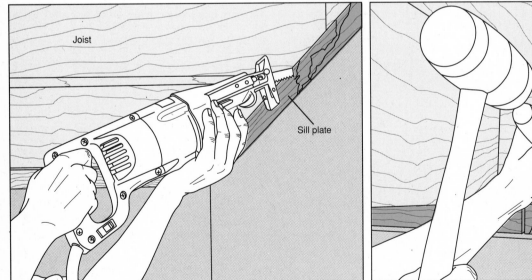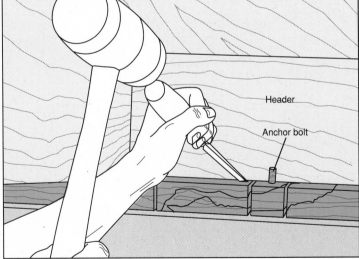

1 **Removing the damaged section.** Working from below the faulty floor section, check the sill plate for signs of rot or insect damage *(page 126)*; for extensive damage, consult a building professional. For minor damage to a small section of the sill plate, replace the damaged section. Wearing safety goggles and a safety helmet, use a pry bar to pull·out any nails holding the damaged section to the header or any joist it supports; also remove the nut and washer from any anchor bolt protruding from the top of it. If the damaged section supports a joist, use a telescoping jack to raise the end of the joist 1/16 inch off it *(page 68)*; to raise the end of more than one joist, set up a jack under a joist at least every 8 feet and use a 4-by-4 longer than the distance between them as a brace on the 2-by-8 pad, temporarily nailing the top plate of the jack to the pad and the pad to the brace. Use a reciprocating saw to cut down at a 90-degree angle through each end of the damaged section *(above, left)*; also cut down the same way on each side of any anchor bolt protruding from the top of it. Then, use a wood chisel and a mallet to chip out the damaged section *(above, right)*, working under the header and any joist supported by it.

REPLACING A SILL PLATE SECTION (continued)

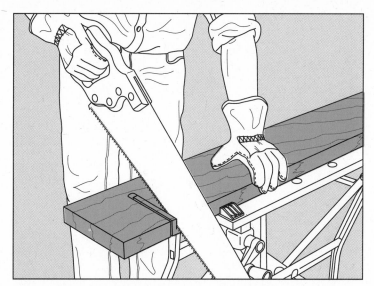

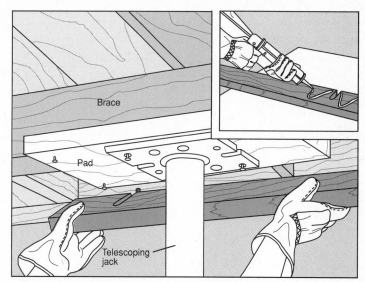

2 **Preparing the replacement section.** Measure the length of the opening in the sill plate, then wear work gloves to cut a piece of pressure-treated lumber of the same dimensions as the sill plate to size. Measure the position of any anchor bolt in the sill plate opening and mark it on the replacement section. Use an electric drill to bore a hole for the anchor bolt at the marked point, then use a saw to cut a notch for it; cut straight to each side of the hole from the edge to be fitted under the header *(above)*. Apply wood preservative to the cut edges of the replacement section.

3 **Installing the replacement section.** Use a caulking gun to apply a bead of acrylic polymeric caulk along the bottom of the replacement section *(inset)*. Wearing safety goggles and a safety helmet, fit the replacement section into position under the header and any joist, aligning any notch in it with the anchor bolt *(above)*; if necessary, use a small sledgehammer to tap it. Remove any telescoping jack. Fit any anchor bolt protruding from the replacement section with a washer and install a nut on it. Use 3-inch box nails to toe-nail *(page 135)* through the header into the replacement section; nail through any joist supported by the replacement section into it the same way.

BRACING A GIRDER WITH SCABS

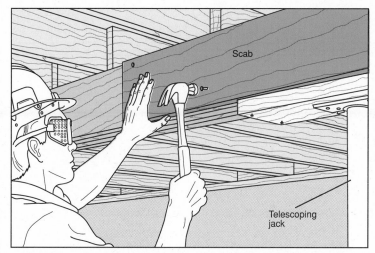

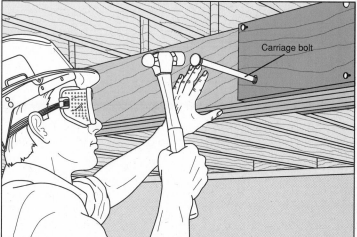

Installing scabs. Working from below the faulty floor section, check for a sagging girder. If a girder is damaged extensively or sags along its entire length, consult a building professional. If the damage to the girder is localized and the sag is slight, reinforce the girder by installing a scab on each side of the damaged section. Use a telescoping jack to raise the girder until it is level as you would a joist *(page 68)*; raise it no more than 1/8 inch per day and 1/2 inch per week. To make each scab, use a saw to cut a piece of lumber of the same grade and dimensions as a joist 6 feet longer than the damaged section. Wearing safety goggles and a safety helmet, position a scab on one side of the girder, centering it on the damaged section; temporarily nail it to the girder with 3-inch

common nails, driving a nail every 12 to 16 inches along it, alternating between the top and the bottom edge *(above, left)*. Position the other scab on the other side of the girder and temporarily nail it in place the same way. Then, bore holes for carriage bolts through the scabs and the girder; plan to use carriage bolts that are 10 inches long. Fit an electric drill with an auger bit of the same diameter as a carriage bolt, then bore a hole every 12 to 16 inches through the scabs and the girder, alternating between the top and the bottom about 2 inches from any edge. Use a ball-peen hammer to tap a carriage bolt into each hole *(above, right)*; then, install a washer and a nut on the threaded end of each carriage bolt, tightening the nuts with a wrench. Remove the telescoping jack.

REPLACING A POST

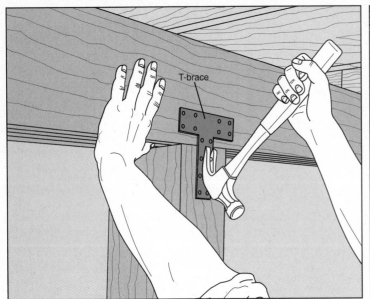

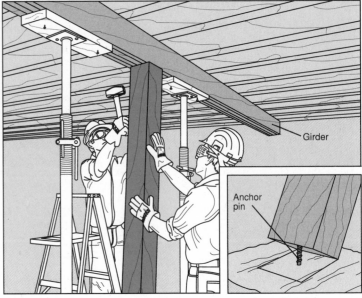

1 **Removing the post.** Working from below the faulty floor section, check for a damaged post. To replace the post, install a telescoping jack within 2 feet of it under the girder on each side of it, supporting the girder as you would a joist *(page 68)*. Wearing safety goggles and a safety helmet, work with a helper to remove the post. If the base of the post is held by a post anchor, have your helper steady the post while you remove the fasteners from the post anchor; if the base of the post rests directly on the footing, trace its outline on the footing. Then, remove the fasteners and any framing anchor holding the top of the post to the girder; to remove the T-brace shown, pull out the

nails *(above, left)*. With your helper steadying the post, use a small sledgehammer to knock the top of it from under the girder *(above, right)*. Then, pull away the post; if the base of it sits on an anchor pin embedded in the footing, lift it off *(inset)*. Check that the girder is level using a carpenter's level; if necessary, extend the jacks until it is level, raising it no more than 1/8 inch per day and 1/2 inch per week. Each time you extend the jacks, have a helper check nearby walls on the stories above the girder for cracks. If a crack develops while raising the girder, consult a building professional. Otherwise, continue extending the jacks the same way, raising the girder until the joists supported by it are level.

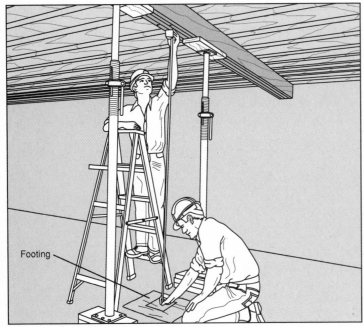

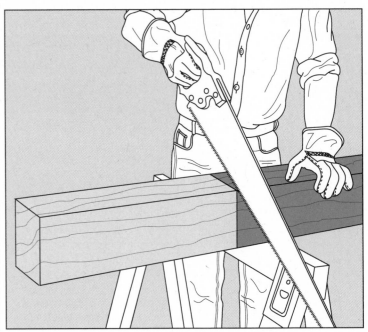

2 **Preparing the replacement post.** To make a replacement post, measure the vertical distance between the bottom of the girder and the footing *(above, left)* or the post anchor where the old post stood. Then, use a handsaw to cut lumber of the same grade and dimensions as the old post to length *(above, right)*. Or, cut lumber of the same grade and dimensions as the joists to length, cutting as many pieces as necessary to make a post of the same thickness as the

girder. To make a post of four 2-by-8s, for example, use 3-inch common nails; fasten one 2-by-8 to another 2-by-8 by driving a nail every 12 to 16 inches along it, alternating between the top and the bottom edges of it, then fasten a 2-by-8 to each side of the fastened 2-by-8s the same way. If the footing for the post has a post anchor or an anchor pin, install the replacement post *(step 4)*; otherwise, first install an anchor pin in the footing *(step 3)*.

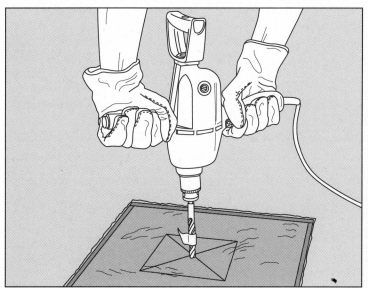

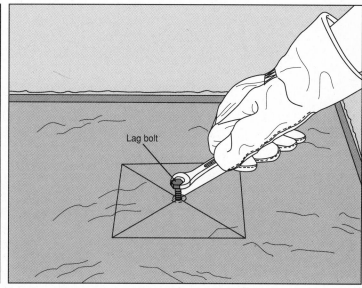

3 **Installing an anchor pin.** For a makeshift anchor pin, use a lag bolt 2 inches long and a shield 1 inch long of the same diameter as the lag bolt. To determine the location for the anchor pin, use the outline of the old post traced on the footing *(step 1)*, marking lines between the corners diagonally opposite to each other. Wearing safety goggles and a dust mask, use a hammer drill to drill a hole for the shield in the footing at the intersection of the marked lines between the corners; drill the hole equal in diameter to the shield and equal in depth to its length *(above, left)*, using masking tape wrapped around the bit to mark the drilling depth. Tap the shield into the hole with a ball-peen hammer, then fit the lag bolt into the shield and use a wrench to turn it *(above, right)* until it protrudes 1 inch from the footing.

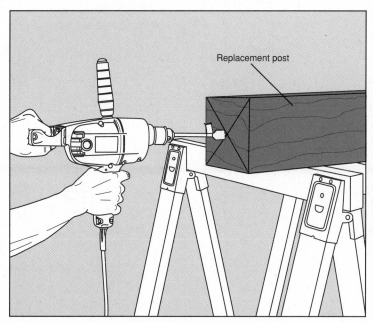

4 **Installing the replacement post.** If there is an anchor pin in the footing, bore a hole for it in the base of the replacement post. Fit an electric drill with a bit of the same diameter as the anchor pin and wrap masking tape around it to mark a drilling depth equal to the amount the anchor pin protrudes from the footing. To determine the location for the hole in the base of the post, mark lines on it between the corners diagonally opposite to each other. Then, bore a hole of the marked depth into the base of the post at the intersection of the marked lines between the corners *(above, left)*. To install the post, work with a helper to stand it upright, fitting the base of it onto the anchor pin or any post anchor; then, slide the top of the post into position under the girder. If the post fits tightly, use a small sledgehammer to tap it into place; if it fits loosely, use a hammer to drive a shim on opposite sides of it between it and the girder. Use a carpenter's level to check that the post is plumb; if necessary, reposition it. When the post is plumb, fasten the top of it to the girder using framing anchors; for example, nail a T-brace to the post and the girder on opposite sides of the girder *(above, right)*. If the base of the post is installed in a post anchor, also fasten the post anchor to the post. Remove the telescoping jacks.

STAIRS

A staircase plays a functional role in everyday life at home, providing easy access between its stories—and an enduring role in the history of house architecture, as a centerpiece of wood joinery and craftsmanship. Two typical staircases are illustrated: the open-closed stringer type *(below, left)*, with an open stringer along the side away from a wall and a closed stringer along the side against a wall; the closed-closed stringer type *(below, right)*, with a closed stringer along the side away from and along the side against a wall. Staircases more elaborate or simpler than these staircases are common, usually different only in the detail or the combination of their features; three varieties of basement staircases are shown on page 79.

The treads and risers of a staircase may be fitted into the routed grooves of a closed stringer and supported in place by wedges; or, they may be set against the cut notches of an open stringer, each tread overhanging it and each riser beveled to fit it. A tread may fit into a routed groove of or butt against the riser above it; it may butt against or have a routed groove to fit the riser its nosing overhangs below it. Glue blocks are typically installed under the staircase along the joint between each tread and the riser below it. A railing assembly comprised of a handrail, a newel post and balusters closes off any side of a staircase away from a wall; a floating handrail is often used on the side of a staircase along a wall.

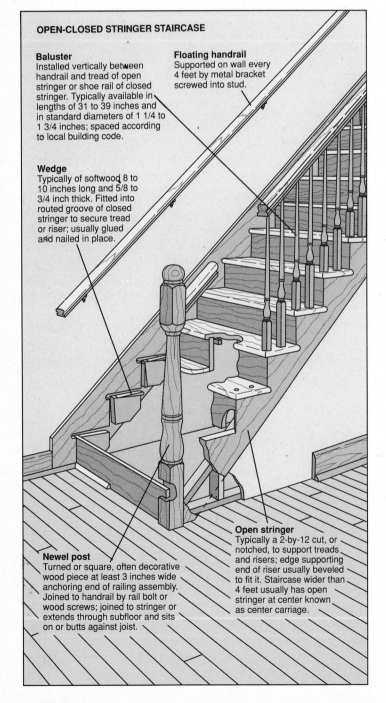

OPEN-CLOSED STRINGER STAIRCASE

Baluster
Installed vertically between handrail and tread of open stringer or shoe rail of closed stringer. Typically available in lengths of 31 to 39 inches and in standard diameters of 1 1/4 to 1 3/4 inches; spaced according to local building code.

Wedge
Typically of softwood 8 to 10 inches long and 5/8 to 3/4 inch thick. Fitted into routed groove of closed stringer to secure tread or riser; usually glued and nailed in place.

Floating handrail
Supported on wall every 4 feet by metal bracket screwed into stud.

Newel post
Turned or square, often decorative wood piece at least 3 inches wide anchoring end of railing assembly. Joined to handrail by rail bolt or wood screws; joined to stringer or extends through subfloor and sits on or butts against joist.

Open stringer
Typically a 2-by-12 cut, or notched, to support treads and risers; edge supporting end of riser usually beveled to fit it. Staircase wider than 4 feet usually has open stringer at center known as center carriage.

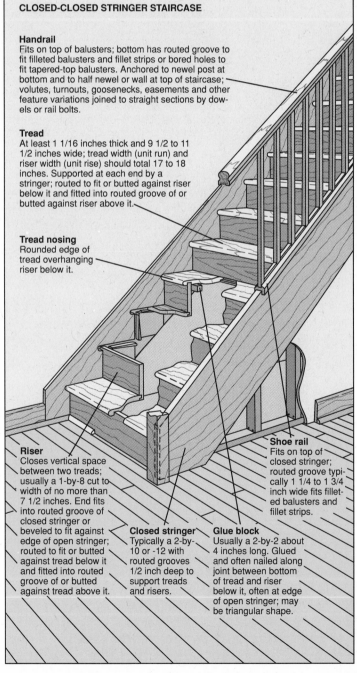

CLOSED-CLOSED STRINGER STAIRCASE

Handrail
Fits on top of balusters; bottom has routed groove to fit filleted balusters and fillet strips or bored holes to fit tapered-top balusters. Anchored to newel post at bottom and to half newel or wall at top of staircase; volutes, turnouts, goosenecks, easements and other feature variations joined to straight sections by dowels or rail bolts.

Tread
At least 1 1/16 inches thick and 9 1/2 to 11 1/2 inches wide; tread width (unit run) and riser width (unit rise) should total 17 to 18 inches. Supported at each end by a stringer; routed to fit or butted against riser below it and fitted into routed groove of or butted against riser above it.

Tread nosing
Rounded edge of tread overhanging riser below it.

Riser
Closes vertical space between two treads; usually a 1-by-8 cut to width of no more than 7 1/2 inches. End fits into routed groove of closed stringer or beveled to fit against edge of open stringer; routed to fit or butted against tread below it and fitted into routed groove of or butted against tread above it.

Closed stringer
Typically a 2-by-10 or -12 with routed grooves 1/2 inch deep to support treads and risers.

Glue block
Usually a 2-by-2 about 4 inches long. Glued and often nailed along joint between bottom of tread and riser below it, often at edge of open stringer; may be triangular shape.

Shoe rail
Fits on top of closed stringer; routed groove typically 1 1/4 to 1 3/4 inch wide fits filleted balusters and fillet strips.

Consult the Troubleshooting Guide on pages 80 and 81 to diagnose and repair the staircase of your home. A staircase properly designed and constructed is rarely beset with a structural problem; nonetheless, everyday wear and tear can take a toll over time. To prolong the beauty of your staircase, maintain the surface finish *(page 82)*. An irritating squeak usually can be silenced quickly by securing the problem tread or riser *(page 93)*, tightening the joints between them and the stringers. Referring to the illustrations of baluster types *(below, left)*, you can tighten any dovetailed *(page 85)*, doweled *(page 86)* or filleted *(page 87)* baluster, or repair *(page 90)* or replace *(page 87)* it; modern balusters are usually the doweled type.

Patience and care are demanded when repairing a staircase to preserve its craftmanship and structural integrity. In some instances, the procedure you will be instructed to follow depends on whether there is access under the staircase; when there is the choice, work from below rather than from above. As a rule, repairs from below the staircase are easiest to perform—carrying the least risk of inadvertent damage since most of the work is out of view. The materials needed for staircase repairs are readily available at a building supply center or lumber yard that specializes in stair parts; the only tools necessary are basic carpentry tools. Before starting a repair, refer to Tools & Techniques *(page 122)* and the Emergency Guide *(page 8)*.

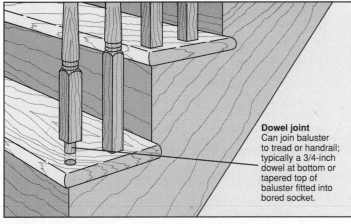

Dowel joint
Can join baluster to tread or handrail; typically a 3/4-inch dowel at bottom or tapered top of baluster fitted into bored socket.

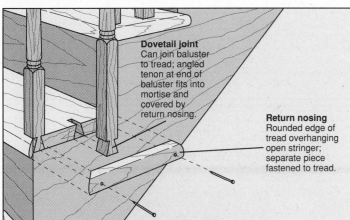

Dovetail joint
Can join baluster to tread; angled tenon at end of baluster fits into mortise and covered by return nosing.

Return nosing
Rounded edge of tread overhanging open stringer; separate piece fastened to tread.

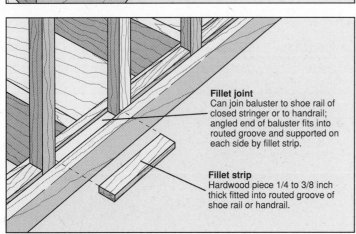

Fillet joint
Can join baluster to shoe rail of closed stringer or to handrail; angled end of baluster fits into routed groove and supported on each side by fillet strip.

Fillet strip
Hardwood piece 1/4 to 3/8 inch thick fitted into routed groove of shoe rail or handrail.

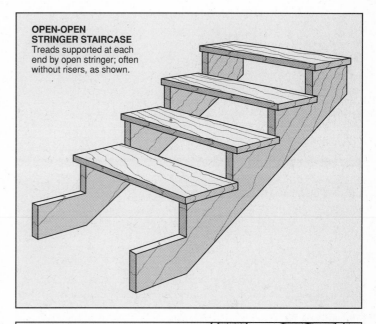

OPEN-OPEN STRINGER STAIRCASE
Treads supported at each end by open stringer; often without risers, as shown.

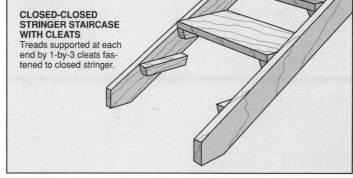

CLOSED-CLOSED STRINGER STAIRCASE WITH CLEATS
Treads supported at each end by 1-by-3 cleats fastened to closed stringer.

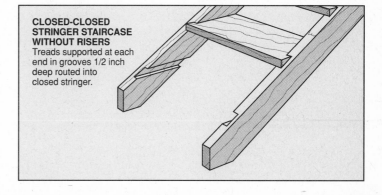

CLOSED-CLOSED STRINGER STAIRCASE WITHOUT RISERS
Treads supported at each end in grooves 1/2 inch deep routed into closed stringer.

TROUBLESHOOTING GUIDE

SYMPTOM	POSSIBLE CAUSE	PROCEDURE
Staircase surface dirty or dull	Everyday wear and tear	Clean staircase (p. 82) □○
	Wax worn; wax build-up	Rewax staircase (p. 84) □◐
Staircase surface stained or discolored	Everyday wear and tear	Clean staircase (p. 82) □○
	Wax worn; wax build-up	Rewax staircase (p. 84) □◐
	Finish scuffed; finish darkened by penetration of water or spilled liquid	Repair finish damage (p. 82) ◨◐
	Finish worn or damaged	Spot-refinish (p. 83) ◨◐ or refinish (p. 84) ◨● staircase
Staircase surface cracked or gouged	Everyday wear and tear; accidental blow or impact	Repair surface damage (p. 82) ◨◐
Staircase wax worn	Everyday wear and tear; lack of regular maintenance	Rewax staircase (p. 84) □◐; maintain surface finish (p. 82) □○
Staircase finish worn or damaged	Everyday wear and tear; lack of regular maintenance	Spot-refinish (p. 83) ◨◐ or refinish (p. 84) ◨● staircase; maintain surface finish (p. 82) □○
Stair runner loose or damaged	Everyday wear and tear; lack of regular maintenance	Troubleshoot carpet (p. 106)
Baluster loose or crooked	Everyday wear and tear; wood shrinkage or shifting of wood joints with age	Tighten dovetailed (p. 85) □○, doweled (p. 86) □○ or filleted (p. 87) □○ baluster
	Baluster damaged	Repair (p. 90) ◨◐ or replace (p. 87) ◨◐ baluster
	Newel post of railing assembly loose or crooked	Secure newel post (p. 91) □○
	Handrail of railing assembly loose at newel post	Secure handrail at newel post (p. 92) □○
	Tread supporting baluster loose or damaged	Secure tread (p. 93) □○; replace tread from below (p. 95) ◼● or from above (p. 97) ◼●
	Stringer supporting baluster damaged	Call staircase professional
Baluster split, cracked or broken	Everyday wear and tear; accidental blow or impact; wood shrinkage or shifting of wood joints with age	Repair (p. 90) ◨◐ or replace (p. 87) ◨◐ baluster
Newel post loose or crooked	Everyday wear and tear; wood shrinkage or shifting of wood joints with age	Secure newel post (p. 91) □○
	Newel post damaged	Call staircase professional
	Floor understructure supporting newel post faulty	Troubleshoot floor understructure (p. 62)
	Stringer supporting newel post damaged	Call staircase professional
Newel post split or cracked	Accidental blow or impact; wood shrinkage or shifting of wood joints with age	Call staircase professional
Handrail loose or sagging	Everyday wear and tear; wood shrinkage or shifting of wood joints with age	Secure handrail at newel post (p. 92) □○; secure floating handrail (p. 104) □○
	Handrail damaged	Call staircase professional
	Baluster supporting handrail loose or damaged	Tighten dovetailed (p. 85) □○, doweled (p. 86) □○ or filleted (p. 87) □○ baluster; repair (p. 90) ◨◐ or replace (p. 87) ◨◐ baluster

DEGREE OF DIFFICULTY: □ **Easy** ◨ **Moderate** ◼ **Complex**
ESTIMATED TIME: ○ **Less than 1 hour** ◐ **1 to 3 hours** ● **Over 3 hours**

SYMPTOM	POSSIBLE CAUSE	PROCEDURE
Handrail loose or sagging (cont'd)	Newel post of railing assembly loose	Secure newel post (p. 91) □○
	Floor understructure supporting staircase faulty	Troubleshoot floor understructure (p. 62)
	Stringer supporting staircase damaged	Call staircase professional
Handrail split or cracked	Accidental blow or impact; wood shrinkage or shifting of wood joints with age	Call staircase professional
Tread slippery	Wax buildup	Rewax staircase (p. 84) □◖
	Stair runner loose or damaged; no stair runner	Troubleshoot carpet (p. 106)
Tread squeaks	Everyday wear and tear; wood shrinkage or shifting of wood joints with age	Work talcum powder into wood joints of tread with balusters, risers and stringers
	Tread loose	Secure tread (p. 93) □○
Tread loose or sagging	Everyday wear and tear; wood shrinkage or shifting of wood joints with age	Secure tread (p. 93) □○
	Tread damaged	Replace tread from below (p. 95) ■● or from above (p. 97) ■●; replace tread of basement staircase (p. 104) □○
	Stringer supporting tread damaged	Call staircase professional; repair stringer of basement staircase (p. 105) ◨◖
Tread nosing split or cracked	Everyday wear and tear; accidental blow or impact; wood shrinkage or shifting of wood joints with age	Repair tread nosing (p. 94) □○
Tread worn, split, cracked or broken	Everyday wear and tear; accidental blow or impact; wood shrinkage or shifting of wood joints with age	Replace tread from below (p. 95) ■● or from above (p. 97) ■●; replace tread of basement staircase (p. 104) □○
Riser loose or crooked	Everyday wear and tear; wood shrinkage or shifting of wood joints with age	Secure riser as you would tread (p. 93) □○
	Riser damaged	Replace riser from below (p. 101) ■● or from above (p. 102) ■●
	Stringer supporting riser damaged	Call staircase professional
Riser split, cracked or broken	Everyday wear and tear; accidental blow or impact; wood shrinkage or shifting of wood joints with age	Replace riser from below (p. 101) ■● or from above (p. 102) ■●
Stringer sagging	Floor understructure supporting stringer faulty	Troubleshoot floor understructure (p. 62)
	Stringer damaged	Call staircase professional; repair stringer of basement staircase (p. 105) ◨◖
Stringer split or cracked	Rot or insect damage	Check for rot and insect damage (p. 126) □○
	Wood shrinkage or shifting of wood joints with age	Call staircase professional; repair stringer of basement staircase (p. 105) ◨◖
Staircase sagging	Floor understructure supporting staircase faulty	Troubleshoot floor understructure (p. 62)
	Stringer supporting staircase damaged	Call staircase professional; repair stringer of basement staircase (p. 105) ◨◖

DEGREE OF DIFFICULTY: □ Easy ◨ Moderate ■ Complex
ESTIMATED TIME: ○ Less than 1 hour ◖ 1 to 3 hours ● Over 3 hours

MAINTAINING THE SURFACE FINISH

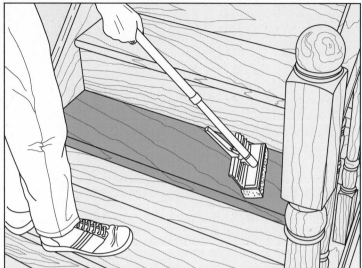

Cleaning the staircase. Vacuum the staircase regularly to keep dirt and grit from being ground into the finish. Use a soft-bristled brush attachment with the vacuum on any surface that is not covered by a stair runner; dust any surface that is hard to reach with the vacuum using a clean, soft cloth. If the staircase has a waxed finish *(page 140)*, touch it up every 4 to 6 months after vacuuming and dusting using a buffing wax of a compatible color; on the handrail, newel posts and balusters, use a paste wax. Following the manufacturer's instructions, wear rubber gloves and apply the wax with a clean cloth, rubbing

vigorously *(above, left)*. If the waxed finish lacks luster, scuffs easily or collects dirt quickly, rewax the staircase *(page 84)*. If the staircase has other than a waxed finish, damp-mop it on a routine basis after vacuuming and dusting to remove any remaining grime; do not soak the finish or let water stand on it. Use a sponge mop lightly dampened with clean, warm water on the treads *(above, right)* and risers; work by hand with a sponge on any surface that is hard to reach with the sponge mop. Wipe the surface dry with a clean cloth. If the finish is damaged, spot-refinish *(page 83)* or refinish *(page 84)* the staircase.

REPAIRING FINISH AND SURFACE DAMAGE

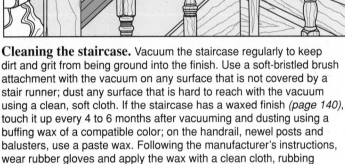

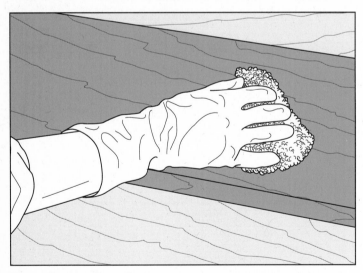

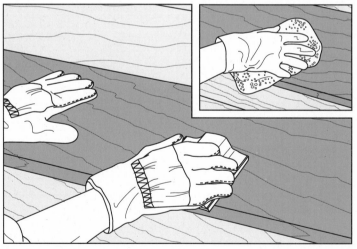

Removing scuff marks. To remove scuff marks from the finish, take off any stair runner in the way *(page 106)* and use a solvent-based wood floor cleaner. Following the manufacturer's instructions, wear rubber gloves and apply a small amount of the cleaner on the damaged surface using fine steel wool, scrubbing gently along the wood grain *(above)* until the scuff marks disappear. Wipe the surface dry with a clean cloth. If the surface has a waxed finish *(page 140)*, rub it vigorously with a dry cloth to restore the luster; if necessary, touch it up with a buffing wax of a compatible color. If the steel wool scratches the surface, spot-refinish it *(page 83)*. Put back any stair runner you removed.

Lightening dark spots. To lighten dark spots in or under the finish, take off any stair runner in the way *(page 106)*. If the surface has a waxed finish *(page 140)*, first try using a solvent-based wood floor cleaner as you would to remove scuff marks *(step left)*. Otherwise, remove the finish from the damaged surface *(page 83)* and use a commercial wood bleach. Following the manufacturer's instructions, wear rubber gloves and safety goggles to apply the bleaching agent using a sponge *(inset)* or a cloth; to stop its action, apply the neutralizing agent. Rinse the surface with water, then wipe it with a cloth and let it dry for about 12 hours. Wearing a dust mask, smooth the surface along the wood grain using fine sandpaper *(above)*, feathering the edges. Brush sanding particles off the surface and wipe it with a tack cloth, then touch up the finish *(page 83)*. Put back any stair runner you removed.

REPAIRING FINISH AND SURFACE DAMAGE (continued)

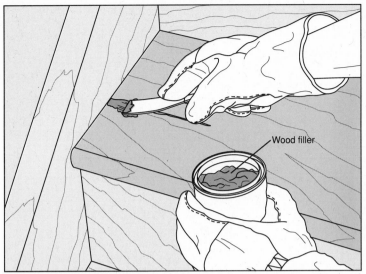

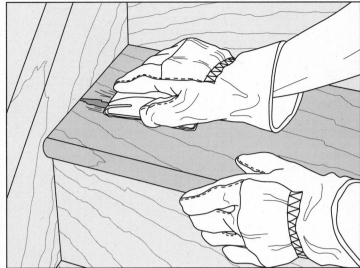

Filling cracks or gouges. To fill a crack or gouge in the surface, take off any stair runner in the way *(page 106)* and remove the finish from the damaged surface *(step 1, below)*. Choose a wood filler of a color that matches the wood and apply it with a putty knife. Following the manufacturer's instructions, wear work gloves and use the putty knife to work the filler into the crack or gouge *(above, left)*; overfill it slightly, then scrape off the excess to level it. Allow the filler to dry, then smooth the surface along the wood grain using fine sandpaper, feathering the edges; on a flat surface such as a tread, work with a sanding block *(above, right)*. Brush sanding particles off the surface and wipe it with a tack cloth, then touch up the finish *(step 2, below)*. Put back any stair runner you removed.

SPOT-REFINISHING THE STAIRCASE

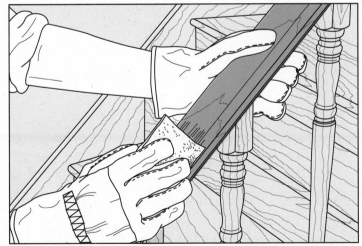

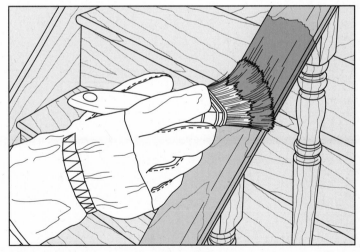

1 Removing the damaged finish. Take off any stair runner in the way *(page 106)*. If the damaged surface has a waxed finish *(page 140)*, strip the wax off it *(page 84)*. Wearing work gloves, smooth the surface along the wood grain using fine sandpaper, feathering the edges. On a turned surface such as the handrail, work by hand with a folded sheet of sandpaper *(above)*; on a flat surface such as a tread, work with a sanding block to ensure even sanding. Work carefully to remove only the damaged finish; avoid sanding off any penetrating stain applied to the wood to color it. Brush sanding particles off the surface and wipe it with a tack cloth. Fill any cracks or gouges in the surface *(step above)* and lighten any dark spots *(page 82)*.

2 Touching up the finish. Choose a finish that matches the original *(page 140)* and follow the manufacturer's instructions to apply it. Wearing work gloves, use a paintbrush to apply a thin, even coat of finish on the surface, working along the wood grain in a smooth stroke *(above)* and feathering the edges; at the end of each stroke, lap back over the surface justed coated. Allow the finish to dry, then smooth the surface lightly with fine sandpaper as you did to remove the damaged finish *(step 1)* and apply another coat of finish. Continue smoothing and applying finish the same way until the surface is uniform, feathering the edges slightly farther each time to help disguise the repair. When the last coat of finish is dry, apply a fresh coat of wax, if necessary *(page 84)*. Put back any stair runner you removed.

REWAXING THE STAIRCASE

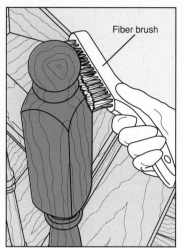
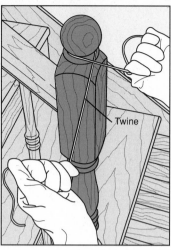

1 **Stripping off the old wax.** If the staircase has a waxed finish *(page 140)*, test it periodically for wax buildup by running the tip of a fingernail lightly across it; if wax scrapes off, take off any stair runner in the way *(page 106)* and rewax the staircase. To strip the wax off the staircase, work on a small section at a time using a solvent-based wood floor cleaner. Following the manufacturer's instructions, wear rubber gloves and apply a small amount of the cleaner on the surface using fine steel wool, scrubbing gently along the wood grain. Work with the cleaner using a soft-bristled brush on a turned surface *(above, left)*; using heavy twine in a tight contour *(above, right)*. Wipe the surface dry with a clean cloth.

2 **Applying a fresh coat of wax.** If any finish under the wax is damaged, spot-refinish *(page 83)* or refinish *(steps below)* the staircase. To apply a fresh coat of wax to the staircase, choose a buffing wax of a compatible color and follow the manufacturer's instructions to apply it; use a paste wax to avoid drips, especially on the handrail, newel posts, balusters and other vertical surfaces. Wearing rubber gloves, work from top to bottom on a small section of the staircase at a time, applying the wax with a clean cloth; rub vigorously with a dry cloth to bring out the luster *(above)*. Continue applying the wax the same way, changing often to clean cloths. After rewaxing the staircase, put back any stair runner you removed.

REFINISHING THE STAIRCASE

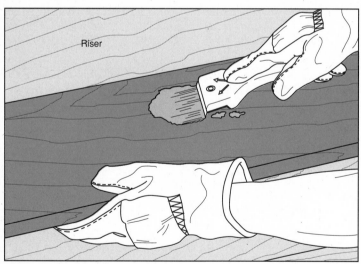
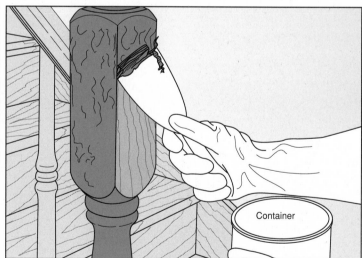

1 **Removing the old finish.** Take off any stair runner in the way *(page 106)*. If the staircase has a waxed finish *(page 140)*, strip the wax off it *(step 1, above)*. To scrape loose or lifting finish off the surface, work as much as possible along the wood grain. Round off the corners on the blade of a paint scraper and a putty knife with a file to keep from gouging the wood; wearing work gloves, use the paint scraper on a flat surface such as a tread *(above, left)* or riser and use the putty knife on a turned surface such as a handrail, newel post or baluster. To strip the entire finish off the surface, work with a chemical stripper following the manufacturer's instructions; use a gel type to avoid drips, especially on the handrail, newel posts, balusters and other vertical surfaces. Ventilate the work area thoroughly, opening windows

and doors to the outdoors; wear a dual-cartridge respirator rated for the stripper, rubber gloves, safety goggles and a long-sleeved shirt. Cover nearby surfaces not to be stripped with dropcloths. Working from top to bottom on a small section of the surface at a time, apply the stripper with a paintbrush. When the finish starts softening and lifting, scrape it off the surface, working as much as possible along the wood grain; use a putty knife with rounded blade corners on a flat surface *(above, right)* and use fine steel wool on a turned surface. Collect the residue taken off the surface in a metal container for safe disposal. After stripping off the finish, wash the surface using the solvent recommended by the stripper manufacturer and a clean cloth, then let it dry. Apply a new finish *(step 3)*, sanding the surface first to smooth it, if necessary *(step 2)*.

REFINISHING THE STAIRCASE (continued)

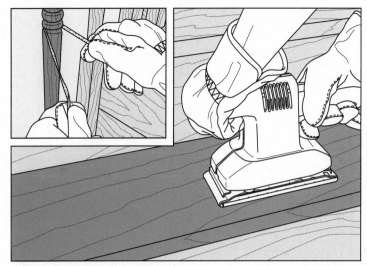

2 **Sanding the surface.** After scraping off loose or lifting finish or stripping off the entire finish, sand the surface along the wood grain with medium sandpaper to smooth it; wear work gloves, a dust mask and safety goggles. On a flat surface such as a tread, work with an orbital sander *(above)* or sanding block to ensure even sanding; on a turned surface such as a baluster, work by hand with a sandpaper strip *(inset)*. Work carefully to avoid sanding off any penetrating stain applied to the wood to color it. Brush sanding particles off the surface and wipe it with a tack cloth. Then, smooth the surface again lightly the same way using fine sandpaper, brushing off particles and wiping with the tack cloth. Fill any cracks or gouges in the surface *(page 83)* and lighten any dark spots *(page 82)*.

3 **Applying the new finish.** Choose a finish that matches the original *(page 140)* and follow the manufacturer's instructions to apply it. Wearing work gloves, apply a thin, even coat of finish with a paintbrush, working along the wood grain in a smooth stroke; lap back at the end of each stroke over the surface just coated. Work from top to bottom on a small section of the surface at a time, applying finish first to the handrail, newel posts and balusters, then to the risers, treads *(above)* and stringers. Allow the finish to dry, then smooth the surface lightly with fine sandpaper *(step 2)* and apply another coat of finish; continue the same way as necessary. When the last coat of finish is dry, apply a fresh coat of wax, if necessary *(page 84)*. Put back any stair runner you removed.

TIGHTENING A DOVETAILED BALUSTER

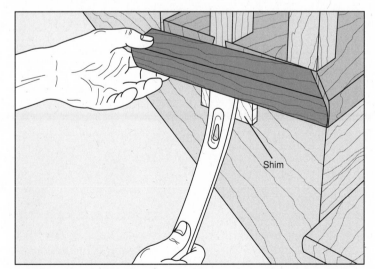

Shim

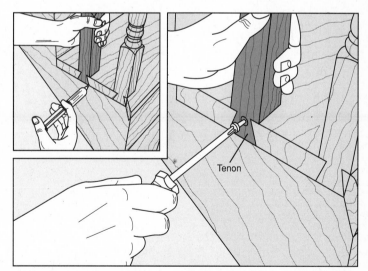

Tenon

1 **Removing the return nosing.** Secure the top of the baluster at the handrail as you would for a doweled *(page 86)* or filleted *(page 87)* baluster. To reach the dovetail joint between the baluster and the tread, take the return nosing off the edge of the tread. Work the blade of a putty knife along the bottom of the return nosing into the joint between it and the tread. Push a wood shim into the joint behind the putty knife and fit the flat end of a pry bar between them, then pull out the putty knife. Gently pry the return nosing away from the tread with the pry bar *(above)*, using the shim as a fulcrum to protect the stringer; work carefully to avoid damaging the return nosing.

2 **Securing the baluster.** Clean any particles out of the dovetail joint using an old knife. Apply wood glue to the dovetail joint on each side of the baluster, forcing it in with a syringe *(inset)* or the applicator tip of the glue container. Fill any gap in the dovetail joint with toothpicks, coating them with glue and pushing them in as far as possible; cut off the protruding ends with a wood chisel. Wearing safety goggles, use an electric drill to bore a pilot hole for countersinking a 2-inch No. 8 wood screw through the tenon of the baluster into the tread; drive in the screw with a screwdriver *(above)*. Wipe off extruded glue using a cloth dampened with water.

TIGHTENING A DOVETAILED BALUSTER (continued)

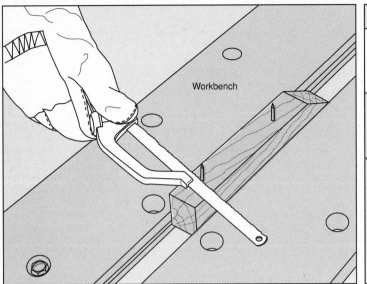

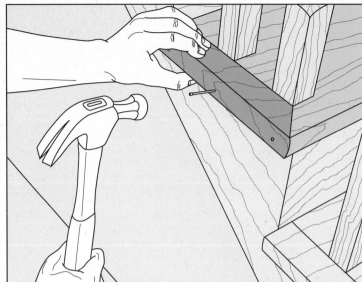

3 **Reinstalling the return nosing.** To remove the nails from the return nosing, secure it in the jaws of a workbench or vise; protect its edges from the jaws with wood blocks, if necessary. Use a hammer and a nail set to drive each nail through the return nosing or use a nail puller to pull each nail out of the back of it; or, wear work gloves and use a mini-hacksaw to cut off the tip of each nail flush with it *(above, left)*. Wearing safety goggles, use an electric drill to bore pilot holes for finishing nails 1/2 inch longer than the thickness of the return nosing; wrap masking tape around the bit to mark the drilling

depth. Position the return nosing on the edge of the tread, then bore through it into the tread about 1 inch from each end and at the center of it. Remove the return nosing and coat the back of it and the edge of the tread with wood glue, then reposition it and use a hammer to drive in the nails *(above, right)*; set each nail head using a nail set. Wipe off extruded glue using a cloth dampened with water. Choose a wax stick of a color that matches the wood and use it to cover the nail heads and fill the old nail holes. Spot-refinish the damaged surface *(page 83)*.

TIGHTENING A DOWELED BALUSTER

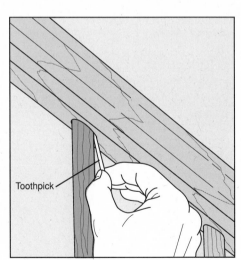

Securing the baluster at the tread. Clean any particles out of the joint between the baluster and the tread using an old knife, then force wood glue into it with a syringe or the applicator tip of the glue container. Wearing safety goggles, use an electric drill to bore a pilot hole for a 1 1/2-inch finishing nail; wrap masking tape around the bit to mark the drilling depth. Holding the drill at a 45-degree angle, bore through one side of the baluster at the bottom of it into the tread *(above, left)*. Use a hammer to drive the nail into the pilot hole *(above, right)*; set the nail head using a nail set. Wipe off extruded glue using a cloth dampened with water. Choose a wax stick of a color that matches the wood and use it to cover the nail head. Spot-refinish the damaged surface *(page 83)*.

Securing the baluster at the handrail. Clean any particles out of the joint between the baluster and the handrail using an old knife, then force wood glue into it with a syringe or the applicator tip of the glue container. Fill any gap in the joint with toothpicks, coating them with glue and pushing them in as far as possible *(above)*; cut off the protruding ends carefully with a wood chisel. Wipe off extruded glue using a cloth dampened with water. Spot-refinish the damaged surface *(page 83)*.

TIGHTENING A FILLETED BALUSTER

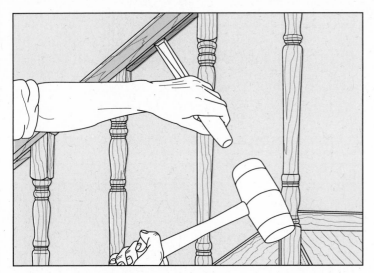

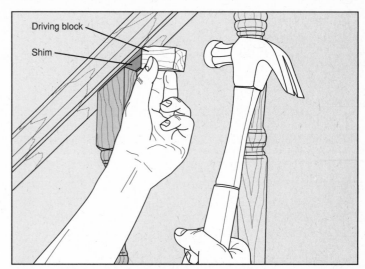

Driving block

Shim

1 **Removing the fillet strip.** First try to secure the baluster at the handrail or shoe rail as you would for a doweled baluster at the handrail *(page 86)*. Otherwise, pry out the fillet strip at the top of the baluster on its highest side to reach the joint between it and the handrail. Wearing safety goggles, work a wood chisel into the handrail groove on one side of the fillet strip, tapping it lightly with a mallet *(above)*; work carefully to avoid damaging the handrail. Continue along the side of the fillet strip the same way, gently prying it out of the handrail groove; if it cannot be removed intact, chisel it out in pieces. Clean any particles out of the joint between the baluster and the handrail using an old knife.

2 **Installing a wood shim.** Force wood glue into the joint with a syringe or the applicator tip of the glue container, then coat a wood shim with glue and drive it into the joint *(above)*; cut off any protruding end with a wood chisel. Pull any nails out of the old fillet strip or cut a new fillet strip to size, then position it and use an electric drill to bore a pilot hole for a 1-inch finishing nail near each end of it. Coat the back and sides of the fillet strip and the handrail groove with glue, then drive in the nails; set each nail head using a nail set. Wipe off extruded glue using a cloth dampened with water. Choose a wax stick of a color that matches the wood and use it to cover the nail heads and fill any old nail holes. Spot-refinish the damaged surface *(page 83)*.

REPLACING A BALUSTER

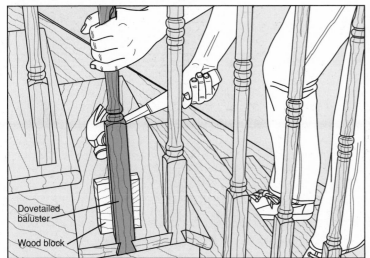

Dovetailed baluster

Wood block

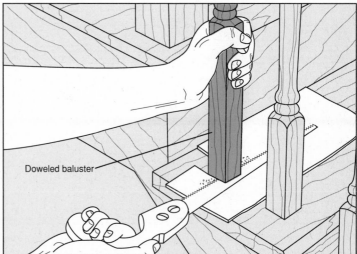

Doweled baluster

1 **Removing the baluster intact.** If a damaged baluster cannot be repaired, remove it in pieces *(step 2)*; otherwise, try to remove any baluster intact. Remove any fillet strip at the top of the baluster on its highest side *(step 1, above)*. For a dovetailed baluster, remove the return nosing from the edge of the tread *(page 85)*, then hammer at the bottom of the baluster to loosen it, cushioning the blows with a wood block *(above, left)*. Pull any nails out of the baluster and continue to work the bottom of it out of the tread the same way, then work the top of it out of the handrail. For a doweled baluster, pull any nails out of the top of it and work it along any exposed handrail groove, then pull the bottom of it out of the tread socket. Otherwise, use a

keyhole saw to cut off the dowel at the bottom of it flush with the tread *(above, right)*; protect the tread with cardboard. Work the baluster back and forth toward the edge of the tread to loosen it, then work it out of the handrail. Clean out the tread socket with a wood chisel. For a filleted baluster, pry out the fillet strip at the bottom on its lowest side, then loosen it by hammering at the top and bottom of it opposite the exposed handrail groove; cushion the blows with a wood block. Pull any nails out of the baluster, then work the top of it out of the handrail and the bottom of it out of the shoe rail. If necessary, repair the baluster *(page 90)*. If the baluster cannot be removed intact, remove it in pieces; otherwise, prepare a replacement baluster *(step 3)*.

REPLACING A BALUSTER (continued)

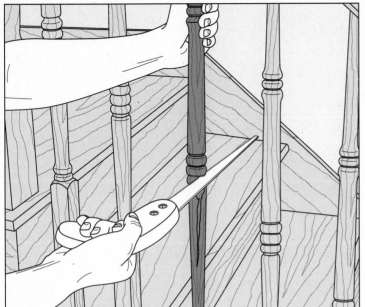

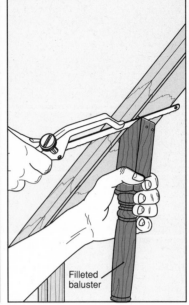

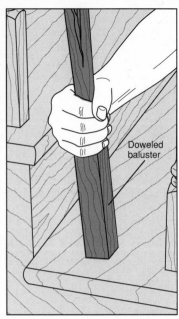

Doweled baluster

Filleted baluster

2 **Removing the baluster in pieces.** If the baluster can be repaired, use a keyhole saw to cut across it near the center at an inconspicuous spot such as the contour of a turning *(above, left)*; otherwise, cut across it a few inches above and below the center to take out a section of it. Work the top of the baluster back and forth to loosen it, then pull it out of the handrail; use a mini-hacksaw to cut through any nails in it, if necessary *(above, near right)*. For the bottom of a dovetailed baluster, remove the return nosing from the edge of the

tread *(page 85)*, then hammer at the bottom of the baluster to loosen it; pull any nails out of it and continue to work it out of the tread the same way. For the bottom of a doweled baluster, work it back and forth to loosen it *(above, far right)*, then remove any nails from it and pull it out of the tread. For the bottom of a filleted baluster, work it back and forth to loosen it, then pull it out of the shoe rail; cut through any nails in it or pull them out of it. When the baluster is removed, repair it *(page 90)* or prepare a replacement baluster *(step 3)*.

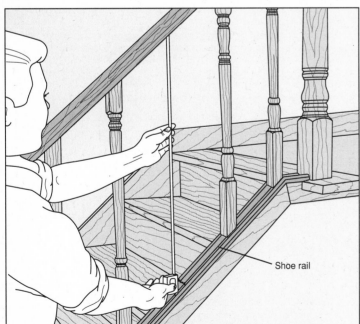

Shoe rail

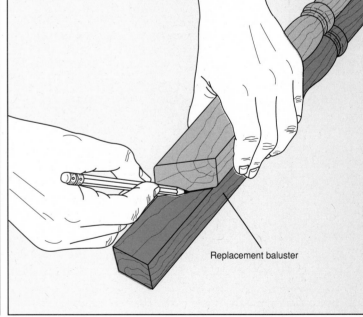

Replacement baluster

3 **Preparing the replacement baluster.** To determine the length of the replacement baluster needed, measure the vertical distance from the handrail to the shoe rail *(above, left)* or tread where the old baluster stood; include the depth of any fillet-strip or dowel socket and dovetail mortise. Purchase an identical replacement baluster at a building supply center that specializes in stair parts; take the old baluster with you. A replacement baluster may have to be

ordered or specially milled. Mark the replacement baluster to length with a pencil; trace any angle necessary onto the top or bottom of it using the ends of the old baluster as a template *(above, right)*. Secure the replacement baluster in the jaws of a workbench or vise, protecting its edges from the jaws with wood blocks. Cut the replacement baluster to size with a backsaw. Then, install the replacement dovetailed *(step 4)*, doweled *(step 5)* or filleted *(step 6)* baluster.

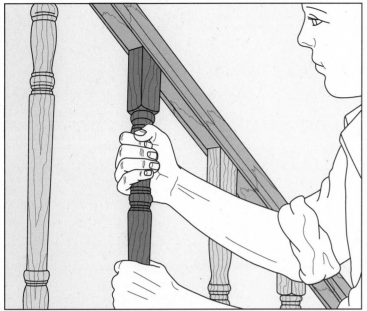

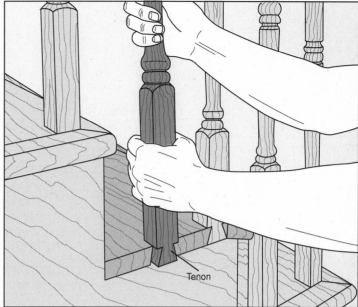

Tenon

4 **Installing a dovetailed baluster.** Remove any fillet strip on the highest side of the handrail socket as you would to install a filleted baluster *(step 6)*. Clean any particles out of the handrail socket and tread mortise with a wood chisel. Test-fit the baluster, working first the top of it into the handrail socket, then the bottom of it into the tread mortise; trim it with a backsaw, a wood chisel or sandpaper as necessary. Coat the handrail socket, tread mortise, and top and bottom of the baluster with wood glue, then fit the top of the baluster into the

handrail *(above, left)* and the bottom of the baluster into the tread *(above, right)*. Wearing safety goggles, use an electric drill to bore a pilot hole for countersinking a 2-inch No. 8 wood screw through the tenon of the baluster into the tread. Drive in the screw, then wipe off extruded glue using a cloth dampened with water. Put back any fillet strip removed from the handrail as you would to install a filleted baluster. Reinstall the return nosing along the edge of the tread *(page 86)*. Spot-refinish any damaged surface *(page 83)*.

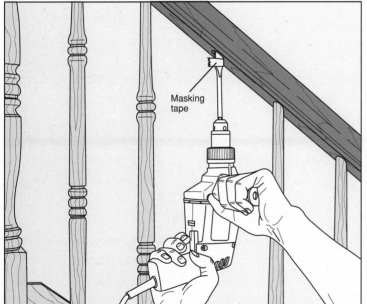

Masking tape

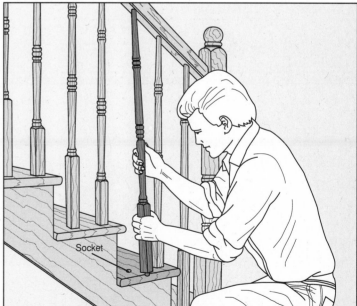

Socket

5 **Installing a doweled baluster.** Remove any fillet strip on the highest side of the handrail socket as you would to install a filleted baluster *(step 6)*. Clean any particles out of the handrail and tread sockets with a wood chisel. Test-fit the baluster, working first the top of it into the handrail socket, then the bottom of it into the tread socket. If necessary, deepen the handrail socket to the length of the dowel at the bottom of the baluster; wearing safety goggles, use an electric drill fitted with a spade bit of the same diameter as the socket *(above, left)*, marking the drilling depth with masking tape. If the

handrail is not thick enough for its socket to be deepened, use a backsaw to trim the dowel at the bottom of the baluster to the depth of the handrail socket. Coat the handrail and tread sockets as well as the top and bottom of the baluster with wood glue, then fit the top of the baluster into the handrail and the bottom of the baluster into the tread *(above, right)*. Wipe off extruded glue using a cloth dampened with water. Put back any fillet strip removed from the handrail as you would to install a filleted baluster, then spot-refinish any damaged surface *(page 83)*.

REPLACING A BALUSTER (continued)

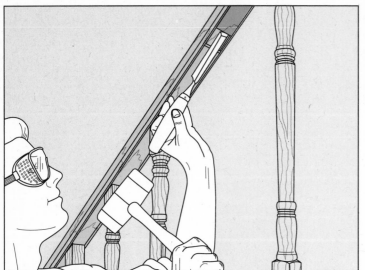

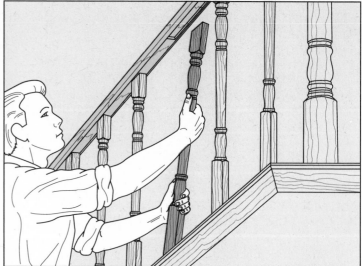

6 **Installing a filleted baluster.** Remove any fillet strip on the highest side of the handrail socket using a wood chisel and a mallet. Wearing safety goggles, work the chisel under the edge of the fillet strip, tapping it lightly with the mallet *(above, left)*. Continue along under the fillet strip, gently prying it out of the handrail groove. Remove the fillet strip on the lowest side of the shoe rail socket the same way. Clean any particles out of the handrail and shoe rail sockets with the chisel. Test-fit the baluster, working the top of it into the handrail socket and the bottom of it into the shoe rail socket; trim it with a backsaw or sandpaper as necessary. Coat the handrail and shoe rail sockets as well as the top and bottom of the baluster with wood glue,

then fit the baluster into the handrail and the shoe rail *(above, right)*. Use an electric drill to bore a pilot hole for a 1-inch finishing nail through the top and bottom of the baluster on the side with the exposed groove; drive in the nails, then set the nail heads with a nail set. To reinstall each fillet strip, pull any nails out of it, then position it and bore a pilot hole for a 1-inch finishing nail near each end of it. Coat the back and sides of the fillet strips as well as the handrail and shoe rail grooves with glue, then drive in the nails and set the nail heads. Wipe off extruded glue using a cloth dampened with water. Choose a wax stick of a color that matches the wood and use it to cover the nail heads and fill any old nail holes. Spot-refinish any damaged surface *(page 83)*.

REPAIRING A BALUSTER

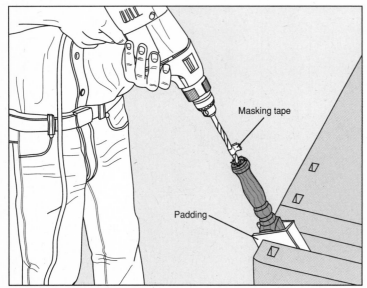

Masking tape

Padding

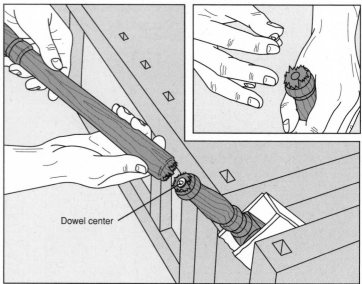

Dowel center

1 **Boring a dowel socket.** If the baluster is split unevenly along its length, apply wood glue to the pieces and clamp them together. If the baluster is broken or cut cleanly across its diameter, remove it *(page 87)* and join the sections using a 1/4- or 3/8-inch dowel. Secure one baluster section in the jaws of a workbench or vise, protecting it from the jaws with padding. Mark two lines across the diameter or opposite corners at the damaged end of the baluster section to locate its center point. Wearing safety goggles, use an electric drill fitted with a

bit of the same diameter as the dowel to bore a hole 3/4 to 7/8 inch deep at the marked center point *(above, left)*; wrap masking tape around the bit to mark the drilling depth. Fit a dowel center into the hole *(inset)*, then locate and mark the center point at the damaged end of the other baluster section; align it with the first baluster section *(above, right)* and press it against the dowel center when it is positioned correctly. Bore a hole 3/4 to 7/8 inch deep into the damaged end of the baluster section at the marked center point.

REPAIRING A BALUSTER (continued)

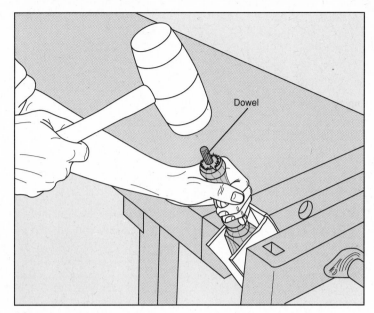

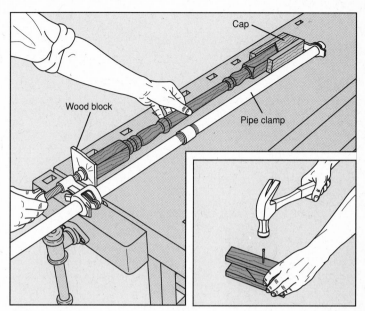

2 **Installing the dowel.** Use a serrated type of dowel or score a standard dowel by drawing it through the serrated jaws of pliers to allow for the movement of wood glue around it as it is driven into the baluster sockets. Cut the dowel 1 1/2 inches long using a backsaw and bevel each end of it slightly with sandpaper. Force wood glue into the baluster sockets using a syringe or the applicator tip of the glue container. Coat the dowel with glue and fit it into one baluster socket, then use a mallet to drive it in *(above)*, forcing glue out around it. Wipe off extruded glue using a cloth dampened with water.

3 **Clamping the baluster sections.** Coat the damaged ends of the baluster sections with wood glue, then align them and fit the dowel into the other baluster socket. Press the baluster sections together, then secure them with a pipe clamp and wood blocks. Fit any angled end of the baluster with a cap, cutting a 2-by-2 at the same angle and nailing a 1-by-2 onto opposite sides of it *(inset)*. Tighten the pipe clamp only enough to close the gap between the baluster sections *(above)*, forcing out a thin bead of glue. Wipe off extruded glue using a cloth dampened with water. Allow the glue to cure, then reinstall the dovetailed, doweled *(page 89)* or filleted *(page 90)* baluster.

SECURING A NEWEL POST

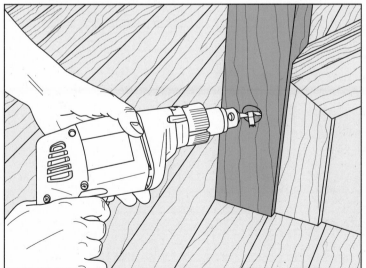

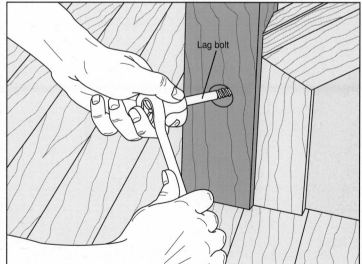

Bolting the newel post to the stringer. If there is access to the newel post from below the floor understructure, bolt it to any joist it butts against *(page 92)*; otherwise, bolt it to the stringer. Wearing safety goggles, use an electric drill fitted with a 1-inch spade bit to bore a hole 1 inch deep into one side of the newel post, centering it in the section joined to the stringer; mark the drilling depth on the bit with masking tape. Then, bore a pilot hole for a 4-inch lag bolt at a 45-degree angle

through the side of the hole in the newel post into the end of the stringer *(above, left)*. Insert the lag bolt into the hole, then tighten it with a wrench *(above, right)*. To fill the hole in the newel post, use a wood plug. Coat the sides of the plug and the hole with wood glue, then seat the plug securely; wipe off extruded glue using a cloth dampened with water. If necessary, install a lag bolt at the bottom or on the opposite side of the newel post the same way. Spot-refinish any damaged surface *(page 83)*.

SECURING A NEWEL POST (continued)

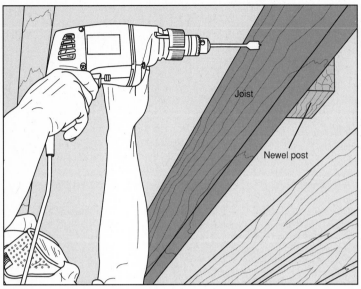

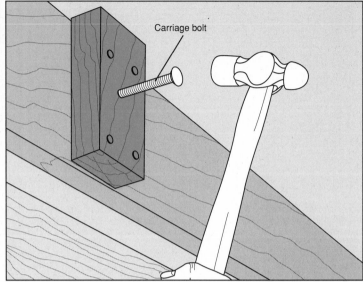

Bolting the newel post to the joist. If there is no access to the newel post from below the floor understructure, bolt it to the stringer *(page 91)*; otherwise, bolt it to any joist it butts against. Having a helper work from above with a carpenter's level to plumb the newel post, work from below to drive nails through it into the joist; use common nails 1 inch longer than the thickness of the section butting against the joist. Wearing safety goggles, use an electric drill fitted with a spade bit to bore a hole for a carriage bolt through the joist and the newel post; work from the side of the joist for greatest maneuvering *(above, left)*. Insert a carriage bolt long enough to fit through the joist and the newel post into the hole, tapping it into place with a ball-peen hammer *(above, right)*. Fit the carriage bolt with a washer and thread a nut onto it; tighten the nut using a wrench.

SECURING THE HANDRAIL

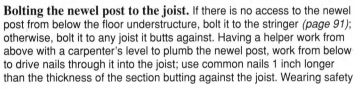

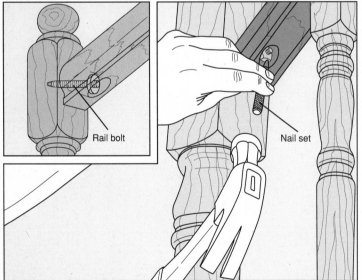

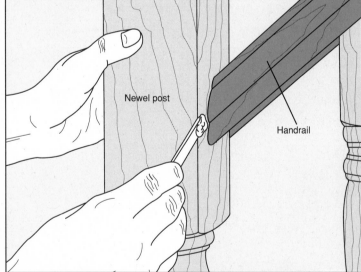

Tightening the handrail to a newel post. Check the bottom of the handrail near the newel post for any wood plug hiding a rail bolt *(inset)* or a wood screw; if there is a fillet strip, remove it *(page 87)*. Wearing safety goggles, remove each plug using a wood chisel and a mallet; work carefully to avoid damaging the handrail or newel post. If the handrail is fastened to the newel post with a rail bolt, loosen the nut using a nail set and a hammer; fit the nail set into a slot and tap it with the hammer *(above, left)*. If the nut is a standard hex or square type, loosen it using a wrench. If the handrail is fastened to the newel post with a screw, remove it. Loosen the handrail enough to clean any particles out of the joint between it and the newel post with a putty knife.

Coat the end of the handrail and the side of the newel post at the joint with wood glue, working it into the joint with a wood stick *(above, right)*; or, force it into the joint using a syringe. To close the joint between the handrail and the newel post, tighten the nut on the rail bolt, forcing out a thin bead of glue; or, drive in a wood screw slightly longer than the one removed. To fill each hole in the bottom of the handrail, use a wood plug of the same diameter; put back any fillet strip removed. Coat the sides of the plug and the hole with glue, then seat the plug securely. Wipe off extruded glue using a cloth dampened with water. Spot-refinish any damaged surface *(page 83)*.

SECURING A TREAD

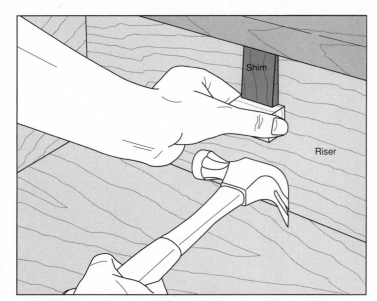

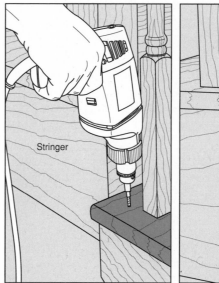

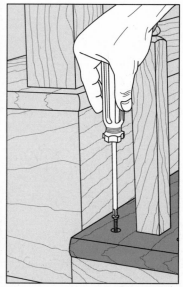

Shimming the tread from above. Work from below to replace any loose or damaged wedge *(step below)* or glue block *(page 94).* Otherwise, take off any stair runner *(page 106)* to reach the tread and the riser below it. If the tread and riser form a butt joint, fasten the tread to the riser and any open stringer *(step right).* If the tread and riser form a rabbet joint, tighten the joint with a thin wood shim about 2 inches wide. Force wood glue into the joint using a syringe or the applicator tip of the glue container, then coat the end of the shim with glue and drive it in using a wood block and a hammer *(above).* Cut off the end of the shim with a wood chisel; work carefully to avoid damaging the riser. Wipe off extruded glue using a cloth dampened with water. Put back any stair runner you removed.

Fastening the tread from above. Work from below to replace any loose or damaged wedge *(step below)* or glue block *(page 94).* Otherwise, take off any stair runner *(page 106)* to reach the tread and the riser below it. If the tread and riser form a rabbet joint, shim the tread *(step left).* If the tread and riser form a butt joint, fasten the tread with 2-inch No. 8 wood screws. Wearing safety goggles, bore a hole for a screw and a wood plug into the tread every 6 inches along the riser and every 3 inches along any open stringer *(above, left),* then drive in the screws *(above, right).* Fit a plug into each hole, coating the sides of it and the hole with wood glue. Wipe off extruded glue using a cloth dampened with water. Spot-refinish any damaged surface *(page 83).* Put back any stair runner you removed.

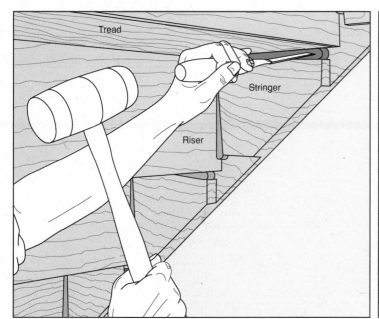

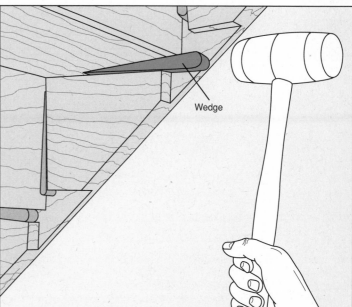

Replacing a wedge from below. If there is no access to the bottom of the tread, work from above to shim it *(step above, left)* or fasten it *(step above, right).* Otherwise, work from below to replace any loose or damaged glue block *(page 94)* or wedge supporting the tread. To remove a wedge, wear safety goggles and work with a wood chisel and a mallet *(above, left);* try to pry it out intact for reinstallation. Pull any nail out of the wedge using a pry bar; clean particles off it and out of the

stringer groove with the chisel. If necessary, cut a replacement wedge of softwood 8 to 10 inches long, about 1 inch wide and 5/8 to 3/4 inch thick at its thickest end; use a very dry wood shingle or 1-by-2. To install the wedge, coat it and the stringer groove with wood glue, then drive it into the groove with the mallet until it fits snugly *(above, right);* avoid driving it in too far to keep from splitting the stringer. Wipe off extruded glue using a cloth dampened with water.

SECURING A TREAD (continued)

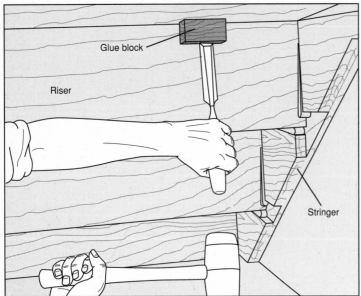

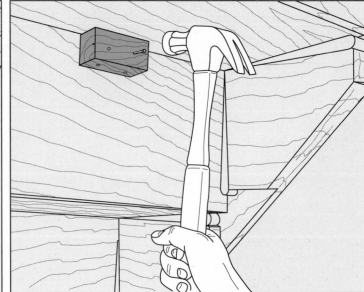

Replacing glue blocks from below. If there is no access to the bottom of the tread, work from above to shim or fasten it *(page 93)*. Otherwise, work from below to replace any loose or damaged wedge *(page 93)* or glue block supporting the tread. To remove a glue block, wear safety goggles and work with a wood chisel and a mallet *(above, left)*; try to pry it out intact for reinstallation. Pull any nail out of the glue block using a pry bar; clean particles off it as well as the tread and riser with the chisel. If necessary, cut replacement glue blocks of very dry 2-by-2 softwood about 4 inches long. To install a glue block, have a

helper working from above stand on the tread to force it down into place; then, position the glue block and use an electric drill to bore pilot holes for 2-inch finishing nails or No. 8 wood screws, marking the drilling depth on the bit with masking tape. Bore a hole near each end of the glue block through it into the tread, then through it into the riser; offset the holes slightly. Coat the contacting sides of the glue block and surfaces of the tread and riser with wood glue, then reposition the glue block and drive in the nails *(above, right)* or screws. Wipe off extruded glue using a cloth dampened with water.

REPAIRING A TREAD NOSING

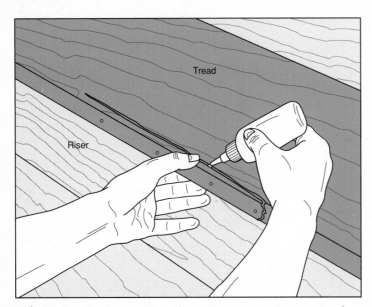

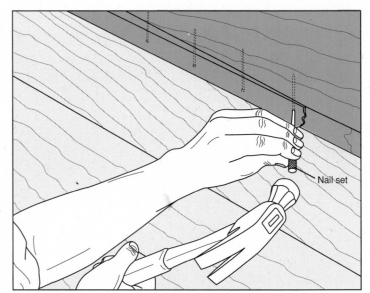

1 **Gluing the damaged section.** Take off any stair runner in the way *(page 106)*. Clean particles out of the damaged section using a soft-bristled brush. Wearing safety goggles, position the damaged section and use an electric drill to bore a pilot hole for a 2-inch finishing nail at a 45-degree angle through it into the tread every 3 to 4 inches along it; mark the drilling depth on the bit with masking tape. Force wood glue into the gap between the damaged section and the tread using the applicator tip of the glue container *(above)* or a syringe.

2 **Nailing the damaged section.** Reposition the damaged section on the tread and drive in the nails with a hammer; use a nail set to set each nail head *(above)*. Wipe off extruded glue using a cloth dampened with water. Choose a wood filler of a color that matches the wood and use a putty knife to cover the nail heads and fill any gap remaining between the damaged section and the tread with it. Spot-refinish the damaged surface *(page 83)*, then put back any stair runner you removed.

REPLACING A TREAD FROM BELOW

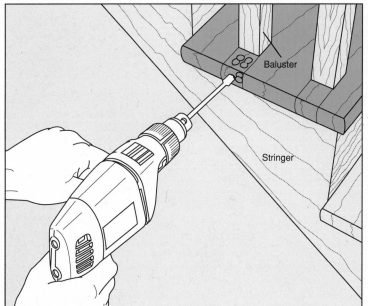

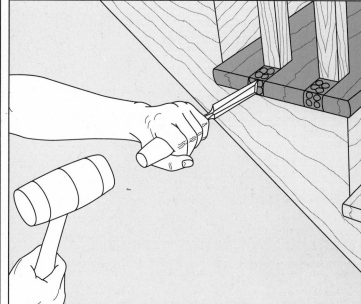

1 Removing the balusters. Take off any stair runner in the way *(page 106)*. If there is no open stringer, work from below to pry out the riser above the tread *(page 101)*, then remove the tread *(step 4)*; if there is no access to the riser from below, work from above to replace the tread *(page 97)*. Otherwise, remove any dovetailed *(page 87)* or doweled baluster from the tread. To remove a doweled baluster, mark a cutting line on the tread from each side of the baluster to the edge of the tread overhanging the stringer. Wearing safety goggles, use an electric drill fitted with a 1/2-inch spade bit to bore a series of holes through the top and edge of the marked tread section *(above, left)*; work carefully to avoid damaging the baluster or stringer. Cut the remaining wood out of the tread section using a wood chisel and a mallet *(above, right)*, clearing a channel as wide as the baluster. Loosen the baluster by working it along the channel, twisting it back and forth; then, pull any nails out of the top of it and work it out of the handrail.

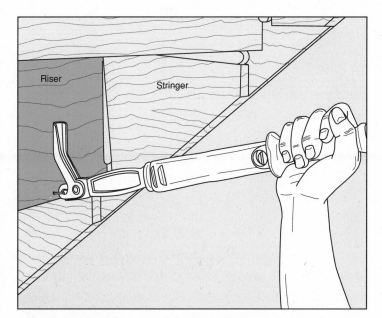

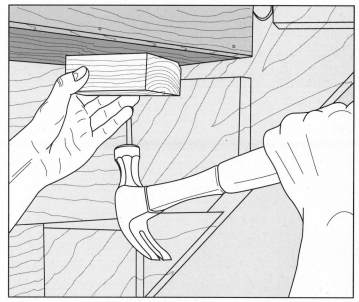

2 Removing the tread fasteners. If there is no access to the tread from below, work from above to replace it *(page 97)*. Otherwise, work from below to remove any wedge *(page 93)* or glue block *(page 94)* supporting the tread. Pull any nails holding the tread out of the bottom of the riser above it using a nail puller *(above)*, a hammer or a pry bar. Work from above to check the tread for any wood plug hiding a fastener holding it to the riser below it or the stringer. Wearing safety goggles, remove any plug from the tread using a wood chisel and a mallet, then take out the fastener.

3 Loosening the tread. Work from below to loosen the tread. Position a wood block against the bottom of the tread near the riser above it and any open stringer, then tap sharply on the block with a hammer *(above)*. If the tread does not loosen, it may form a rabbet joint with the riser above it; wearing safety goggles, use a wood chisel and a mallet to pry apart the tread and riser *(page 101)*, working carefully from below and above to avoid damaging the riser. Continue loosening the tread the same way, working along it near the riser above it and toward the riser below it.

REPLACING A TREAD FROM BELOW (continued)

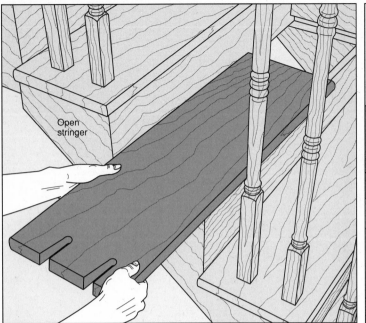

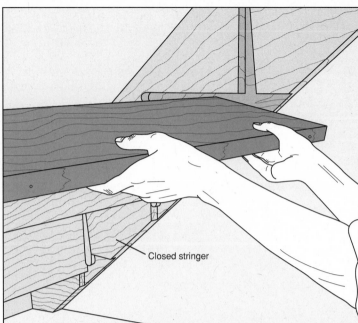

4 **Removing the tread.** If there is no closed stringer, work from above to lift the tread off the riser below it, then lift or slide it off the stringers. If there is an open stringer and a closed stringer, work from above to slide the tread out of the closed stringer and raise it off the riser below it, then slide it off the open stringer *(above, left)*; if necessary, loosen it from the closed stringer by scraping along the joint with a putty knife. If there is no open stringer, work from below to raise the tread off the riser below it, then slide it at an angle out of the stringers *(above, right)*; if necessary, loosen it from the riser by tapping on the bottom of it along the joint using a hammer, cushioning the blows with a wood block. After removing the tread, clean particles off the contacting surfaces of the risers and stringers with a wood chisel.

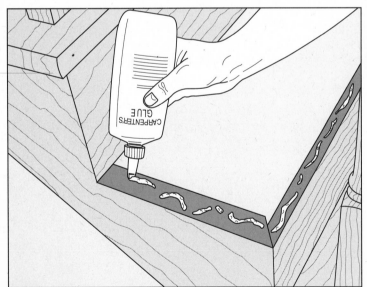

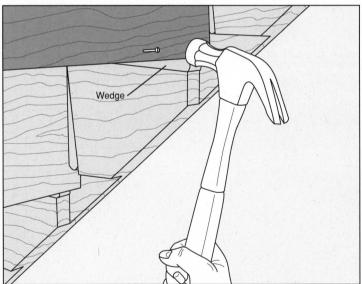

5 **Installing a replacement tread.** Purchase an identical replacement tread at a building supply center that specializes in stair parts; take the old tread with you, ensuring its nosing and any groove are duplicated. Cut the tread to size using a circular saw or saber saw fitted with a fine crosscut blade. Test-fit the tread, reversing the procedure used to remove the old one *(step 4)*; trim it carefully with a rasp, a wood chisel or sandpaper as necessary to fit it into any closed stringer or any groove in the riser above it. Prepare the tread for any doweled *(page 99)* or dovetailed *(page 100)* baluster removed. Take out the tread to coat the contacting surfaces of it, the risers and the stringers with wood glue *(above, left)*. Reposition the tread and put back any wedge removed *(page 93)*; if you removed the riser above the tread, reinstall it *(page 102)*. Wearing safety goggles, use an electric drill to bore a pilot hole for a 2-inch finishing nail or No. 8 wood screw every 6 inches through the bottom of the riser above the tread into the tread; mark the drilling depth on the bit with masking tape. Drive in the nails *(above, right)* or screws, then put back any glue block removed *(page 94)*. Work from above to bore a hole for a 2-inch No. 8 wood screw and a wood plug into the tread every 3 to 4 inches along any open stringer, then drive in the screws. Fit a plug into each hole, coating the sides of it and the hole with glue. Wipe off extruded glue using a cloth dampened with water. Reinstall any doweled or dovetailed baluster removed *(page 89)*. Spot-refinish any damaged surface *(page 83)*. Put back any stair runner you removed.

REPLACING A TREAD FROM ABOVE

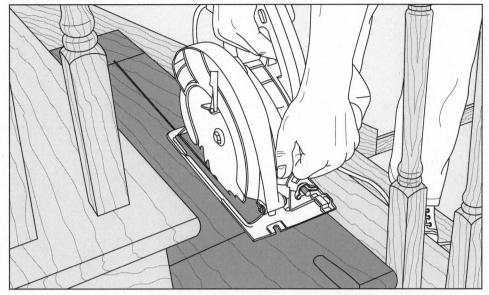

1 **Cutting out the tread.** Take off any stair runner in the way *(page 106)*. Work from below to replace the tread if there is access to the bottom of it *(page 95)*; otherwise, remove any baluster from it *(page 95)*, then work from above to replace it. Wearing safety goggles and a dust mask, cut out as large a section of the tread between the stringers as possible using a circular saw; set its cutting depth equal to the tread thickness. Check the tread for any wood plug hiding a fastener and avoid cutting through it. Make a cut across the width of the tread from its nosing to the riser above it at each end of it. Then, cut along the length of the tread, making a plunge cut at one stringer 3 to 4 inches from the nosing and continuing to the other stringer *(left)*; make another cut as close as possible to the riser above the tread the same way.

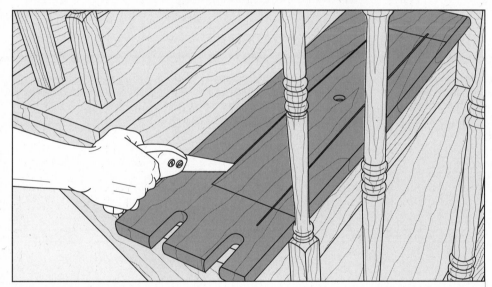

2 **Finishing the cuts with a handsaw.** To prevent the cut tread section from falling below the staircase, bore a hole through the center of it large enough for a finger to fit into and support it; wearing safety goggles, use an electric drill fitted with a 1-inch spade bit. Then, use a keyhole saw to finish the ends of each cut made with the circular saw *(left)*; support the cut tread section as you finish the ends of the last cut, fitting your finger into the hole in the center of it. Pull out the cut tread section, working carefully to avoid dropping it. Loosen the tread section from the riser below it by tapping on the bottom of it along each side of the riser with a hammer, then lift it off.

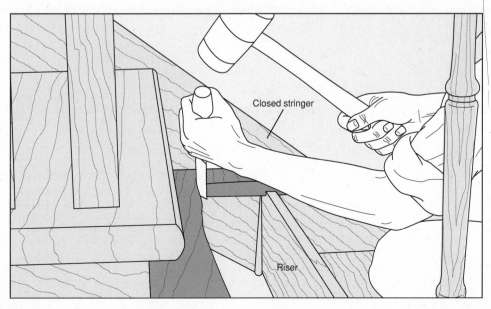

3 **Chiseling out the remaining tread.** To cut out the remaining tread or loosen any joint between it and a stringer or a riser, use a wood chisel and a mallet; work carefully, cutting along the wood grain as much as possible. Cut along the remaining tread to any closed stringer from the corner of the opening *(left)*, then pry the cut section out of the stringer and off the riser below it. Chisel any wood plug out of the remaining tread and remove the fastener under it. Pry the remaining tread out of any riser groove and any closed stringer; work carefully to avoid damaging any wedge supporting it. Chisel off any wedge or glue block supporting the tread; keep it for reinstallation. After removing the remaining tread, clean particles off the contacting surfaces of the risers and stringers with the chisel; remove any fasteners from the bottom of the riser above the opening.

Closed stringer

Riser

REPLACING A TREAD FROM ABOVE (continued)

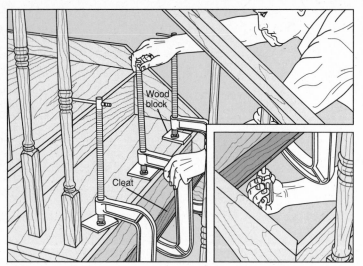

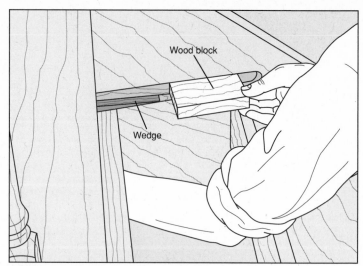

4 **Installing a cleat.** Measure the bottom of the riser between the stringers, then cut a 1-by-3 to length for a cleat to support the replacement tread. Test-fit the cleat, positioning its 1-inch edge flush with the back of the riser, then coat the contacting surfaces of it and the riser with wood glue. Secure each end and the center of the cleat using a 10-inch C clamp, tightening it against the tread above the opening *(above)* to force out a thin bead of glue along the joint; protect the tread with a wood block. Wearing safety goggles, use an electric drill to bore a pilot hole for a 2-inch No. 8 wood screw every 6 inches along the bottom of the cleat into the riser. Drive in the screws *(inset)*, then remove the C clamps. Wipe off extruded glue using a cloth dampened with water.

5 **Positioning a wedge.** If there is no closed stringer, prepare a replacement tread *(step 6)*. Otherwise, use a wood block of the same thickness as a tread to position a wedge at each closed stringer. Clean particles off the old wedge and out of the stringer groove with a wood chisel. If necessary, cut a replacement wedge of softwood 8 to 10 inches long, about 1 inch wide and 5/8 to 3/4 inch thick at its thickest end; use a very dry wood shingle or 1-by-2. Coat the bottom of the wedge and the stringer groove with wood glue. Positioning the wood block as you would a tread, slide the wedge along the stringer groove *(above)* until it fits snugly under the bottom of the wood block. Remove the wood block, then wipe off extruded glue using a cloth dampened with water. Allow the glue to cure.

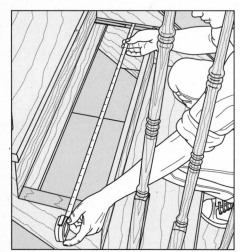

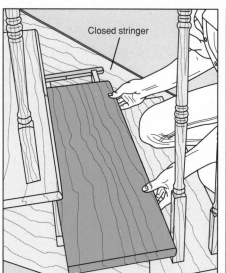

6 **Preparing a replacement tread.** To determine the dimensions of the replacement tread needed, use a tape measure; include any stringer groove in the length *(above)* and any riser groove in the width. Use a remaining tread or section of the old tread as a measuring guide. Purchase an identical replacement tread at a building supply center that specializes in stair parts; take sections of the old tread with you to ensure its nosing and any groove are duplicated. Wearing safety goggles and a dust mask, cut the tread to size using a circular saw or saber saw fitted with a fine crosscut blade.

7 **Test-fitting the replacement tread.** If there is no closed stringer, slide the tread onto the stringers, fitting it into any groove in the riser above it and onto the riser below it. If there is an open stringer and a closed stringer, slide it onto the open stringer *(above, left)*, then fit it into the closed stringer and any groove in the riser above it, and onto the riser below it. If there is no open stringer, cut an amount equal to the depth of a stringer groove off one end of the tread, then mark an amount equal to half the depth of a stringer groove partway across each end of the tread. Fit two opposite corners of the tread into the stringers *(above, right)*, then rotate it into place, fitting it into any groove in the riser above it and onto the riser below it; use the marked lines to center it. Trim the tread carefully with a rasp, a wood chisel or sandpaper as necessary to fit it; tap it into place using a hammer, cushioning the blows with a wood block. Prepare the tread for any doweled *(page 99)* or dovetailed *(page 100)* baluster removed.

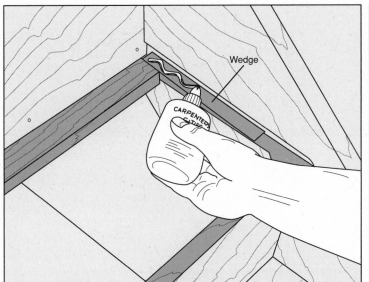

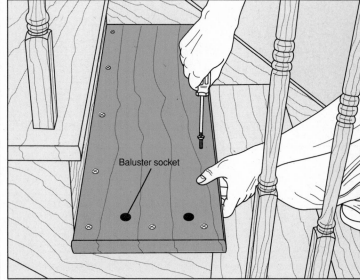

8 **Installing the replacement tread.** Take out the tread, reversing the procedure used to test-fit it *(step 7)*. Coat the contacting surfaces of the tread, the stringers, the risers and the cleat with wood glue *(above, left)*, then reposition the tread. Wearing safety goggles, use an electric drill to bore a hole for a 2-inch No. 8 wood screw and a wood plug into the tread every 6 inches along the cleat and the

riser and every 3 inches along any open stringer; then, drive in the screws *(above, right)*. Fit a plug into each hole, coating the sides of it and the hole with glue. Wipe off extruded glue using a cloth dampened with water. Reinstall any doweled or dovetailed baluster removed *(page 89)*. Spot-refinish any damaged surface *(page 83)*. Put back any stair runner you removed.

PREPARING A TREAD FOR DOWELED BALUSTERS

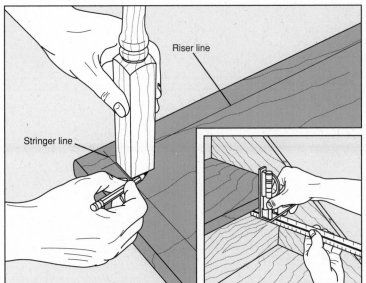

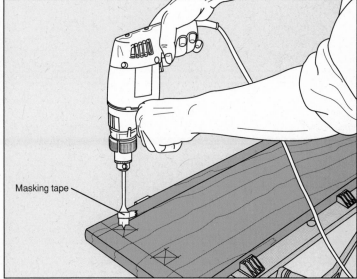

Locating and boring dowel sockets. With the tread in position, mark onto the top of it the edge of the riser below it and the open stringer using a combination square. Butt the end of the square's blade against the riser, then lock its head against the tread nosing *(inset)*. Turn the square 180 degrees, resting its blade on the tread with its head locked against the nosing. Keeping the square's head locked against the nosing, hold a pencil against the end of its blade and draw it along the tread to the open stringer, marking the edge of the riser. Mark the edge of the open stringer onto the tread the same way. Secure the tread to a workbench and use the corner of the riser and stringer lines to locate the first baluster, tracing its outline *(above, left)* or measuring and trans-

ferring its dimensions. Mark a line on the tread parallel to the riser line half way between it and the back edge of the tread; use the corner of this line and the stringer line to locate the second baluster, working on the side of it closest to the back edge of the tread. Locate the center of each baluster outline by marking diagonal lines across its opposite corners. Wearing safety goggles, use an electric drill fitted with a spade bit of the same diameter as a baluster dowel to bore a hole 1/16 inch deeper than its length at the center of each baluster outline *(above, right)*; mark the drilling depth on the bit with masking tape. Vacuum particles out of the holes.

PREPARING A TREAD FOR DOVETAILED BALUSTERS

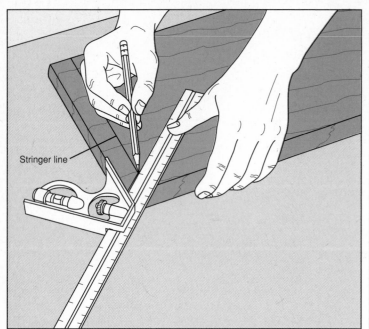

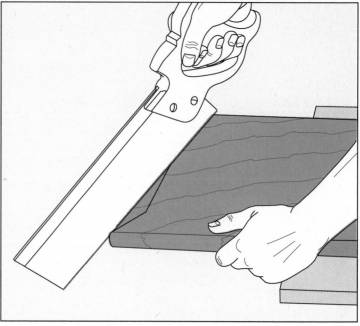

1 **Marking and cutting for the return nosing.** With the tread in position, mark onto the top of it the edge of the open stringer using a combination square as you would to locate a dowel socket *(page 99)*. Then, secure the tread to a workbench and use the square to mark a line at a 45-degree angle from the front corner of the tread to the stringer line *(above, left)*. Cut the tread along the 45-degree angle line using a backsaw *(above, right)*, stopping at its point of intersection

with the stringer line. Use a saber saw and a cutting guide to cut the tread along the stringer line; work from the end of the stringer line at the back edge of the tread and stop at its point of intersection with the cut along the 45-degree angle line. Test-fit the return nosing against the tread; trim the tread carefully with a rasp, a wood chisel or sandpaper as necessary for the return nosing to fit it neatly.

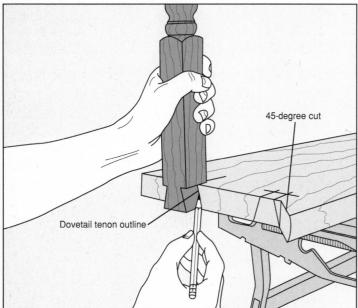

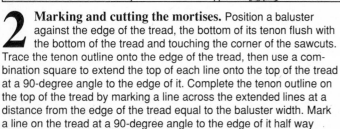

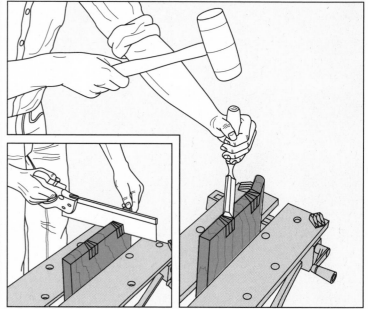

2 **Marking and cutting the mortises.** Position a baluster against the edge of the tread, the bottom of its tenon flush with the bottom of the tread and touching the corner of the sawcuts. Trace the tenon outline onto the edge of the tread, then use a combination square to extend the top of each line onto the top of the tread at a 90-degree angle to the edge of it. Complete the tenon outline on the top of the tread by marking a line across the extended lines at a distance from the edge of the tread equal to the baluster width. Mark a line on the tread at a 90-degree angle to the edge of it half way

between the corner of the sawcuts and the back edge of it; use this line to trace the tenon outline of the second baluster, working on the side of it closest to the back edge of the tread and aligning the baluster edge with it *(above, left)*. Secure the tread on end in a workbench, then trace the tenon outlines onto the bottom of it and use a backsaw to make a series of cuts within the sides of each mortise *(inset)*. Wearing safety goggles, use a wood chisel and a mallet to cut each mortise; work first on the top and bottom of the tread between the ends of the sawcuts, then into the edge of it *(above, right)*. Test-fit each baluster periodically.

REPLACING A RISER FROM BELOW

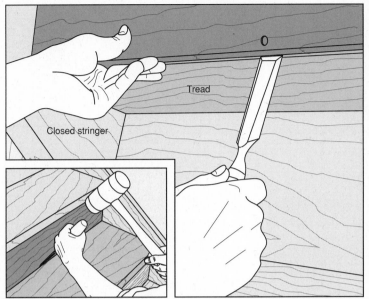

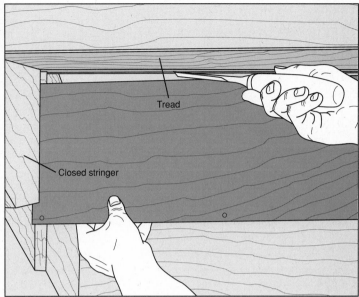

1 **Prying apart the riser and tread.** Take off any stair runner in the way *(page 106)*. If there is no closed stringer or no access to the riser from below, work from above to replace the riser *(page 102)*. Otherwise, work from below to remove any wedge *(page 93)* or glue block *(page 94)* supporting the riser as you would for a tread. Pull out any nails holding the bottom of the riser to the tread below it. Work from above to check the tread above the riser for any wood plug hiding a fastener holding it to the riser; wearing safety goggles, remove any plug using a wood chisel and a mallet, then take out the fastener. Work from below starting at any closed stringer to loosen the riser, pulling it

away from the tread below it with the chisel *(above, left)*. If the riser does not loosen, it may form a rabbet joint with the tread below it; use the chisel and mallet to pry apart the riser and tread, working carefully along the joint from below and above *(inset)*. Continue loosening the riser the same way, also working from below along the tread above it *(above, right)*. To remove the riser, pull it down out of any closed stringer; twist it to clear any open stringer, working from above to pull out any nails holding it to the open stringer. If you cannot loosen or remove the riser, work from above to replace it. After removing the riser, clean particles off the contacting surfaces of the treads and stringers with the chisel.

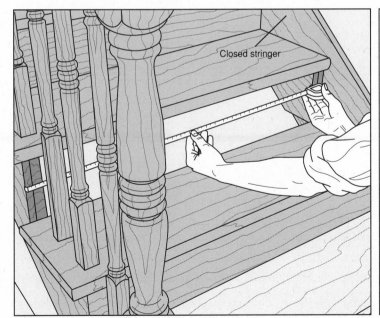

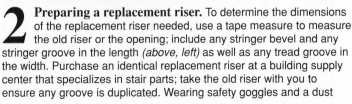

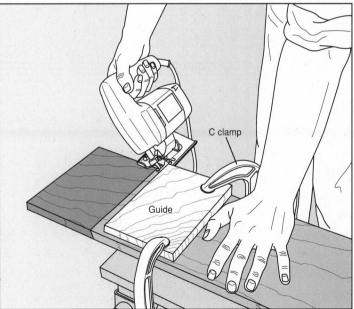

2 **Preparing a replacement riser.** To determine the dimensions of the replacement riser needed, use a tape measure to measure the old riser or the opening; include any stringer bevel and any stringer groove in the length *(above, left)* as well as any tread groove in the width. Purchase an identical replacement riser at a building supply center that specializes in stair parts; take the old riser with you to ensure any groove is duplicated. Wearing safety goggles and a dust

mask, cut the riser to size using a saber saw or a circular saw fitted with a fine crosscut blade. Secure a wood block to the riser as a cutting guide with C clamps to cut a 45-degree angled bevel across any end of it to be joined with a beveled open stinger *(above, right)*; use an electric drill to bore a pilot hole for a 2-inch finishing nail at the top and bottom as well as the center of the beveled end of it.

REPLACING A RISER FROM BELOW (continued)

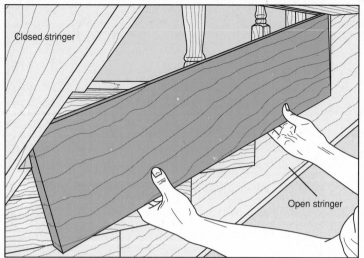

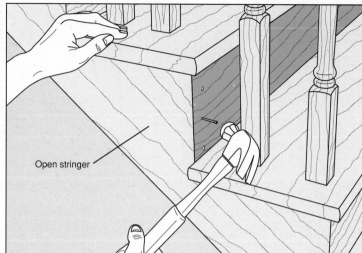

3 **Installing the replacement riser.** Work from below to test-fit the riser, twisting it to fit it against any open stringer *(above, left)*; push it up into any closed stringer, fitting it into any groove in the tread above it and against the tread below it. Trim the riser carefully with a rasp, a wood chisel or sandpaper as necessary to fit it; if there is an open stringer and a closed stringer, you may need to trim 1/16 inch off the end at the closed stringer. Take out the riser to coat the contacting surfaces of it, the treads and the stringers with wood glue, then reposition it and put back any wedge removed as you would for a tread *(page 93)*. Wearing safety goggles, use an electric drill to bore a pilot hole for a 2-inch finishing nail or No. 8 wood screw every 6 inches through the bottom of the riser into the tread below it; mark the drilling depth on the bit with masking tape. Drive in the nails or screws, then put back any glue block removed as you would for a tread *(page 94)*. Work from above to drive 2-inch finishing nails through any end of the riser at an open stringer *(above, right)*; use a nail set to set the nail heads. Wipe off extruded glue using a cloth dampened with water. Choose a wax stick of a color that matches the wood and use it to cover the nail heads. Spot-refinish any damaged surface *(page 83)*. Then, put back any stair runner you removed.

REPLACING A RISER FROM ABOVE

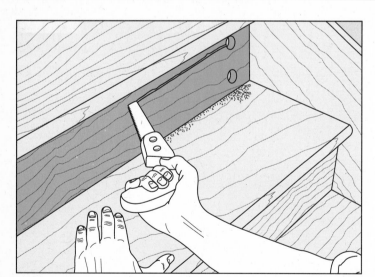

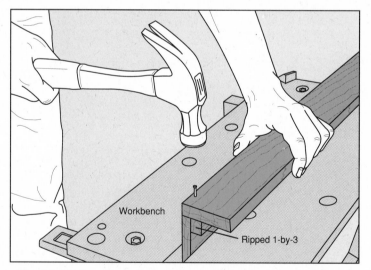

1 **Cutting out the riser.** Take off any stair runner in the way *(page 106)*. Work from below to replace the riser if there is access to the bottom of it and there is a closed stringer *(page 101)*. Otherwise, use an electric drill fitted with a 1-inch spade bit to bore a hole at each corner of the riser about 3 inches from the stringer and 1 inch from the tread; wear safety goggles. Use a keyhole saw to cut between the holes, working along the length *(above)* and across the width of the riser; fit your finger into a hole as you finish the last cut. Pull out the cut riser section, working carefully to avoid dropping it. Cut out the remaining riser and any wedge or glue block supporting it using a wood chisel and a mallet; work along the wood grain. Use a mini-hacksaw to cut off any fastener holding the remaining riser.

2 **Making a tread cleat.** Fit the opening with a tread cleat to support the replacement riser. Use a tape measure to measure the length of the opening between the stringers, then use a backsaw to cut three 1-by-3s to length. Measure the thickness of the tread below the opening and cut one of the 1-by-3s to a width equal to it; use a saber saw and a cutting guide to make the rip cut along the length of the 1-by-3. To make the cleat, form a butt joint with the two 1-by-3s and fit the ripped 1-by-3 along the inside edges of it. Coat the contacting surfaces of the 1-by-3s with wood glue, then drive a 1 1/2-inch box nail every 3 inches along one 1-by-3 into the ripped 1-by-3; nail the other 1-by-3 to the first 1-by-3 the same way *(above)*. Wipe off extruded glue using a cloth dampened with water.

REPLACING A RISER FROM ABOVE (continued)

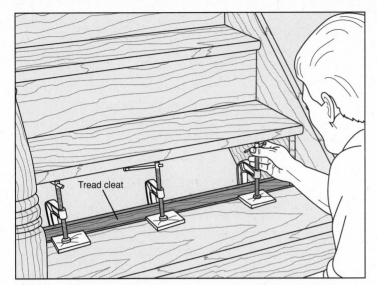

Tread cleat

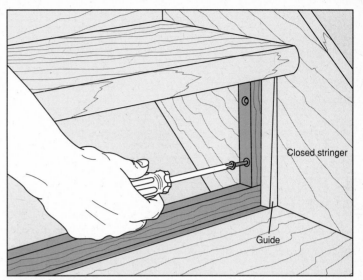

Closed stringer

Guide

3 **Installing the tread cleat.** Test-fit the tread cleat, positioning the ripped 1-by-3 flush with the tread below the opening; trim it carefully with a rasp, a wood chisel or sandpaper as necessary. Take out the cleat to coat the contacting surfaces of it and the tread with wood glue, then reposition it. Secure each end and the center of the cleat using a 6-inch C clamp, tightening it against the tread *(above)* to force out a thin bead of glue along the joint; protect the tread with a wood block. Wearing safety goggles, use an electric drill to bore a pilot hole for a 3-inch finishing nail every 6 inches along the back of the cleat into the tread. Drive in the nails, then remove the C clamps. Wipe off extruded glue using a cloth dampened with water.

4 **Installing a stringer cleat.** If there is no closed stringer, install a replacement riser *(step 5)*; otherwise, fit any closed stringer with a cleat. Measure the height of the opening along the stringer between the tread cleat and the tread above it, then use a backsaw to cut a 1-by-2 to length. Position the cleat against the stringer, setting a section of the old riser in place as a guide. Wearing safety goggles, use an electric drill to bore a pilot hole for a 2 1/2-inch No. 8 wood screw at the top and bottom of the cleat. Coat the contacting surfaces of the cleat, the stringer, the tread and the tread cleat with wood glue, then drive in the screws *(above)*. Wipe off extruded glue using a cloth dampened with water.

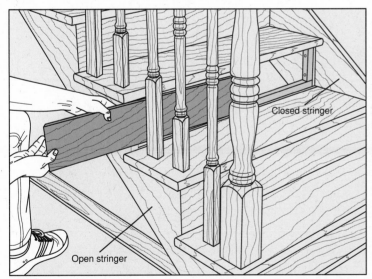

Closed stringer

Open stringer

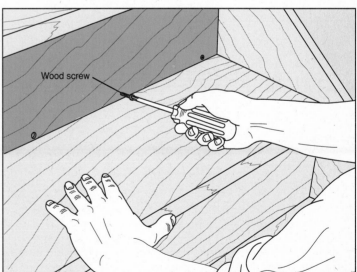

Wood screw

5 **Installing a replacement riser.** To determine the dimensions of the replacement riser needed, measure the opening; include any stringer groove or bevel in the length and any tread groove in the width. Purchase an identical replacement riser at a building supply center that specializes in stair parts. Wearing safety goggles and a dust mask, cut the riser to size using a saber saw or a circular saw fitted with a fine crosscut blade; bevel any end to be joined with an open stringer at a 45-degree angle. Test-fit the riser, trimming it carefully with a rasp, a wood chisel or sandpaper as necessary; tap it into place using a hammer, cushioning the blows with a wood block. Slide the riser into place on any open stringer *(above, left)*, fitting it into any closed stringer and any groove in the tread above it. If there is no open stringer, cut an

amount equal to the depth of a stringer groove off one end of the riser, then fit it into place and center it. Take out the riser to coat the contacting surfaces of it and the stringers, tread and tread cleat with wood glue, then reposition it. Use an electric drill to bore a hole for a 1 1/2-inch No. 8 wood screw and a wood plug every 6 inches through the bottom of the riser into the tread cleat, then drive in the screws *(above, right)* and install the plugs with glue; fasten the riser every 2 to 3 inches to any stringer cleat the same way. Use the same procedure to fasten the riser to any open stringer with 2-inch finishing nails; set the nail heads using a nail set and cover them with a wax stick of a color that matches the wood. Wipe off extruded glue using a cloth dampened with water. Spot-refinish any damaged surface *(page 83)*. Put back any stair runner you removed.

SECURING A FLOATING HANDRAIL

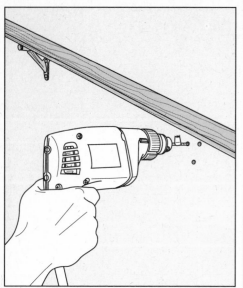

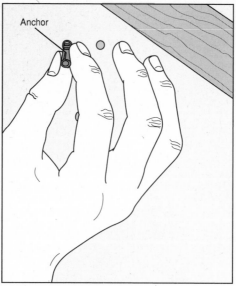

Anchor

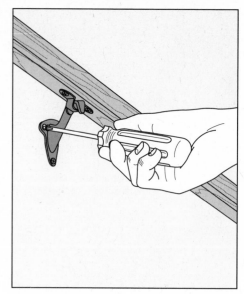

1 **Boring holes for a wall bracket.** To secure the handrail, tighten any loose bracket screws; or, replace them with ones slightly longer. If necessary, install additional brackets; at least one is needed every 4 feet along the handrail. To install a bracket, locate a stud behind the wall; use an electronic density sensor or tap along the wall and listen for a change from a hollow to a solid sound every 16 inches. Position the bracket under the handrail at the stud and mark its screw holes. Wearing safety goggles, use an electric drill to bore pilot holes for the bracket screws *(above, left)*, ensuring at least two enter the wall at the stud; if one misses, enlarge it enough to fit in an anchor for the screw *(above, right)*.

2 **Installing the wall bracket.** Position the bracket against the wall under the handrail; if necessary, have a helper support it in place. Using a screwdriver, first drive the bracket screws into the handrail, then drive the bracket screws into the wall *(above)*; ensure each screw is installed tightly.

REPLACING A TREAD (BASEMENT STAIRCASE)

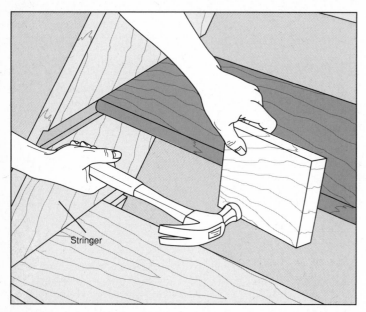

Stringer

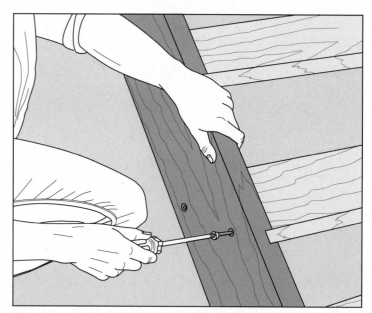

1 **Removing the damaged tread.** Remove any nails or screws holding the tread; on a typical staircase without risers, check for fasteners at each end of the tread and along the outside edge of each stringer. If the tread is fitted between closed stringers, drive it out of them using a hammer; hold a wood block against the tread nosing and strike it *(above)*, distributing the force of the blows. If the tread is seated on open stringers, lift it off them.

2 **Installing a replacement tread.** Purchase an identical replacement tread at a building supply center that specializes in stair parts. Wearing safety goggles and a dust mask, cut the tread to size using a circular saw or a saber saw. Position the tread and secure it to the stringers. Use an electric drill to bore holes for counter-sinking 3-inch No. 8 wood screws every 3 to 4 inches: through each closed stringer into the end of the tread; through each end of the tread into any cleat or open stringer. Drive in the screws *(above)*, then cover the screw heads with a wax stick.

REPAIRING A STRINGER (BASEMENT STAIRCASE)

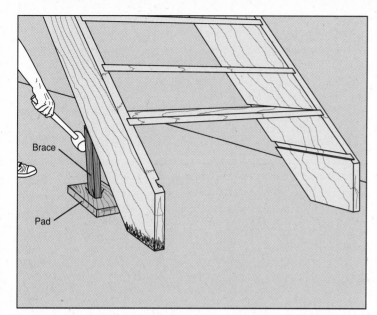

1 Bracing the damaged stringer. To repair a stringer that is damaged at its base, support it in position with a wood brace and cut off the damaged section. Take off the bottom tread as you would to remove a damaged tread *(page 104)*. For the brace, use a 2-by-8 about 2 feet long as the base and a 2-by-4; cut the 2-by-4 to a length of about 2 feet, holding it against the stringer to mark it. Drive the brace under the stringer using a small sledgehammer until it is supported in position *(above)*; use a carpenter's level to check that the treads are horizontal.

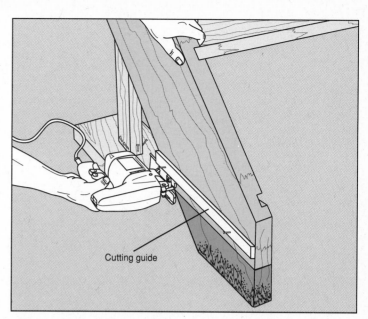

2 Cutting off the damaged section. To determine the extent of the damaged section, use an awl to poke into the stringer; work up the stringer from its base, continuing as far as the wood is easily penetrated. When solid wood is reached, mark a horizontal line across the stringer above the damaged section of it using a carpenter's level. Wearing safety goggles and a dust mask, cut off the damaged section of the stringer using a saber saw *(above)*; temporarily nail a board to the stringer as a cutting guide. Remove the damaged section of the stringer and the cutting guide.

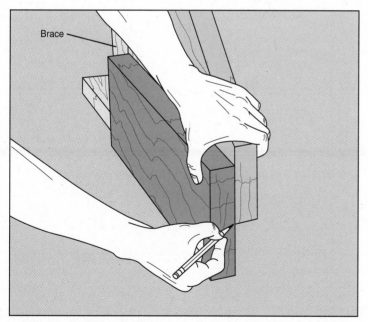

3 Marking and cutting a replacement section. Use a length of 2-by-6 or 2-by-8 to make a replacement section, positioning it flat on the floor and flush against the side and front edges of the undamaged stringer to mark it. Use the bottom edge of the undamaged stringer to mark the height of the replacement section *(above)*; use the back edge of the undamaged stringer to mark the angle of the replacement section. Wearing safety goggles and a dust mask, use a saber saw to cut the replacement section to size.

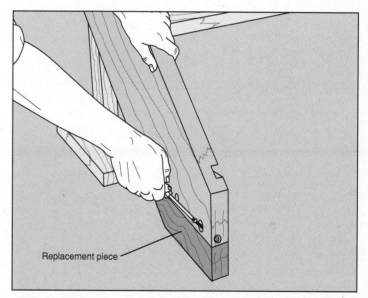

4 Installing the replacement section. Position the replacement section under the undamaged stringer. Wearing safety goggles, use an electric drill to bore holes for countersinking 2 1/2-inch No. 8 wood screws at an angle through the undamaged stringer into the replacement section: one hole at the front and at the back; two holes on each side. Remove the replacement section to coat the top of it and the bottom of the undamaged stringer with wood glue, then reposition it and drive in the screws *(above)*; cover the screw heads with a wax stick. Wipe off extruded glue using a cloth dampened with water. Remove the brace from under the stringer, then reinstall the bottom tread as you would any replacement tread *(page 104)*.

CARPETS

Sturdy fabrics, a wide range of colors and luxuriant textures make the wall-to-wall carpet a popular flooring choice for almost every room in the house—combining "barefoot" warmth with "hard-heeled" sturdiness. Two principal types are shown: glue-down *(below)* and stretch-in *(page 107)*. A glue-down carpet or stair runner typically has a cushion layer of foram backing and is secured directly to the subfloor or stairs with latex adhesive. A stretch-in carpet or stair runner has a separate undercushion stapled to the subfloor or stairs onto which it is placed; it is stretched and hooked onto tackless strips nailed to the edges of the subfloor or stairs. A glue-down or stretch-in carpet can be installed the same way on top of finish flooring. And while both types of carpets are still equally common, the glue-down carpet is often favored over the stretch-in carpet by the do-it-yourselfer because few special tools are required to repair or replace it.

Glue-down and stretch-in carpets are comprised of a top layer of cut pile or loop pile. The yarn that makes up the pile is stitched to a primary backing of fabric, then a secondary backing is bonded with latex to the bottom of the primary backing. With a carpet that is cut pile, the stitched yarn is cut for a surface of straight-standing yarn ends. With a carpet that is loop pile, the stitched yarn is left uncut to form a surface of continuous yarn loops. Whether your carpet or stair runner is glue-down or stretch-in of cut pile or loop pile, you should undertake repairs to it as soon as a problem is apparent—both to maintain the beauty and life of it as well as to help prevent damage to the floor understructure. Vacuum the carpet regularly *(page 109)* to keep dirt and grit from being ground into the pile and the backing. Remove a stain *(page 110)* as soon as you notice it. Refurbish flattened pile *(page 111)* to keep the carpet looking tidy and even-textured.

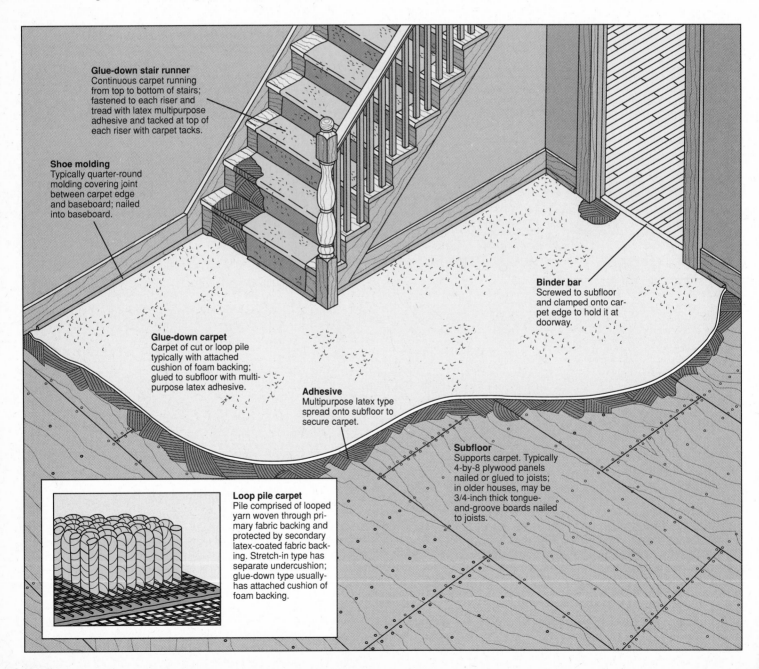

Glue-down stair runner
Continuous carpet running from top to bottom of stairs; fastened to each riser and tread with latex multipurpose adhesive and tacked at top of each riser with carpet tacks.

Shoe molding
Typically quarter-round molding covering joint between carpet edge and baseboard; nailed into baseboard.

Glue-down carpet
Carpet of cut or loop pile typically with attached cushion of foam backing; glued to subfloor with multi-purpose latex adhesive.

Adhesive
Multipurpose latex type spread onto subfloor to secure carpet.

Binder bar
Screwed to subfloor and clamped onto carpet edge to hold it at doorway.

Subfloor
Supports carpet. Typically 4-by-8 plywood panels nailed or glued to joists; in older houses, may be 3/4-inch thick tongue-and-groove boards nailed to joists.

Loop pile carpet
Pile comprised of looped yarn woven through primary fabric backing and protected by secondary latex-coated fabric backing. Stretch-in type has separate undercushion; glue-down type usually has attached cushion of foam backing.

Consult the Troubleshooting Guide *(page 108)* to help you diagnose any carpet problem. If routine cleaning with a vacuum fails to spruce up a soiled or faded carpet or stair runner, use a water-extraction carpet cleaner to revive it *(page 109)*. Repairs to a glue-down carpet usually are simple and can be made using common household tools. A small tear in a glue-down carpet can be quickly reglued *(page 111)*; a damaged section can be replaced *(page 112)*. Similar repairs can be made to a stretch-in carpet, but they typically are more time-consuming and require special tools. For a repair to any type of carpet, the biggest problem can be finding a replacement piece; even a saved remnant of the original installation may not match exactly if it has not been exposed to the same conditions. Often, you may need to replace the glue-down carpet *(page 113)* or stair runner *(page 120)* or the entire stretch-in carpet *(page 118)* or stair runner *(page 121)*.

The materials and supplies necessary for carpet repairs are readily available at a carpet dealer or a building supply center. Refer to Tools & Techniques *(page 122)* for information on many of the common household tools you are likely to need. Any of the special tools you may require, especially for work with a stretch-in carpet, can be rented at a tool rental agency: a knee-kicker, a power stretcher, a wall trimmer or a seaming iron. When you are renting any special tool, ask to see the manufacturer's operating instructions for it; if possible, have the tool demonstrated before you take it home. Practice working with any special tool on old pieces of carpet until you are comfortable using it and perfect your technique. Before beginning any carpet repair, carefully review the step-by-step instructions provided in the chapter. Also read the Emergency Guide *(page 8)*; work carefully and follow all safety precautions.

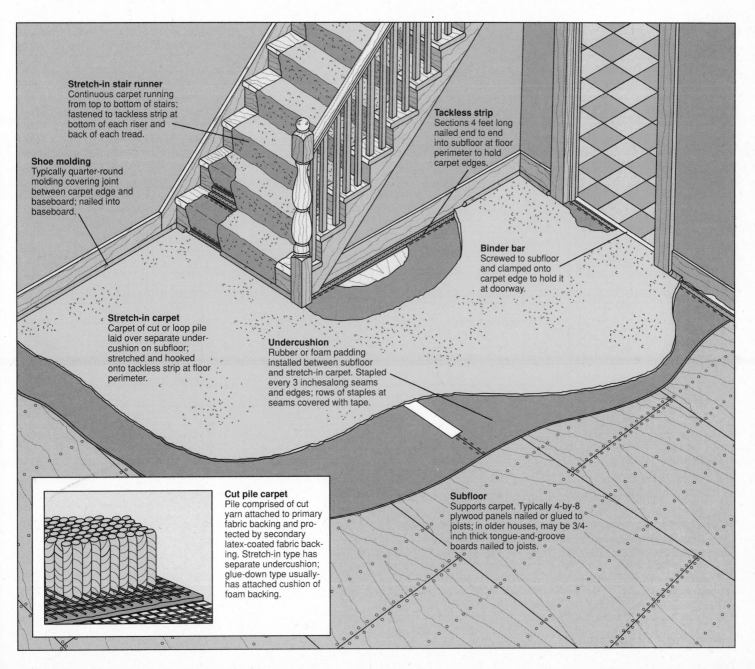

Stretch-in stair runner
Continuous carpet running from top to bottom of stairs; fastened to tackless strip at bottom of each riser and back of each tread.

Shoe molding
Typically quarter-round molding covering joint between carpet edge and baseboard; nailed into baseboard.

Tackless strip
Sections 4 feet long nailed end to end into subfloor at floor perimeter to hold carpet edges.

Binder bar
Screwed to subfloor and clamped onto carpet edge to hold it at doorway.

Stretch-in carpet
Carpet of cut or loop pile laid over separate undercushion on subfloor; stretched and hooked onto tackless strip at floor perimeter.

Undercushion
Rubber or foam padding installed between subfloor and stretch-in carpet. Stapled every 3 inches along seams and edges; rows of staples at seams covered with tape.

Cut pile carpet
Pile comprised of cut yarn attached to primary fabric backing and protected by secondary latex-coated fabric backing. Stretch-in type has separate undercushion; glue-down type usually has attached cushion of foam backing.

Subfloor
Supports carpet. Typically 4-by-8 plywood panels nailed or glued to joists; in older houses, may be 3/4-inch thick tongue-and-groove boards nailed to joists.

TROUBLESHOOTING GUIDE

SYMPTOM	POSSIBLE CAUSE	PROCEDURE
GLUE-DOWN		
Carpet dirty or soiled	Everyday wear and tear; lack of maintenance	Vacuum carpet (p. 109) □○; maintain carpet (p. 109) □◐▲
	Fabric deterioration with age	Replace carpet section (p. 112) ◪◐ or replace carpet (p. 113) ◪●; stair runner (p. 120) ◪●
Carpet emits odor	Everyday wear and tear; lack of maintenance	Vacuum carpet (p. 109) □○; maintain carpet (p. 109) □◐▲
Carpet static	Low house humidity	Increase house humidity
Carpet stained or discolored	Everyday wear and tear; food or liquid spill; sunlight	Remove stain (p. 110) □○; shield carpet from sunlight
	Carpet damaged; fabric deterioration with age	Replace pile section (p. 114) □◐; replace carpet section (p. 112) ◪◐ or replace carpet (p. 113) ◪●; stair runner (p. 120) ◪●
Carpet burned	Dropped cigarette; spark from fireplace	Replace pile section (p. 114) □◐ or replace carpet section (p. 112) ◪◐; keep fireplace screened
Carpet pile flattened	Everyday wear and tear	Refurbish carpet pile (p. 111) □○
Carpet sheds pile tufts	Normal wear of new carpet	Vacuum carpet (p. 109) □○
	Carpet damaged; fabric deterioration with age	Replace pile section (p. 114) □◐; replace carpet section (p. 112) ◪◐ or replace carpet (p. 113) ◪●; stair runner (p. 120) ◪●
Carpet torn	Accidental damage caused by sharp object	Repair carpet (p. 111) □○ or replace carpet section (p. 112) ◪◐
Carpet worn	Everyday wear and tear; fabric deterioration with age	Replace pile section (p. 114) □◐; replace carpet section (p. 112) ◪◐ or replace carpet (p. 113) ◪●; stair runner (p. 120) ◪●
Carpet springy; sagging or bulged	Finish flooring faulty	Troubleshoot wood flooring (p. 14) or resilient flooring (p. 36)
	Floor understructure faulty	Troubleshoot floor understructure (p. 62)
STRETCH-IN		
Carpet dirty or soiled	Everyday wear and tear; lack of maintenance	Vacuum carpet (p. 109) □○; maintain carpet (p. 109) □◐▲
	Fabric deterioration with age	Replace carpet section (p. 116) ◪◐▲ or replace carpet (p. 118) ■◐▲; stair runner (p. 121) ◪◐▲
Carpet emits odor	Everyday wear and tear; lack of maintenance	Vacuum carpet (p. 109) □○; maintain carpet (p. 109) □◐▲
Carpet static	Low house humidity	Increase house humidity
Carpet stained or discolored	Everyday wear and tear; food or liquid spill; sunlight	Remove stain (p. 110) □○; shield carpet from sunlight
	Carpet damaged; fabric deterioration with age	Replace pile section (p. 114) □◐; replace carpet section (p. 116) ◪◐▲ or replace carpet (p. 118) ■◐▲; stair runner (p. 121) ◪◐▲
Carpet burned	Dropped cigarette; spark from fireplace	Replace pile section (p. 114) □◐ or replace carpet section (p. 116) ◪◐▲; keep fireplace screened
Carpet pile flattened	Everyday wear and tear	Refurbish carpet pile (p. 111) □○
Carpet sheds pile tufts	Normal wear of new carpet	Vacuum carpet (p. 109) □○
	Carpet damaged; fabric deterioration with age	Replace pile section (p. 114) □◐; replace carpet section (p. 116) ◪◐▲ or replace carpet (p. 118) ■◐▲; stair runner (p. 121) ◪◐▲
Carpet loose	Carpet edge detached; tackless strip damaged	Secure carpet edge (p. 116) □○▲
Carpet torn	Accidental damage caused by sharp object	Replace carpet section (p. 116) ◪◐▲
Carpet worn	Everyday wear and tear; fabric deterioration with age	Replace pile section (p. 114) □◐; replace carpet section (p. 116) ◪◐▲ or replace carpet (p. 118) ■◐▲; stair runner (p. 121) ◪◐▲
Carpet springy; sagging or bulged	Carpet edge detached; tackless strip damaged	Secure carpet edge (p. 116) □○▲
	Finish flooring faulty	Troubleshoot wood flooring (p. 14) or resilient flooring (p. 36)
	Floor understructure faulty	Troubleshoot floor understructure (p. 62)

DEGREE OF DIFFICULTY: □ Easy ◪ Moderate ■ Complex
ESTIMATED TIME: ○ Less than 1 hour ◐ 1 to 3 hours ● Over 3 hours   ▲ Special tool required

MAINTAINING A CARPET

1 **Vacuuming the carpet.** To remove loose dirt and keep the pile fresh and upright, vacuum the carpet regularly. If the carpet has an odor, sprinkle baking soda on it before vacuuming; for greasy dirt, apply a commercial powdered carpet cleaner following the manufacturer's instructions. Use a canister or upright vacuum cleaner with rotary brushes; empty or change the dust bag if it is more than half full. Starting at a corner and working back toward the door, vacuum one small carpet section at a time; move the vacuum slowly back and forth in overlapping strokes to agitate the pile, making several passes over a high-traffic section.

2 **Preparing to clean the carpet.** If the carpet remains soiled after vacuuming, rent a water-extraction carpet cleaner at a tool rental agency; to clean a stair runner, also rent an upholstery cleaning nozzle. Ensure that the carpet cleaner is equipped with a sufficient length of hose for the job and buy enough of the recommended shampoo for your carpet. Clear the carpet and remove any stains from it *(page 110)*. On any spot of the carpet that is heavily soiled, apply a commercial carpet soil remover following the manufacturer's instructions; spray enough of the soil remover onto the spot to cover it *(above)*, without saturating the carpet.

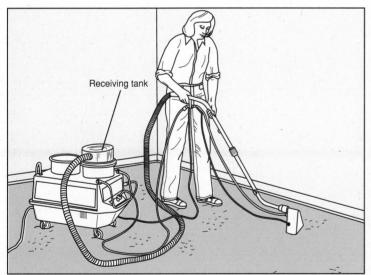

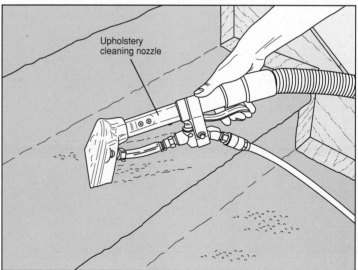

3 **Cleaning the carpet.** Mix enough shampoo and water to fill the supply tank of the carpet cleaner following the manufacturer's instructions. Test the solution by applying a small amount on an inconspicuous spot on the carpet; if the dye runs, dilute the solution with water or use a milder shampoo. Raise the pile of a deep-pile carpet before cleaning it by brushing against the pile with a long-handled brush. To clean the carpet, start at a corner and work back toward the door, shampooing one section 3 feet square at a time. Depress the spray trigger and move the nozzle of the carpet cleaner slowly back and forth over the section in overlapping strokes; then, release the spray trigger and move the nozzle back over your strokes to extract the

shampoo and dirt. Continue the same way *(above, left)*, overlapping each section slightly. When the supply tank of the carpet cleaner empties, stop and empty the receiving tank; refill the supply tank to continue. To clean a stair runner, fit the carpet cleaner with the upholstery cleaning nozzle following the manufacturer's instructions. Working from the top to the bottom of the stairs, shampoo a riser and tread *(above, right)* section of the runner at a time. Raise the pile of a deep-pile carpet again after cleaning it. Allow the carpet to dry to the touch, usually overnight, before moving furniture onto it. To prevent furniture legs from staining a slightly damp carpet, slip aluminum foil or waxed paper under them; leave the foil or paper for several days until the carpet is completely dry.

REMOVING STAINS

STAIN-LIFTING PROCEDURES

Stain	Cleaning agent
General food or beverage: for example, alcoholic drink, wine, beer, coffee, tea, chocolate, milk or ice cream	1 teaspoon of mild household detergent per cup of warm water 1 tablespoon of ammonia per cup of water 1 cup of white vinegar per cup of water Hydrogen peroxide
Acidic food or beverage: for example, catsup, mustard, soft drink, lemonade, excrement or vomit	Dry baking soda 1 teaspoon of powdered enzyme laundry detergent per cup of warm water Powdered carpet cleaner*
Oil or grease: for example, makeup, tar, shortening, furniture polish, cooking oil or butter	Non-flammable dry cleaning fluid*
Chewing gum	Lay ice pack on gum until it is hard and brittle; then, pick hardened gum off carpet
Blood or urine	1 teaspoon of dishwashing detergent per cup of warm water 1 tablespoon of ammonia per cup of water 1 cup of white vinegar per cup of water
Candle wax or crayon	1 teaspoon of dishwashing detergent per cup of warm water Non-flammable dry cleaning fluid*
Unknown origin	1 teaspoon of mild household detergent per cup of warm water 1 tablespoon of ammonia per cup of water 1 cup of white vinegar per cup of water Non-flammable dry cleaning fluid* Hydrogen peroxide

* Available at grocery store or building supply center

Choosing a cleaning agent. Remove a stain as soon as you notice it—and be patient; repeated applications of a cleaning agent may be necessary. Following any specific procedures on stain removal recommended by the carpet manufacturer, consult the chart at left to choose an appropriate cleaning agent for the type of stain; apply the general techniques for lifting out a stain suited to the cleaning agent you are using *(step below)*. Always start with the mildest cleaning agent recommended for the stain, listed first in the chart; if it does not remove the stain, try the next cleaning agent recommended, continuing as necessary. Before applying any cleaning agent, test it on an inconspicuous spot of the carpet or a scrap piece of it; if the cleaning agent discolors or otherwise damages it, use another cleaning agent. If a stain defies all cleaning agents recommended, consult a professional carpet cleaner. Or, try refurbishing the pile *(page 111)* or replacing a section of it *(page 114)*; otherwise, replace the glue-down *(page 112)* or stretch-in *(page 116)* carpet section.

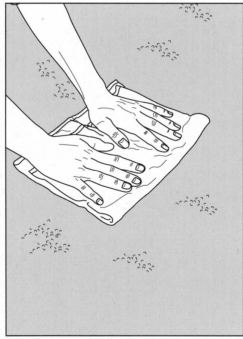

Lifting out a stain. If there is solid material embedded in the carpet, remove it. For a dried solid, use an old toothbrush to make short, gentle strokes across the area, dislodging the material; then, vacuum it. For a semi-liquid solid, use a plastic spatula to scoop up as much of the material as possible *(above, left)* without scraping the area; then, blot it with paper towels. To apply a liquid cleaning agent, moisten a clean, white cloth with it and dab the stain, working in from the perimeter; never rub or scour. To lift out the stain, lay a clean, dry cloth or paper towels on it and press down firmly *(above, center)*, soaking up the liquid; repeat with dry cloths or paper towels until the stain is lifted. To rinse the area after applying a liquid cleaning agent, use a sponge dampened with water to dab it, then blot it with paper towels. To apply a powdered cleaning agent, follow the manufacturer's instructions; in general, sprinkle a light coat of it on the stain *(above, right)*, then gently work it into the area using a soft-bristled brush. Wait for the time recommended by the manufacturer, then vacuum the area thoroughly.

REFURBISHING A SECTION OF PILE

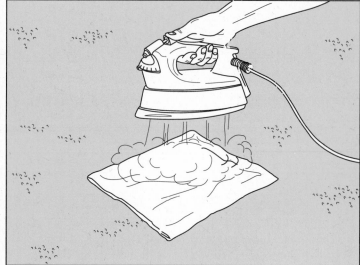

Raising flattened carpet pile. If a section of pile is flattened, use a coin to try raising it. Making short, brisk strokes, scrape the coin against the pile of the flattened section *(above, left)* to lift it upright; alternately, try raising the pile using an old hair comb, brushing it the same way. If you cannot raise the pile with a coin or a hair comb, use a steam iron set to its lowest steam setting. Lay a clean cloth on the flattened section of pile, then hold the steam iron a few inches above it and depress the steam button a few times, releasing short bursts of steam *(above, right)*.
Caution: Do not place a hot iron directly onto the carpet. Set aside the iron and cloth, then use the coin or hair comb to try raising the pile again. If necessary, use the cloth and steam iron again, repeating the same procedure as necessary until the flattened section of pile is raised.

REPAIRING A GLUE-DOWN CARPET

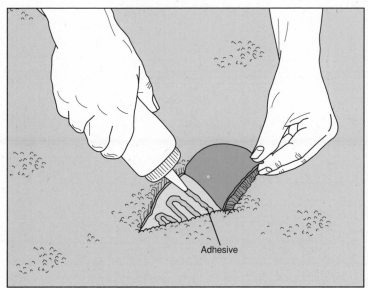

Adhesive

Regluing a torn carpet. For a large tear, replace the damaged section *(page 112)*. For a small tear, repair it using latex multipurpose adhesive. Gently lift up the edge of the torn carpet and fold it back. Apply a thin, even bead of adhesive along the base of the pile around the lifted carpet edges. When the adhesive is dry to the touch, apply a thin, even coat of adhesive on the bottom of any unadhered carpet edge around the opening and in the opening under the lifted carpet *(above, left)*. Fold the lifted carpet carefully into place, pressing it into the opening; if any pile catches, free it using the tip of an awl. Dab the pile with a clean cloth to blot any extruded adhesive. Place a weight such as a telephone book on the repaired carpet *(above, right)* and let the adhesive set for the time specified by the manufacturer—usually 12 hours. Remove the weight, then gently rub any flattened pile to raise it.

REPLACING A SMALL GLUE-DOWN CARPET SECTION

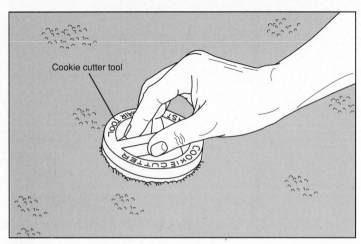

Cookie cutter tool

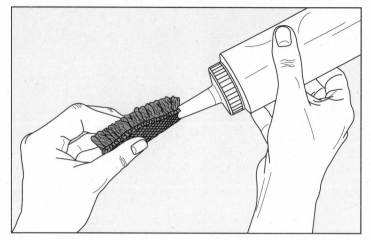

1 **Removing the damaged section.** Buy a cookie cutter tool and latex multipurpose adhesive at a flooring supply store; also have on hand a matching carpet remnant for a replacement section. Position the cookie cutter tool on the carpet with its pin protruding into the center of the damaged section. Pressing down firmly on the cookie cutter tool, turn it clockwise to cut through the carpet around the damaged section *(above)*. To remove the damaged section, pull out as many layers of it as you can by hand; use a small putty knife to scrape any adhered foam backing and adhesive out of the opening. Use the cookie cutter tool to cut a replacement section.

2 **Installing the replacement section.** Apply a thin, even bead of adhesive along the base of the pile around the edges of the replacement section *(above)* and the opening. When the adhesive is dry to the touch, apply a thin, even coat of adhesive in the opening. Fit the replacement section carefully into place, pressing it into the opening; if any pile catches, free it using the tip of an awl. Dab the pile with a clean cloth to blot any extruded adhesive. Place a weight on the replacement section and let the adhesive set for the time specified by the manufacturer—usually 12 hours. Remove the weight, then gently rub any flattened pile to raise it.

REPLACING A LARGE GLUE-DOWN CARPET SECTION

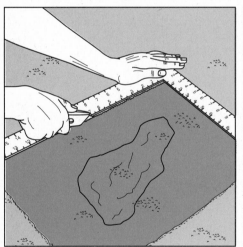

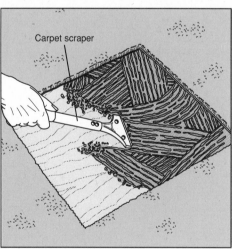

Carpet scraper

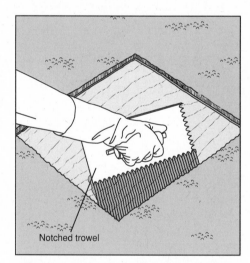

Notched trowel

1 **Removing the damaged section.** Buy latex multipurpose adhesive at a flooring supply store; also have on hand a matching carpet remnant for a replacement section. Lay a carpenter's square on the carpet, framing two edges of the damaged section parallel to the floor edges. Pressing down lightly to steady the square without flattening the pile, part the tufts of pile along the inside edges of the square. Use a utility knife to score repeatedly along each inside edge of the square, cutting through the carpet *(above, left)* along two adjacent edges of the damaged section. Reposition the square to frame the other two edges of the damaged section, then part the tufts of pile and cut along the inside edges of it the same way. Pull out as many layers of the damaged section as you can by hand. Wearing safety goggles, use a carpet scraper to remove any adhered foam backing and adhesive out of the opening; holding the scraper at a 45-degree angle, push it forward to scrape the opening clean *(above, right)*. Vacuum particles out the opening. Make a template of the opening out of cardboard or kraft paper and trace it on the back of the carpet remnant; then, cut the remnant to size with the utility knife.

2 **Installing the replacement section.** Apply a thin, even bead of adhesive along the base of the pile at the edges of the replacement section and the opening; when it is dry to the touch, coat the opening with adhesive using a notched trowel *(above)*. Press the replacement section in place; if any pile catches, free it using an awl. Blot extruded adhesive with a clean cloth. Place a weight on the replacement section and let the adhesive set for the time specified by the manufacturer—usually 12 hours. Remove the weight, then gently rub any flattened pile to raise it.

REPLACING A GLUE-DOWN CARPET

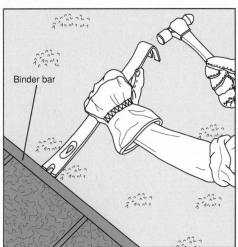

Binder bar

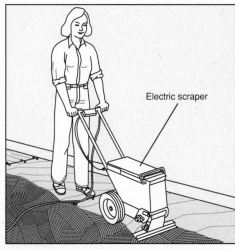

Electric scraper

1 **Preparing to install a new carpet.** Measure the floor *(above)* and buy new carpet to fit at a carpet dealer; also buy enough latex multipurpose adhesive. If you need two carpet pieces, have the dealer cut the pieces for a seam in a low-traffic area perpendicular to a window; have the edge of each piece for the seam marked. To make the seam, buy a glue-down carpet seam sealer; for a loop pile carpet, also a loop pile cutter.

2 **Removing the old carpet.** Rent an electric scraper at a tool rental agency. Remove any shoe molding *(page 133)* and loosen the carpet edge from any binder bar holding it at a doorway. Wearing safety goggles and work gloves, use a ball-peen hammer and a pry bar to work along the binder bar, prying its lip off the carpet edge *(above, left)*; then, use the tip of an old screwdriver to pry the carpet edge out of it. To remove the carpet, grab the freed edge and work along it, then across the room, pulling up as much of the carpet by hand as possible. To remove any adhered foam backing and adhesive remaining on the floor, use the electric scraper. **Caution:** Keep children and pets away. Starting at a corner, scrape the floor in parallel strips, pushing the scraper slowly along the floor from one end to the other and back again *(above, right)*. Vacuum particles off the floor.

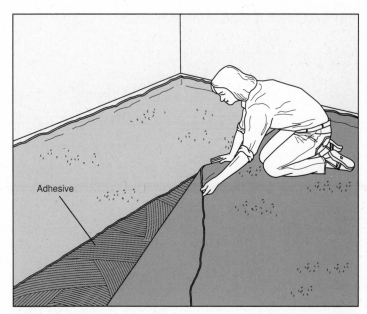

Adhesive

3 **Laying out the new carpet.** To install a single carpet piece, lay it on the floor with its edges lapped up the walls, then adhere it and use a utility knife to trim off the excess *(step 5)*. To install more than one carpet piece, trim each store-marked edge to make a seam. For a loop pile carpet, fit the notch of a loop pile cutter onto the carpet and push forward to trim a 1-inch strip off it *(inset)*. For a cut pile carpet, lay the piece pile-down and snap a chalk line 1 inch from the edge on it *(above)*; then, cut along the line with a utility knife and straightedge. Lay the pieces on the floor with their cut edges butted together and their outer edges lapped up the walls. Then, adhere the carpet seam *(step 4)*.

4 **Adhering a carpet seam.** Fold the carpet on one side of the seam back 18 inches, then apply a bead of carpet seam sealer to the base of the pile along the edge of it. Repeat the procedure with the carpet on the other side of the seam. Wearing rubber gloves, use a notched trowel to spread a thin, even coat of adhesive on the exposed floor. Starting at one end of the seam and working along it, roll the carpet on one side of it onto the adhesive, smoothing it toward the seam with your hand; repeat the procedure with the carpet on the other side of the seam, pressing down on the butted edges to secure the seam *(above)*. If any pile catches in the seam, use the tip of an awl to free it. Blot any extruded adhesive with a clean cloth.

REPLACING A GLUE-DOWN CARPET (continued)

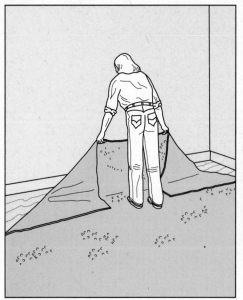

5 **Adhering the carpet.** Adhere one half of the carpet at a time starting along one edge; if there is a seam, start along an edge parallel to it. Fold back the carpet at each corner, then fold it back toward the center of the floor *(above, left)*, stopping at any adhered section along a seam. Wearing rubber gloves, use a notched trowel to spread a thin, even coat of adhesive on the exposed floor, working from the perimeter toward the center of it *(above, center)*.

Then, roll the carpet one fold at a time onto the adhesive; use a 2-by-4 to smooth out and press down each unfolded section. Use the same procedure to adhere the other half of the carpet, then trim off the excess with a utility knife. At any doorway or wall opening, fit the carpet edge snugly into the groove of any binder bar; then, hold a 2-by-4 against the lip of the binder bar and strike it, bending the lip down onto the carpet edge *(above, right)*. Reinstall any shoe molding you removed.

REPLACING A SECTION OF PILE

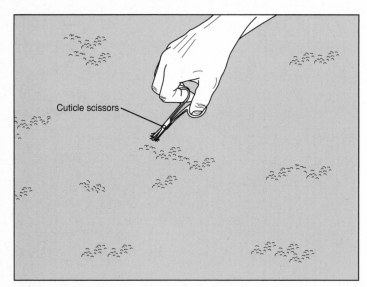

Cuticle scissors

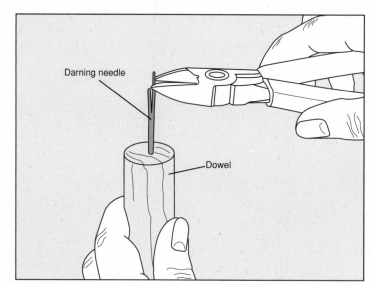

Darning needle

Dowel

1 **Removing the damaged tufts.** For superficial damage to a tiny section of cut pile carpet, try replacing the damaged pile; otherwise replace the glue-down *(page 112)* or stretch-in *(page 116)* carpet section. If only the pile tips are damaged, use a pair of cuticle scissors to trim them. For deeper damage to the pile, use the cuticle scissors to sever each damaged tuft of pile at the primary backing of the carpet *(above)*; then, vacuum particles out of the area. Use tweezers to pull replacement tufts of pile out of a matching carpet remnant or an inconspicuous spot in the carpet, gripping each tuft firmly at its base and tugging it free of the primary backing.

2 **Making a tuft setter.** To install the replacement pile, make a tuft setter out of a wood dowel 3/4 inch in diameter and a darning needle. Wearing safety goggles, cut the dowel about 4 inches long, then use an electric drill to bore a hole about 1 1/2 inches deep for the darning needle in one end of it. Insert the needle into the dowel with its eye protruding out of the hole; if it protrudes more than a few inches, remove it and trim off the bottom of it using diagonal-cutting pliers. Reinsert the needle tightly into the dowel, then use the pliers to cut off the upper portion of its eye *(above)*, making a two-pronged tip for holding and installing the replacement tufts of pile.

REPLACING A SECTION OF PILE (continued)

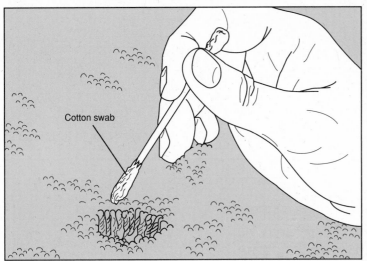

3 **Installing the replacement tufts.** To install replacement tufts of pile, use the tuft setter to insert them one at a time into the backing in the opening. Dip the end of a cotton swab into latex multipurpose adhesive and dab the adhesive into a hole in the backing *(above, left)*. Fit the top of a replacement tuft into the base of the tuft setter prongs; then, jab the tuft setter into the glued hole in the backing *(above, right)*, pushing its prongs far enough to seat the base of the replacement tuft in the glued backing. Continue to apply adhesive and insert replacement tufts until the opening is filled, fitting the tufts as close together as possible. Let the adhesive set for 24 hours; then, if necessary, use cuticle scissors to trim the replacement tufts level with the surrounding pile.

USING A KNEE-KICKER

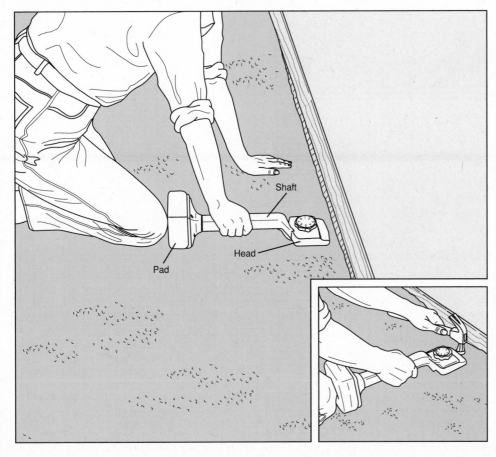

Setting up and using a knee-kicker. Use a knee-kicker to secure or detach a stretch-in carpet edge. Rent a knee-kicker at a tool rental agency and follow the manufacturer's instructions to select the correct tooth depth for the carpet thickness; then, test the depth by using the knee-kicker on a matching carpet remnant. If the teeth penetrate through the remnant, decrease their depth; if they do not grip, increase their depth. To use the knee-kicker to secure a carpet edge to a tackless strip, lay it on the carpet perpendicular to the edge with its head a few inches from the edge. Holding the knee-kicker shaft firmly with one hand, thrust a knee against the pad *(left)* to bite the carpet with the teeth, pushing the carpet edge forward to seat it on the tackless strip; if necessary, thrust again. Keeping your knee against the knee-kicker pad to hold it steady, run the face of a hammer along the carpet edge *(inset)* to secure it to the tackless strip under it. Repeat the procedure along the carpet edge as necessary to secure it. To use the knee-kicker to detach a carpet edge from a tackless strip, follow the same procedure, pushing the carpet edge forward to loosen it from the tackless strip, then using an awl to pull the loosened edge free.

SECURING A STRETCH-IN CARPET

 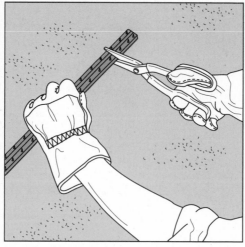 

Replacing a tackless strip. If a carpet edge has pulled away from or is buckled near a wall, remove the shoe molding *(page 133)* from the wall. Using a knee-kicker *(page 115)*, try hooking the carpet edge back onto the tackless strip along the floor edge; if a section of tackless strip is damaged, use the knee-kicker to detach enough of the carpet to fully expose it—a section is usu- ally 4 feet long. Wearing work gloves and safety goggles, use a pry bar and a ball-peen hammer to pry out the damaged section *(above, left)*. Buy a length of matching tackless strip at a carpet dealer; if necessary, trim it to fit the opening *(above, center)*. Position the replacement tackless strip in the opening with its pins facing up and angled toward the wall, then hammer it into place *(above, right)*. Use the knee-kicker to stretch the carpet edge onto the tackless strip, then reinstall or replace the shoe molding.

REPLACING A STRETCH-IN CARPET SECTION

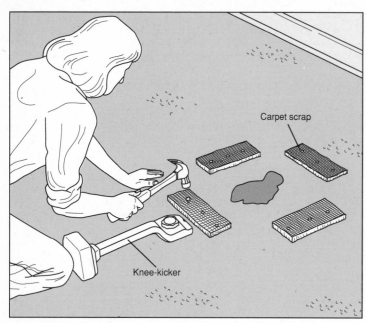

Carpet scrap

Knee-kicker

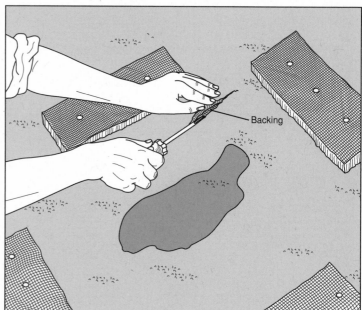

Backing

1 **Preparing to remove the damaged section.** Find a matching carpet remnant for a replacement section. To facilitate removal of the damaged section, use a knee-kicker *(page 115)* to slacken the tension of the carpet on each side of the damaged section. Position the knee-kicker on the carpet 8 inches from one side of the damaged section. Steadying the knee-kicker with one hand, thrust it with your knee to slide the carpet forward toward the damaged section. Holding the knee-kicker steady with your knee, lay a carpet scrap upside down just ahead of it; nail through the carpet scrap to temporarily hold the slackened carpet. Repeat the procedure to slacken and hold the carpet on the other sides of the damaged section *(above, left)*. To prepare the carpet for cutting, mark a square-cornered outline around the damaged section; use the tip of an old screwdriver to work along each side of the damaged section between two rows of pile tufts, separating them to expose the line of backing under them *(above, right)*.

REPLACING A STRETCH-IN CARPET SECTION (continued)

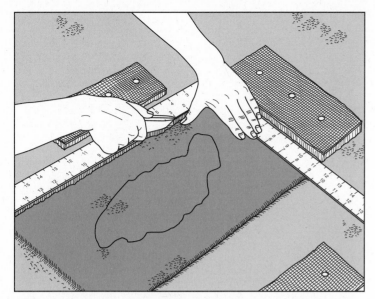

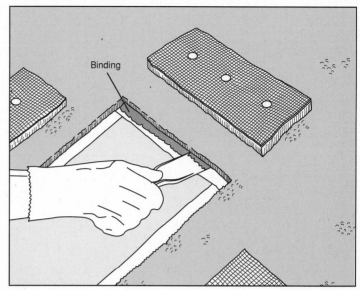

Binding

2 **Removing the damaged section.** Lay a carpenter's square on the carpet, aligning it with two adjacent marked lines of the outline around the damaged section. Pressing down on the square, part the tufts of pile along the inside edges of it and use a utility knife to score repeatedly along them *(above)*, cutting through the carpet backing along two adjacent edges of the damaged section. Use the same procedure to cut along the other two adjacent marked lines, then pull out the damaged section. Cut out any damaged section of undercushion with the utility knife. Fit a replacement section of matching undercushion in the opening and staple it in place every 3 inches along each edge of it with a 3/8-inch staple; also staple each edge of the undercushion around it.

3 **Preparing to install the replacement section.** Make a template of the opening out of cardboard and trace it onto the back of the carpet remnant, then cut the replacement section to size with a utility knife. Apply a bead of latex seam adhesive to the base of the pile along each edge of the replacement section and the opening, then let it dry. Fit a strip of 2-inch cloth binding along each edge of the opening, centering it under the undamaged carpet; buy cloth binding at a fabric store and cut it to size. Wearing rubber gloves, use a spatula to apply latex multipurpose adhesive on each binding strip. Lift each edge of the undamaged carpet in turn to coat the binding strip under it, then press the undamaged carpet into place and coat the binding strip exposed in the opening *(above)*.

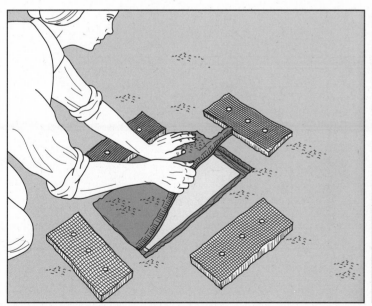

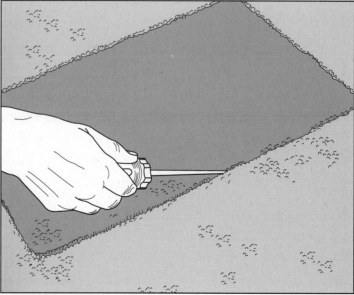

4 **Installing the replacement section.** Press the replacement section carefully into place, its pile aligned with the surrounding carpet *(above, left)*; if any pile catches, free it using the tip of an old screwdriver *(above, right)* or an awl. Blot any extruded adhesive with a clean cloth. Place a weight on the replacement section and let the adhesive set for the time specified by the manufacturer—usually 12 hours. Remove the weight and pry off the carpet scraps nailed along each edge of the replacement section, then gently rub any flattened pile to raise it.

REPLACING A STRETCH-IN CARPET

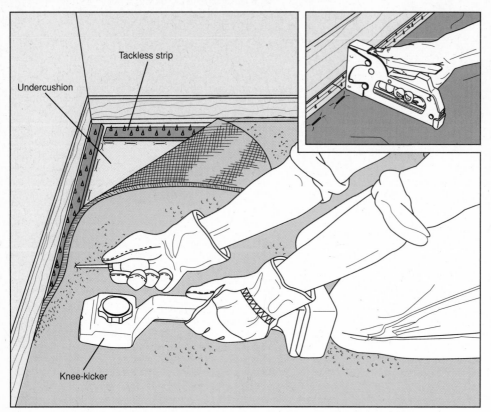

Undercushion

Tackless strip

Knee-kicker

1 Preparing to install a new carpet.
Measure the floor and buy new carpet to
fit at a carpet dealer. If you need two carpet pieces, have the dealer cut the pieces for a
seam in a low-traffic area perpendicular to a
window; have the edge of each piece for the
seam marked. To make the seam, buy latex
seam adhesive and hot-melt seam tape; for a
loop pile carpet, also a loop pile cutter. Rent
the tools you need at a tool rental agency: a
knee-kicker, a power stretcher and a wall trimmer or a stair tool; for any seam, also a seaming iron. Remove any shoe molding *(page 133)*
and loosen the carpet edge from any binder bar
holding it at a doorway. Wearing safety goggles
and work gloves, use the knee-kicker *(page
115)* and an awl to pull the carpet off the tackless strip under each edge of it *(left)*, then roll it
up. Cut out any damaged section of undercushion with a utility knife and pull any staples out
of it. Fit a replacement section of matching undercushion in the opening and staple it in place
every 3 inches along each edge of it with a 3/8-
inch staple *(inset)*; also staple each edge of the
undercushion around it and cover the seams
with duct tape. Replace any damaged tackless
strip *(page 116)*.

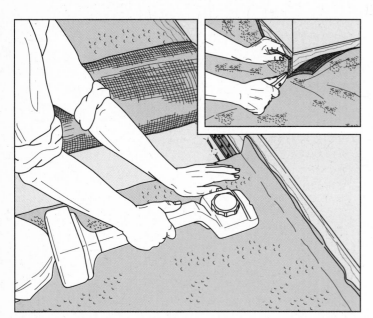

2 Laying out the carpet. If there are two carpet pieces, cut them
for a seam *(step 3)*. To lay out the carpet, center it on the floor
with any excess lapped up the walls; ensure any edges for a
seam butt snugly. Using a knee-kicker *(page 115)*, temporarily secure
the center 2 feet of a carpet edge to a tackless strip; secure a 1-foot
section on each side of any seam *(above)*. Secure the opposite carpet
edge the same way. Using a utility knife, make a relief cut in the excess
carpet at each corner *(inset)* and obstruction to lay the carpet flat. Using
the knee-kicker, unhook the temporarily-secured edges. Make any
carpet seam *(step 4)*; otherwise, stretch-in the carpet *(step 5)*.

Undercushion

3 Cutting carpet pieces for a seam. Before laying out carpet
pieces for a seam, trim the store-marked edge of each piece for
it. To trim the edge of a loop pile carpet for a seam, fit the notch
of the loop pile cutter onto the carpet and push forward to trim a 1-inch
strip off it. To trim the edge of a cut pile carpet for a seam, lay the piece
pile-down and snap a chalk line along it 1 inch from the edge *(above)*;
then, cut along the line using a utility knife and a straightedge. When
the edge of each carpet piece for the seam is trimmed, lay out the
carpet *(step 2)*.

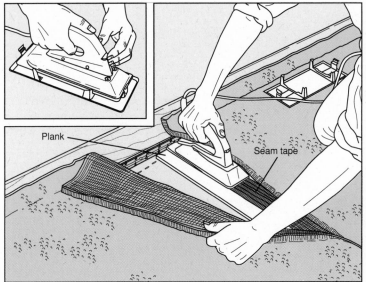

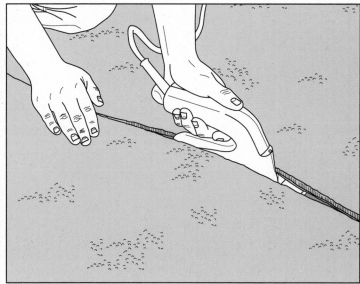

4 **Making a carpet seam.** Measure the length of the seam and cut a strip of hot-melt seam tape to size. Roll back the carpet 18 inches from each side of the seam and apply a bead of seam adhesive to the base of the pile along the carpet edge; allow the seam adhesive to dry to the touch. Lay the strip of hot-melt seam tape on the undercushion between the carpet edges, centering it along the seam with its glue side facing up. Hook the seam tape onto the tackless strip at each end of the seam to keep it from moving, then slip a plank several feet long between it and the undercushion at one end of it. Set up the seaming iron, following the manufacturer's instructions to select the proper heat setting *(inset)*. Starting at the end of the seam with the

plank, set the iron squarely on the seam tape; wait 10 seconds, then slowly glide the iron forward along the seam tape *(above, left)* at a rate of 2 to 3 feet per minute. Pause every 12 inches and use your free hand to press down the carpet edges onto the seam tape behind the iron *(above, right)*; for a loop pile carpet, lay a telephone book on the secured seam, then move it along the seam behind you as you go. If the carpet curls, stop and lower the iron temperature. When you reach the end of the plank, slide it ahead under the seam tape and continue. When you reach the other end of the seam, remove the iron and press down the carpet edges. Roll back the carpet from the wall to remove the plank.

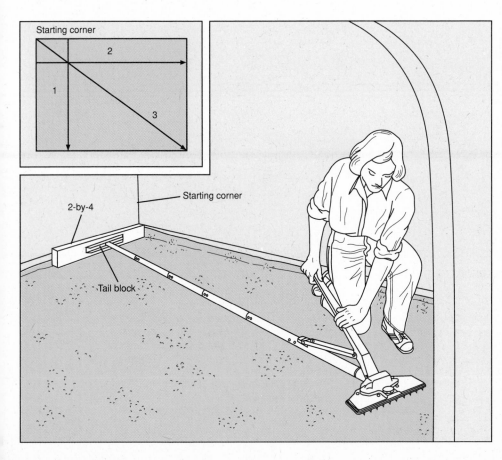

5 **Stretching-in the new carpet.** Use the knee-kicker and power stretcher to hook the carpet onto the tackless strip along each edge of the floor. Follow the manufacturer's instructions to set up the power stretcher and adjust its tooth depth; in general, set it at a 90-degree angle to a wall with its head 8 inches from the tackless strip and its tail block braced with a wood block against the opposite wall. To power-stretch the carpet, set the power stretcher lever at a 45-degree angle to the floor and push it down, stretching the carpet forward and onto the tackless strip; run a hammer face along the carpet to secure it. To stretch-in the carpet, select a starting corner and use the knee-kicker *(page 115)* to hook an 18-inch section of carpet on each side of it. Then, power-stretch the carpet in turn from each hooked section to the wall directly opposite it *(inset, 1 and 2)*. Use the knee-kicker to hook an 18-inch section of the carpet on each side of the corners adjacent to the starting corner, then the carpet between the starting corner and the corners adjacent to it. Power-stretch the carpet from the starting corner to the corner diagonally opposite *(inset 3)* and hook it on each side of the corner. Then, power-stretch the carpet from points along the wall on one side of the starting corner to hook it along the opposite wall, angling the power stretcher slightly *(left)*; power-stretch the carpet from points along the wall on the other side of the starting corner to hook it along the final wall.

REPLACING A STRETCH-IN CARPET (continued)

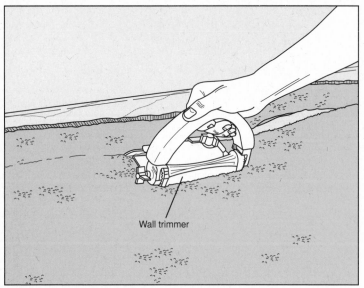

Wall trimmer

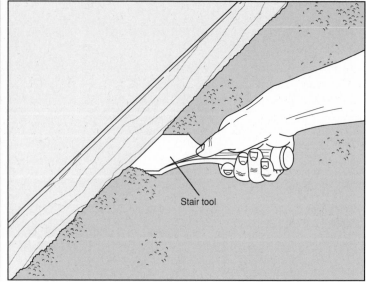

Stair tool

6 **Trimming the carpet.** To trim off the excess along the carpet edges, use the wall trimmer. Follow the manufacturer's directions to set the trimmer to the cutting depth recommended for the pile thickness of the carpet. Trim along one edge of the carpet at a time, starting at one end of it. Holding the trimmer at a 45-degree angle to the floor and pressing its guide bar against the excess carpet, cut down through the excess until the base of the trimmer is flat on the floor;

then, push forward to cut straight along the excess and sever it from the carpet *(above, left)*. After trimming the carpet edge, use the tip of the guide bar on the trimmer to tuck it behind the tackless strip along the baseboard. Alternately, use a utility knife and a straightedge to trim off the excess carpet; then, use a stair tool to tuck in the edges *(above, right)*. At a doorway or wall opening, fit the carpet edge into any binder bar. Then, reinstall any shoe molding you removed.

REPLACING A GLUE-DOWN STAIR RUNNER

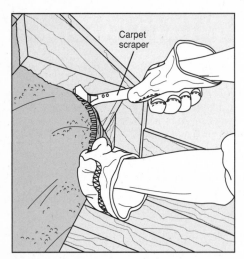

Carpet scraper

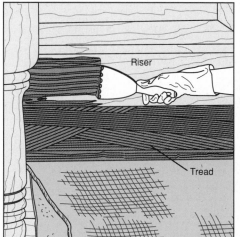

Riser

Tread

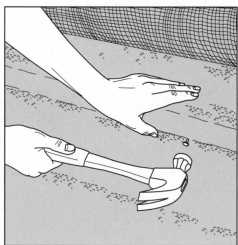

1 **Removing the stair runner.** Wearing work gloves, start at the bottom of the runner and use a carpet scraper to work under an edge and loosen it, then pull up as much of it as you can *(above)*. Work to the top of the runner the same way, prying loose and pulling it up; then, roll up and dispose of it. Use the carpet scraper to scrape any foam backing and adhesive off the stairs, then vacuum them. To measure for a new runner, measure down each riser and across each tread from the top to the bottom of the stairs.

2 **Installing the stair runner.** Buy a new runner to fit at a carpet dealer and have it rolled up in the direction of the pile; also buy enough latex multipurpose adhesive and No. 18 carpet tacks. To install the runner, start at the bottom of the stairs. Lay the runner on the floor, centering it between the sides of the stairs. Use a notched knife to apply adhesive on the first riser, coating it from the bottom to the top within 1 inch of the runner edges. Unroll the runner up to the first tread, then align its end with the bottom of the riser and press it into place. Drive tacks at 2-inch intervals through the runner along the top of the riser; rub the pile to hide the tacks. Roll back the runner to apply adhesive on the first tread and second riser *(above, left)*, then unroll it up to the second tread to press it into place and tack it along the top edge of the riser *(above, right)*. Work up the stairs adhering and tacking the runner the same way; if necessary, use a utility knife and a straightedge to trim off any excess.

REPLACING A STRETCH-IN STAIR RUNNER

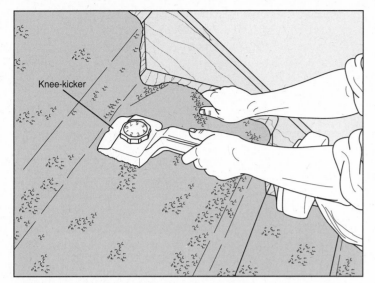

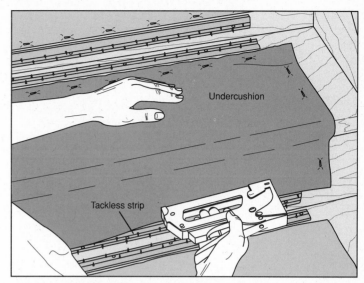

1 **Removing the stair runner.** Use a knee-kicker *(page 115)* to remove the runner, loosening it from the first few treads at the bottom of the stairs. Position the knee-kicker on the tread about 2 inches from the riser above it and near an edge of the runner. Steadying the knee-kicker with one hand, thrust forward with your knee to loosen the runner, then pull it off the tackless strip under it *(above)*. When the runner is free of the first few treads, work from the bottom to the top of the stairs to pull it off, then roll it up and dispose of it. Replace any damaged undercushion or tackless strip *(step 2)*; otherwise, install a new runner *(step 3)*.

2 **Replacing undercushion or a tackless strip.** If the under-cushion covering a tread and riser is damaged, pull the staples out of it with pliers and dispose of it. Position a replacement piece of matching undercushion on the tread and riser, then use a staple gun to drive a 3/8-inch staple every 3 inches along each edge of it, securing it to the tread and riser *(above)*. If a tackless strip is damaged, use a pry bar to pull it off. Buy a length of matching tackless strip at a carpet deal-er; if necessary, trim it to fit the opening. Position the replacement tack-less strip in the opening with its pins facing up and angled toward the joint of the tread and the riser, then hammer it into place.

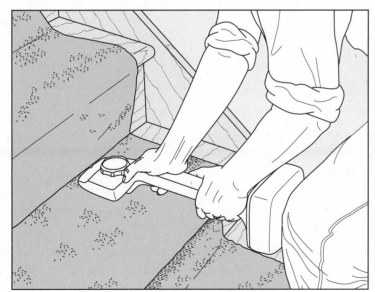

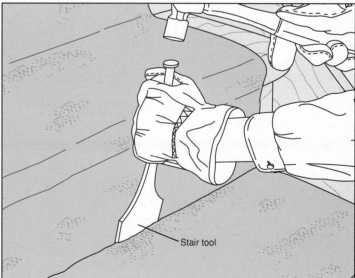

3 **Installing the stair runner.** Buy a new runner to fit at a carpet dealer and have it rolled up in the direction of the pile; also buy No. 18 carpet tacks. To install the runner, start at the bottom of the stairs. Lay the runner on the floor, centering it between the sides of the stairs. Unroll the runner up to the last riser and temporarily nail it. Align the bottom end of the runner with the bottom of the first riser and press it into place on the tackless strip using the face of the hammer. Using the knee-kicker *(page 115)*, start at the bottom of the stairs to secure the runner to the tackless strips on each tread and the riser above it. Position the knee-kicker on the tread about 2 inches from the

riser above it and near an edge of the runner. Steadying the knee-kicker with one hand, thrust forward with your knee to stretch the runner onto the tackless strips *(above, left)*, then run the face of the hammer along it to secure it. Use a stair tool and and a ball-peen hammer to tuck the run-ner into the joint between the tackless strips on the tread and the riser *(above, right)*. Continue the same way until you reach the last tread, then secure the end of the runner to the top of the riser above it every 2 inch-es with carpet tacks; if necessary, use a utility knife and a straightedge to trim off any excess.

TOOLS & TECHNIQUES

This section introduces tools and techniques that are basic to repairing floors, stairs, and carpets such as using abrasives (*page 127*), boring or drilling with an electric drill (*page 129*), and cutting using power saws and handsaws (*page 130*). Also included is information on identifying and applying finishes (*page 140*), and on using telescoping jacks (*page 137*). The charts on abrasives, fasteners and finishes are designed for easy reference to help you select the required material.

You can handle most repairs to floors, stairs and carpets with the basic kit of tools and supplies shown below and on pages 123 to 125. Special tools you may need, such as telescoping jacks, a drum sander, a demolition hammer, a commercial floor polisher, a tile cutter and a power stretcher, can be obtained at a tool rental agency. For the best repair results, always use the right tool for the job—and be sure to use it correctly. When shopping for tools, buy the highest-quality ones you can afford.

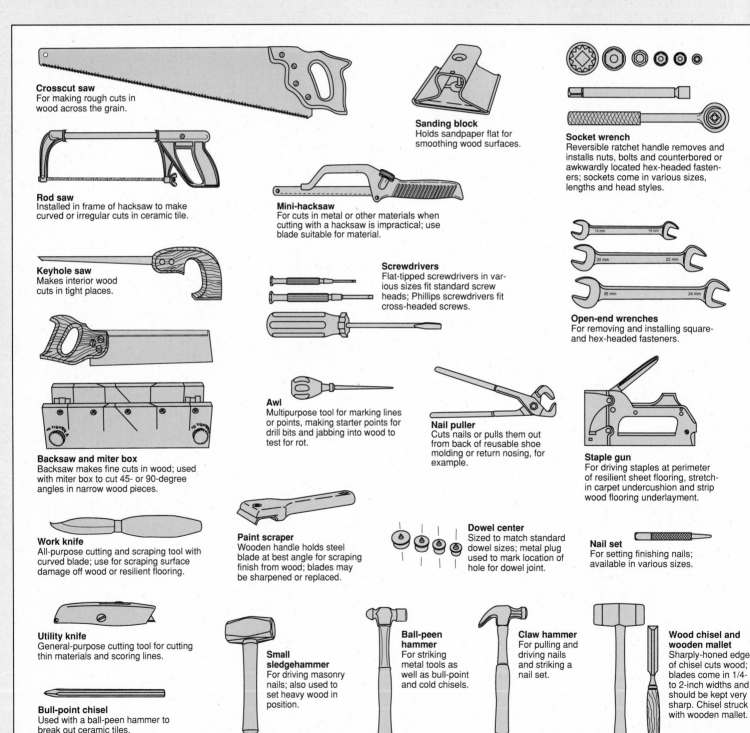

Crosscut saw
For making rough cuts in wood across the grain.

Rod saw
Installed in frame of hacksaw to make curved or irregular cuts in ceramic tile.

Keyhole saw
Makes interior wood cuts in tight places.

Backsaw and miter box
Backsaw makes fine cuts in wood; used with miter box to cut 45- or 90-degree angles in narrow wood pieces.

Work knife
All-purpose cutting and scraping tool with curved blade; use for scraping surface damage off wood or resilient flooring.

Utility knife
General-purpose cutting tool for cutting thin materials and scoring lines.

Bull-point chisel
Used with a ball-peen hammer to break out ceramic tiles.

Sanding block
Holds sandpaper flat for smoothing wood surfaces.

Mini-hacksaw
For cuts in metal or other materials when cutting with a hacksaw is impractical; use blade suitable for material.

Screwdrivers
Flat-tipped screwdrivers in various sizes fit standard screw heads; Phillips screwdrivers fit cross-headed screws.

Awl
Multipurpose tool for marking lines or points, making starter points for drill bits and jabbing into wood to test for rot.

Nail puller
Cuts nails or pulls them out from back of reusable shoe molding or return nosing, for example.

Paint scraper
Wooden handle holds steel blade at best angle for scraping finish from wood; blades may be sharpened or replaced.

Dowel center
Sized to match standard dowel sizes; metal plug used to mark location of hole for dowel joint.

Small sledgehammer
For driving masonry nails; also used to set heavy wood in position.

Ball-peen hammer
For striking metal tools as well as bull-point and cold chisels.

Claw hammer
For pulling and driving nails and striking a nail set.

Socket wrench
Reversible ratchet handle removes and installs nuts, bolts and counterbored or awkwardly located hex-headed fasteners; sockets come in various sizes, lengths and head styles.

Open-end wrenches
For removing and installing square- and hex-headed fasteners.

Staple gun
For driving staples at perimeter of resilient sheet flooring, stretch-in carpet undercushion and strip wood flooring underlayment.

Nail set
For setting finishing nails; available in various sizes.

Wood chisel and wooden mallet
Sharply-honed edge of chisel cuts wood; blades come in 1/4- to 2-inch widths and should be kept very sharp. Chisel struck with wooden mallet.

Take the time to care for and store your tools properly. To avoid damaging a cutting tool, for example, check for hidden fasteners before starting a cut. When a saw blade becomes dull, buy and install a replacement or have it sharpened by a professional. Keep a handsaw on its side when not in use to avoid damaging a finish floor. Inspect a tool before using it. Tighten loose handles or screws and replace damaged parts. Clean and lubricate power tools according to the manufacturer's instructions.

To clean metal hand tools, use a cloth moistened with a few drops of light machine oil—but never oil their handles. Wipe wood resin and dirt off metal tools using a clean cloth dipped in mineral spirits. To remove rust, rub the tool with fine steel wool, then apply a few drops of light machine oil with a soft cloth to keep the tool rust-free. Store tools on a shelf safely away from children in a locked metal or plastic tool box; or, hang up tools well out of their reach.

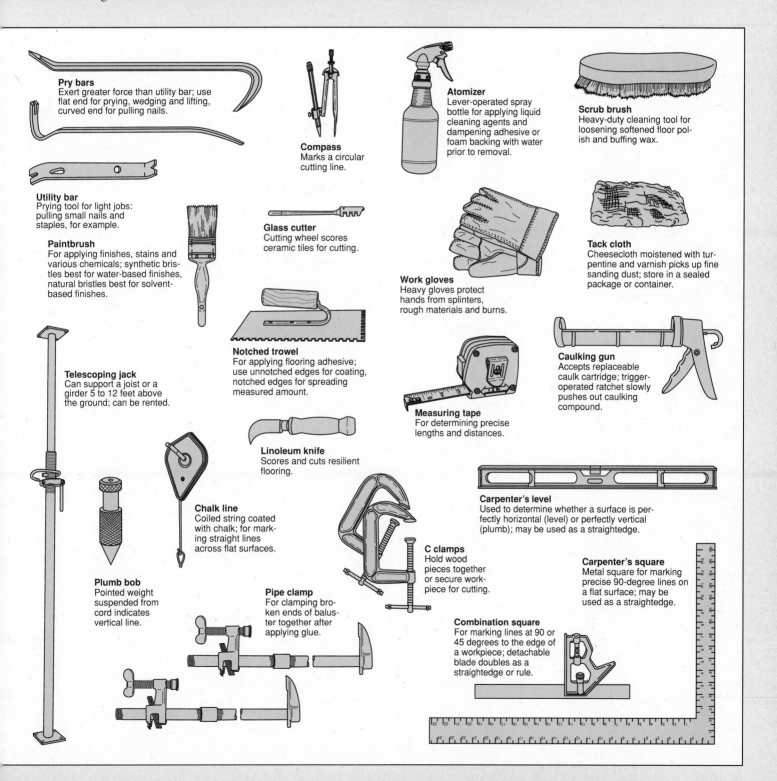

Pry bars
Exert greater force than utility bar; use flat end for prying, wedging and lifting, curved end for pulling nails.

Compass
Marks a circular cutting line.

Atomizer
Lever-operated spray bottle for applying liquid cleaning agents and dampening adhesive or foam backing with water prior to removal.

Scrub brush
Heavy-duty cleaning tool for loosening softened floor polish and buffing wax.

Utility bar
Prying tool for light jobs: pulling small nails and staples, for example.

Glass cutter
Cutting wheel scores ceramic tiles for cutting.

Tack cloth
Cheesecloth moistened with turpentine and varnish picks up fine sanding dust; store in a sealed package or container.

Paintbrush
For applying finishes, stains and various chemicals; synthetic bristles best for water-based finishes, natural bristles best for solvent-based finishes.

Work gloves
Heavy gloves protect hands from splinters, rough materials and burns.

Notched trowel
For applying flooring adhesive; use unnotched edges for coating, notched edges for spreading measured amount.

Caulking gun
Accepts replaceable caulk cartridge; trigger-operated ratchet slowly pushes out caulking compound.

Telescoping jack
Can support a joist or a girder 5 to 12 feet above the ground; can be rented.

Measuring tape
For determining precise lengths and distances.

Linoleum knife
Scores and cuts resilient flooring.

Carpenter's level
Used to determine whether a surface is perfectly horizontal (level) or perfectly vertical (plumb); may be used as a straightedge.

Chalk line
Coiled string coated with chalk; for marking straight lines across flat surfaces.

C clamps
Hold wood pieces together or secure workpiece for cutting.

Carpenter's square
Metal square for marking precise 90-degree lines on a flat surface; may be used as a straightedge.

Plumb bob
Pointed weight suspended from cord indicates vertical line.

Pipe clamp
For clamping broken ends of baluster together after applying glue.

Combination square
For marking lines at 90 or 45 degrees to the edge of a workpiece; detachable blade doubles as a straightedge or rule.

While most materials and supplies can be obtained at a building supply center, consult a flooring dealer when shopping for replacement flooring. In addition to offering specific advice and expertise suited to your requirements, a flooring dealer should be able to supply you with the right type and amount of adhesives, finishes and other supplies. Bring with you the exact dimensions of the floor along with a scaled diagram of the room layout showing any doorways or openings and any floor obstructions.

Before removing any damaged component of your floor, stairs or carpet, try to determine whether you can obtain a matching replacement. Many styles of flooring materials remain available for decades; others may be nearly impossible to find. Weigh the costs and benefits of an imperfect match against replacing an entire finish floor, taking the expected life-span of the flooring into consideration. If in doubt about your ability to complete a repair, do not hesitate to consult a professional.

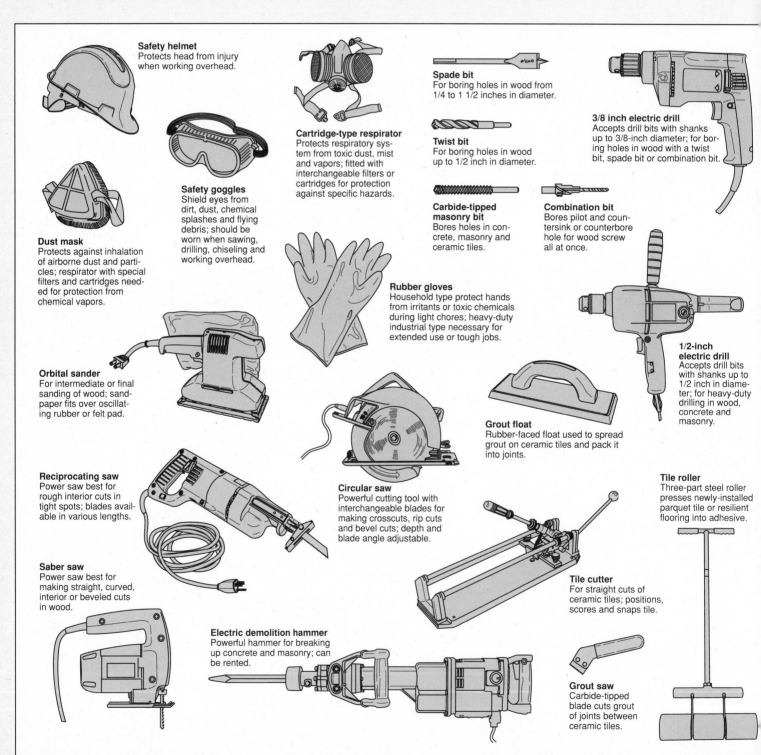

Safety helmet
Protects head from injury when working overhead.

Cartridge-type respirator
Protects respiratory system from toxic dust, mist and vapors; fitted with interchangeable filters or cartridges for protection against specific hazards.

Spade bit
For boring holes in wood from 1/4 to 1 1/2 inches in diameter.

Twist bit
For boring holes in wood up to 1/2 inch in diameter.

3/8 inch electric drill
Accepts drill bits with shanks up to 3/8-inch diameter; for boring holes in wood with a twist bit, spade bit or combination bit.

Safety goggles
Shield eyes from dirt, dust, chemical splashes and flying debris; should be worn when sawing, drilling, chiseling and working overhead.

Carbide-tipped masonry bit
Bores holes in concrete, masonry and ceramic tiles.

Combination bit
Bores pilot and countersink or counterbore hole for wood screw all at once.

Dust mask
Protects against inhalation of airborne dust and particles; respirator with special filters and cartridges needed for protection from chemical vapors.

Rubber gloves
Household type protect hands from irritants or toxic chemicals during light chores; heavy-duty industrial type necessary for extended use or tough jobs.

1/2-inch electric drill
Accepts drill bits with shanks up to 1/2 inch in diameter; for heavy-duty drilling in wood, concrete and masonry.

Orbital sander
For intermediate or final sanding of wood; sandpaper fits over oscillating rubber or felt pad.

Grout float
Rubber-faced float used to spread grout on ceramic tiles and pack it into joints.

Reciprocating saw
Power saw best for rough interior cuts in tight spots; blades available in various lengths.

Circular saw
Powerful cutting tool with interchangeable blades for making crosscuts, rip cuts and bevel cuts; depth and blade angle adjustable.

Tile roller
Three-part steel roller presses newly-installed parquet tile or resilient flooring into adhesive.

Saber saw
Power saw best for making straight, curved, interior or beveled cuts in wood.

Tile cutter
For straight cuts of ceramic tiles; positions, scores and snaps tile.

Electric demolition hammer
Powerful hammer for breaking up concrete and masonry; can be rented.

Grout saw
Carbide-tipped blade cuts grout of joints between ceramic tiles.

Prevent minor problems from developing into major ones by undertaking repairs as soon as a problem is detected. Throughout this book, various repair options may be presented for a specific problem. A problem can have a number of solutions, the best of which will depend on your specific circumstances and individual preference. In many instances, damaged finish flooring can be repaired, but if it is badly or extensively damaged, the section or entire floor should be replaced.

Using many of the various chemicals presented in this book, including wood finishes, flooring adhesives, cleaning solutions and chemical strippers, can release toxic or flammable vapors into the air as solvents evaporate. Be especially cautious when working on an entire floor. Follow the precautions for working with chemicals *(page 139)*, as well as all safety precautions printed on the label of the product you are using. Always wear appropriate protective clothing and recommended safety gear.

Knee-kicker
Stretches carpet to hook it onto tackless strip; adjustable for thickness of carpet.

Cookie cutter tool
Cuts circular patches out of carpet.

Loop pile cutter.
For cutting edge of loop pile carpet for a seam.

Carpet scraper
For removing carpet adhesive and foam backing from small areas of subfloor.

Sheet flooring seam sealer applicator
For fusing sheet flooring seams; T-shaped tip spreads seam slightly and dispenses thin bead of liquid sealer.

Carpet adhesive dispenser
Applies seam sealer to glue-down carpet and adhesive to stretch-in along edges where fibers join backing.

Wall trimmer
For tailoring carpets to fit at a wall.

Stair tool
Tucks stretch-in stair runner into groove between tackless strips of tread and riser.

Floor edger
Sanding tool used to remove finish from perimeter of wood floors. Can be rented; different grades of sanding disks supplied by tool rental agent.

Power stretcher
Stretches carpet; with tail block braced against wall, lever used to apply tension to head, gripping carpet and stretching it onto tackless strip along opposite wall.

Residential floor polisher
For polishing buffing wax on wood flooring and buffing resilient flooring.

Power scraper
Heavy-duty machine for removing carpet adhesive and foam backing from large areas of subfloor; can be rented.

Seam iron
Used to seal stretch-in carpet seams by heating hot-melt tape; adjustable temperature dial.

Floor nailer and mallet
For driving flooring cleats when installing floorboards; can be rented.

Drum sander
Heavy-duty sander used to remove finish from wood floors. Can be rented; different grades of sandpaper supplied by tool rental agent.

Commercial floor polisher
Heavy-duty machine used on wood flooring with sanding screen to roughen finish before recoating and with scrubbing pad between coats of new finish; can be rented.

Vacuum cleaner
For removing dust and dirt; used with brush attachment for resilient, rigid and wood flooring, power head for carpets.

Water extraction carpet cleaner
Injects hot water and cleaning solution into carpet to dissolve dirt, then vacuums it up; available with upholstery attachment for stair runners. Can be rented.

INSPECTING WOOD FOR ROT AND INSECT DAMAGE

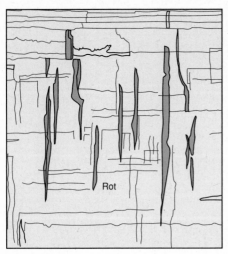 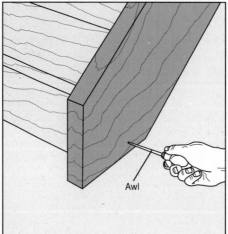 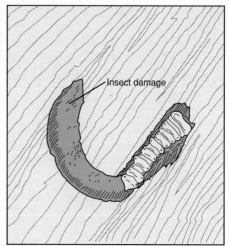

Identifying wood damage. To check for rot and insect damage, closely inspect any wood flooring and the wooden components of your floor understructure that are accessible *(page 62)*; wood near plumbing fixtures or in contact with a concrete foundation or basement floor is especially vulnerable. Include in your check the subfloor, the headers, the sill plates, the outside ends of joists, the bottom of posts and the base of stringers. Spongy wood fibers and gray or dark discoloration are telltale signs of rot; look for wood that is damp, split, or cracking across the grain *(above, left)*. Wood suffering from rot may also exhibit no visible signs of a problem. To test for rot, press the point of an awl as deeply as possible into the wood *(above, center)*. If the wood is soft and gives way, crumbling instead of splintering, it is weakened by rot. If the wood is pitted or powdery, riddled with tiny holes or tunnels *(above, right)* or supporting long, gray tubes, suspect insect damage and consult a pest control professional.

CHISELING

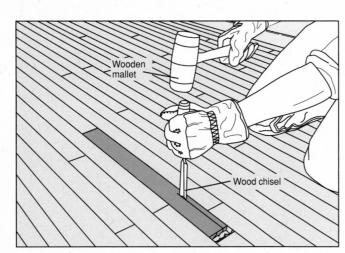 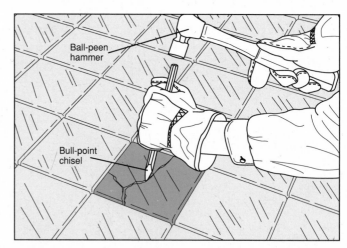

Using a wood chisel. Use a wood chisel to cut and remove wood or separate wood pieces held together by a glue joint. Inspect the chisel before using it; if the blade is dull, sharpen it. Wear safety goggles when using the chisel; ensure that the workpiece is secured. To cut into a damaged board, hold the chisel at a 90-degree angle to it with the cutting edge pointing away from you, the bevel facing the waste. Strike the handle of the chisel with a wooden mallet *(above)*, cutting into the wood. Work from end to end of the damaged board the same way.

Using a bull-point chisel. Use a bull-point chisel to chip a damaged ceramic tile out of a rigid floor. Wear safety goggles and work gloves when using the chisel. To chip out the damaged tile, hold the chisel firmly with its tip at the center of the tile. Strike the handle of the chisel lightly with a ball-peen hammer *(above)*, applying only enough force to crack the tile; striking too hard can "telegraph" vibrations to adjacent tiles, damaging them. Work from the center of the tile toward its edges the same way, chipping it into small pieces.

USING ABRASIVES

ABRASIVE	GRIT	GRADE	USES
SANDPAPER			
Very coarse	36	2	Removes heavy coats of finish and fine layer of wood. Used with drum sander and floor edger for first pass on wood floor in poor condition
	40	1 1/2	
	50	1	
Coarse	60	1/2	Removes finish and smooths rough wood; levels deep depressions and scratches. Used with drum sander and floor edger for second pass on wood floor in poor condition or for only pass on wood floor in average condition; used for spot repairs with orbital sander or sanding block
	80	1/0 (or 0)	
Medium	100	2/0	Smooths wood prior to applying a finish. Used with orbital sander or sanding block
	120	3/0	
Fine	150	4/0	For final smoothing of wood before applying a finish and abrading surface between finish coats. Used with orbital sander or sanding block
	180	5/0	
Very fine	220	6/0	For final hand-smoothing of turned wood surfaces prior to applying a finish
	240	7/0	
SANDING SCREEN			
Medium	100		Smooths wood and removes sanding marks of drum sander and floor edger; abrades finish of wood floor in good condition for refinishing. Used with commercial floor polisher
	120		
SCRUBBING PAD			
			Abrades surface between finish coats. Used with commercial floor polisher
STEEL WOOL			
Medium		1	Wipes residue off wood stripped with chemical stripper
Fine		0	Removes stains, scuff marks and worn finish from wood
Extra-fine		000	Removes excessive gloss from finish

Choosing an abrasive. Use sandpaper, a sanding screen, a scrubbing pad or steel wool as an abrasive to groom a wood surface. The chart at left lists appropriate uses for sandpaper grits or grades and steel wool grades. When you are using an abrasive, wear a dust mask to avoid inhaling particles. Replace an abrasive when it tears or clogs and no longer cuts well. After using an abrasive, vacuum the dust or brush it off the surface using a whisk broom; wipe the surface with a tack cloth.

When there is a choice between two grades of an abrasive, start with the finer and observe its effects; switch to the coarser if work progresses slowly. If you are sanding a wood floor *(page 22)* that is in poor condition, progress from very coarse to coarse to medium sandpaper, choosing the grade at the same end of each category: 36- or 40-grit sandpaper to 60-grit sandpaper to a 100-grit sanding screen; or, 50-grit sandpaper to 80-grit sandpaper to a 120-grit sanding screen.

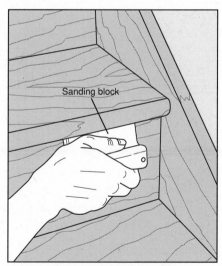

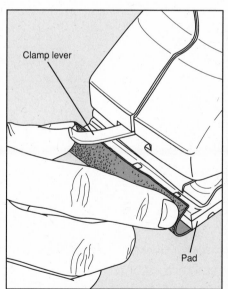

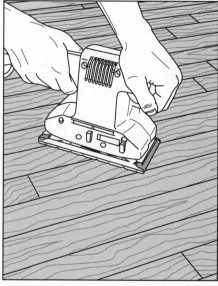

Using a sanding block. To sand a small, flat wood surface by hand, use a sanding block; buy one or make one by rounding the corners of a 1-by-4. Cut a sheet of sandpaper to fit the sanding block using scissors or a utility knife. Clamp the sandpaper in the sanding block; if it is homemade, hold the sandpaper tightly around it. Sand along the grain as much as possible, applying even, moderate pressure *(above)*.

Using an orbital sander. To sand a large, flat wood surface, use an orbital sander. Load the sander with sandpaper following the manufacturer's instructions, cutting it to size using scissors or a utility knife, then fitting it snugly around the pad *(above, left)* and locking each clamp lever. To use the sander, grip it firmly with both hands and lift it to depress the trigger switch. When the sander is running at full speed, gently set it down flat on the surface *(above, right)* and immediately move it slowly back and forth in long, smooth, overlapping strokes; work in the direction of the wood grain as much as possible. When any dust bag is half full, empty it *(page 128)*. To stop sanding, lift the sander off the surface, then release the trigger switch; let the pad stop moving before setting the sander down.

USING ABRASIVES (continued)

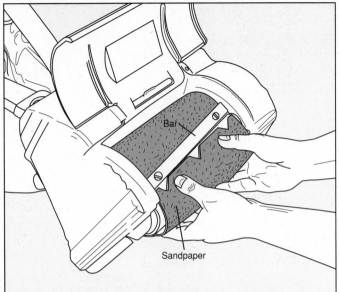

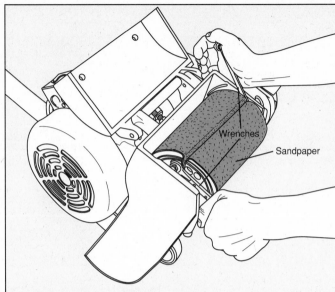

Using a drum sander. To sand an entire wood floor, use a drum sander—available at a tool rental agency. Load the sander with sandpaper following the manufacturer's instructions, tilting it back and resting it on its handles. For a sander with a bar-type clamping mechanism *(above, left)*, loosen the bar screws and feed the sandpaper around the drum, orienting the arrows on the back of it up and toward the front of the sander. Slide the ends of the sandpaper under the bar, as shown, then hold the sandpaper snugly against the drum and tighten the bar screws. For a sander with a slot-type clamping mechanism *(above, right)*, loosen the bolt at each end of the slot using the wrenches supplied with the sander; continue until the X marked on each bolt is visible. Fit the ends of the sandpaper into the slot, then tighten the bolts with the wrenches, as shown, until the sandpaper is held snugly around the drum. Use the sander to sand the wood floor *(page 22)*, stopping when the dust bag is half full to empty it *(step below, right)*.

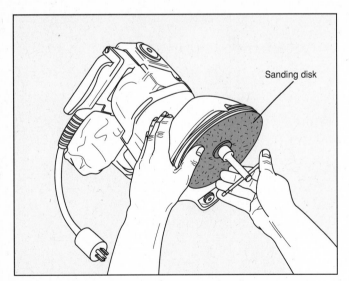

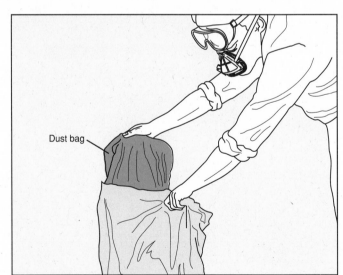

Using a floor edger. To sand the perimeter of a wood floor, use a floor edger—available at a tool rental agency. Load the edger with a sanding disk following the manufacturer's instructions, using the wrench supplied with it to remove the bolt and take off the washer. Position the sanding disk on the edger and seat the washer, its concave side facing out; then, thread the bolt through the washer and the sanding disk by hand. Tighten the bolt securely using the wrench *(above)*. Use the edger to sand the perimeter of the wood floor *(page 22)*, stopping when the dust bag is half full to empty it *(step right)*.

Emptying a dust bag. Empty the dust bag of an orbital sander, a drum sander or a floor edger when it is half full, turning off and unplugging the tool. Detach the dust bag from the tool following the manufacturer's instructions, then gently set it upright on the floor. Pull an opened garbage bag down over and around the dust bag nearly to the floor. Gather the garbage bag around the dust bag and hold it, then grab the bottom of the dust bag and upend the bags together. Holding the garbage bag around the dust bag to seal it, shake the sanding particles out of the dust bag into the garbage bag *(above)*.

DRILLING

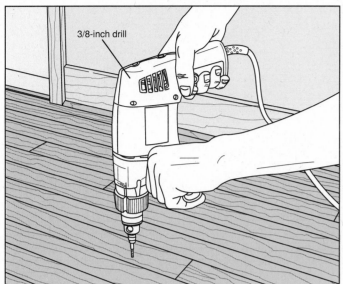

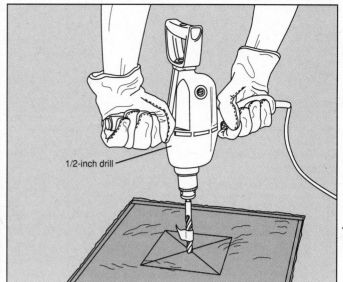

Using a drill. Use an electric drill to bore into wood and to drill into concrete or other materials. An electric drill is sized by the largest diameter bit shank its chuck can hold. For most drilling purposes, a 3/8-inch variable-speed drill is sufficient; for heavy-duty drilling, use a 1/2-inch drill. Always use a drill with the proper bit for the material: a twist bit, spade bit or auger bit for wood; a carbide-tipped masonry bit for concrete or ceramic tile, for example. The type and size of bit to use depends on the hole you are making *(step below, right)*. To install a bit, use the chuck key supplied with the drill to open the chuck jaws enough to insert its shank. Tighten the chuck jaws securely around the bit with the chuck key, fitting it in turn into each chuck hole and turning it clockwise. If necessary, mark the bit to an exact drilling depth *(step below, left)*. Wear safety goggles when operating a drill. If you are boring into wood with a 3/8-inch drill, grip the drill firmly with both hands; apply light pressure and depress the trigger switch *(above, left)*, then gradually increase pressure. Withdraw the bit from the hole before releasing the trigger switch. If you are drilling into concrete with a 1/2-inch drill, use the same procedure *(above, right)*; withdraw the bit frequently from the hole to keep it from overheating.

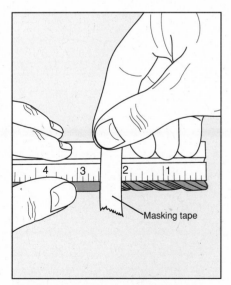

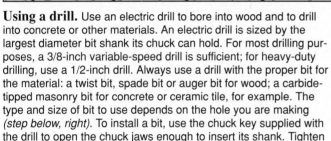

Drilling to an exact depth. Measure the drilling depth from the tip of the bit. To mark the drilling depth on the bit, wrap a strip of masking tape around it *(above)* or tighten a stop collar on it using the hex wrench supplied. When drilling, withdraw the bit when the masking tape or stop collar just touches the surface.

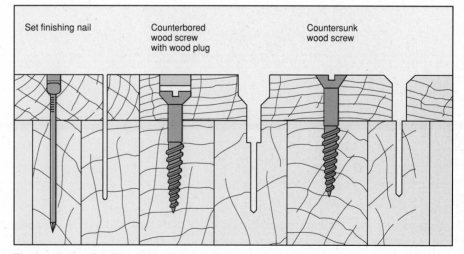

Boring holes for fasteners. Use an electric drill to bore or drill holes for fasteners. To bore a pilot hole for a nail, use a twist bit slightly smaller than its shank in diameter and bore to a depth equal to 2/3 its shank length *(above, left)*; shown is a finishing nail set below the surface with a nail set. To bore a hole for a wood screw and a wood plug, use a combination bit equal to 2/3 the screw shank diameter and bore to a depth equal to the plug thickness and the screw shank length if the wood is hardwood *(above, center)*; equal to the plug thickness and 1/2 the screw shank length if the wood is softwood. To bore a hole for countersinking a wood screw, use a combination bit equal to 2/3 its shank in diameter and bore to a depth equal to its shank length if the wood is hardwood *(above, right)*; equal to 1/2 its shank length if the wood is softwood.

CLAMPING

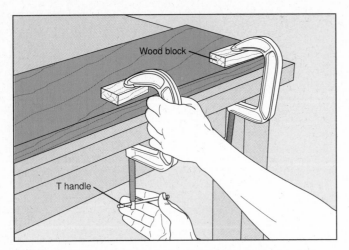

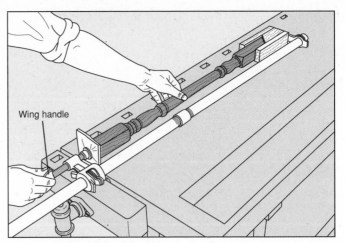

Using C clamps. For pressure or holding power over a span of up to 12 inches, use C clamps—available with reaches from 1 to 12 inches. To secure a workpiece onto a work table, as shown, open the jaws of a C clamp enough to fit loosely around them. Protecting the surface of the workpiece with a wood block, hold the C clamp by the frame and turn the T handle to tighten the jaws against the workpiece and the work table; continue until the jaws fit snugly, then give an extra 1/4 turn. Install a C clamp every 6 to 8 inches along the workpiece the same way *(above)*.

Using a pipe clamp. For pressure or holding power over a span of more than 12 inches, use a pipe clamp. To secure two sections of a broken baluster together after applying glue, as shown, slide the movable jaw far enough from the stationary jaw to fit loosely around the ends of the baluster. Protecting each end of the baluster with a cardboard pad or wooden cap, align the movable jaw with the stationary jaw and turn the wing handle to tighten the jaws *(above)*; apply only enough clamping pressure as necessary to hold the baluster sections together.

USING POWER SAWS

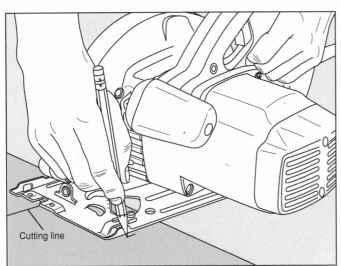

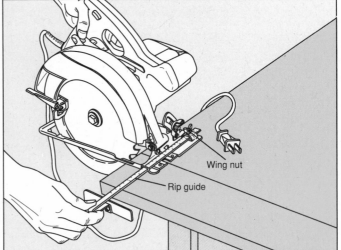

Setting up a cutting guide. Use a cutting guide to ensure a straight crosscut (across the wood grain) or rip cut (along the wood grain) with a circular saw or saber saw. Butt the saw against the end of the cutting line, the baseplate notch aligned with it. Holding the saw steady, mark a point at the edge of the baseplate *(above, left)*. Measure the distance between the marked point and the cutting line, then mark a point at the same distance from the cutting line at the other end of it using a carpenter's square. Align the edge of a straight-edged board with the marked points and secure it with C clamps or temporarily nail it in place. For a rip cut, you can buy a rip guide; follow the manufacturer's instructions to install it on the saw. With the saw butted against the end of the cutting line, slide the arm of the guide through the baseplate slots *(above, right)* until it fits snugly, then tighten the wing nut.

USING POWER SAWS (continued)

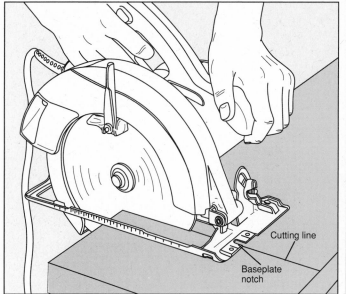

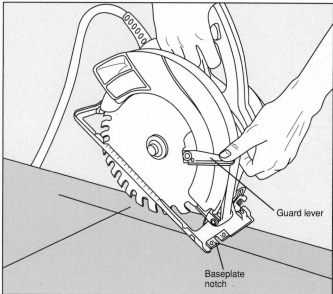

Using a circular saw. For crosscuts (across the wood grain) and rip cuts (along the wood grain), use a circular saw with a combination blade. Following your owner's manual instructions, install the blade on the saw and set the cutting depth: for a standard cut, about 1/2 inch deeper than the wood thickness; for a plunge cut, equal to the wood thickness. Set the baseplate of the saw to the angle desired. Wear safety goggles and a dust mask when operating the saw. To make a standard cut, align the baseplate notch with the cutting line. Gripping the saw firmly with both hands, stand to one side of the cutting line and depress the trigger switch, then slowly guide the saw forward *(above, left)*; shown is a crosscut. To make a plunge cut, retract the lower blade guard and align the baseplate notch with the cutting line, the blade as close to an end of it as possible *(above, right)*. Gripping the saw firmly, depress the trigger switch and slowly lower the saw; when the baseplate rests flat, let go of the lower blade guard and slowly guide the saw forward.

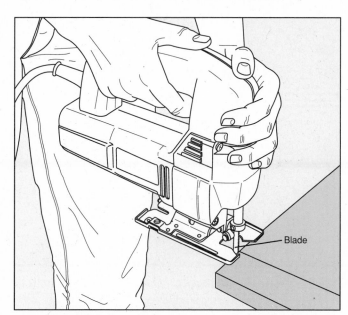

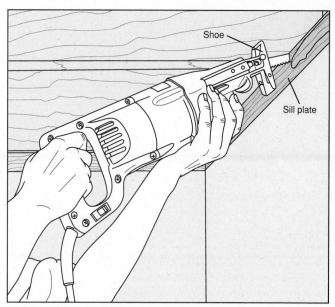

Using a saber saw. For almost any cut in wood, use a saber saw with a suitable blade. Following your owner's manual instructions, install the blade on the saw. Set the baseplate of the saw to the angle desired. Wear safety goggles and a dust mask when operating the saw. To make a standard cut, align the blade with the cutting line. Gripping the saw firmly with both hands, stand to one side of the cutting line and depress the trigger switch, then slowly guide the saw forward *(above)*; shown is a crosscut.

Using a reciprocating saw. For rough, interior or awkward-angled cuts, use a reciprocating saw with a suitable blade. Following your owner's manual instructions, install the blade on the saw. Wear safety goggles and a dust mask when operating the saw. To cut a sill plate section, as shown, align the blade with the cutting line. Gripping the saw firmly with both hands, rest it on its shoe with the blade raised slightly and depress the trigger switch, then slowly lower the saw, guiding the blade into the cutting line *(above)*.

USING HANDSAWS

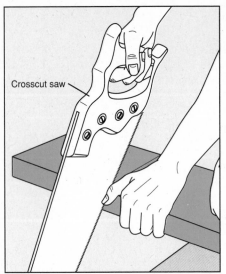

Crosscut saw

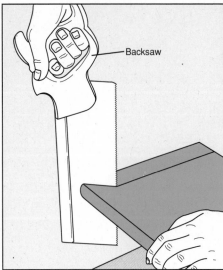

Backsaw

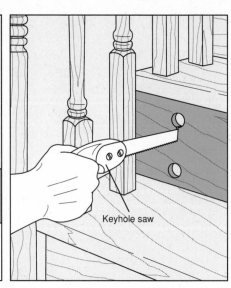

Keyhole saw

Cutting wood with a handsaw. For quick, rough wood cuts across the grain, use a crosscut saw. To start the cut, hold the saw almost perpendicular to the workpiece at the end of the cutting line and draw the blade slowly toward you several times. Lower the angle of the saw to about 45 degrees and cut along the cutting line on the downstroke *(above, left)* until you are about 1 inch from the end of it. To finish the cut, grip the waste side with one hand and raise the saw almost perpendicular to the workpiece, then use

short up-and-down strokes. For fine wood cuts, use a backsaw the same way *(above, center)*; shown is a cut into a tread at a 45-degree angle for a return nosing. For wood cuts within the interior, in a tight corner or at an awkward angle, use a keyhole saw the same way. For a cut within the interior of a riser, as shown, first use an electric drill fitted with a spade bit to bore starter holes for the blade of the saw, then use the saw to cut along the cutting line, making short, rapid strokes with the blade toe *(above, right)* or heel.

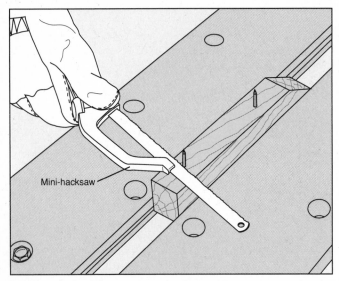

Mini-hacksaw

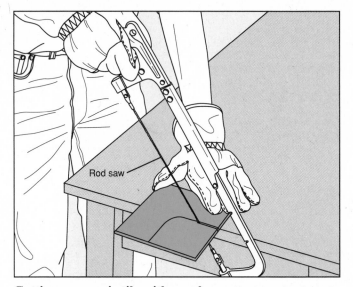

Rod saw

Cutting nails with a mini-hacksaw. For cuts in metal or other materials such as ceramic, concrete and plastic, use a hacksaw; use a mini-hacksaw when cutting with a standard hacksaw is impractical: the workpiece is small, as shown, or access to it is obstructed, for example. Use a blade suitable for the material—a metal-cutting or tungsten-carbide type. Install the blade on the frame of the saw following the manufacturer's instructions, ensuring that the teeth are facing away from the handle. Gripping the saw firmly, butt the blade against any cutting line and cut using short, smooth strokes *(above)*; if necessary, apply pressure to bend the blade slightly.

Cutting a ceramic tile with a rod saw. For curved or irregular cuts in ceramic, use a tungsten-carbide rod saw; install it in a hacksaw frame as you would any other hacksaw blade, following the manufacturer's instructions. Wear safety goggles and work gloves when using the saw. Hold the saw almost perpendicular to the workpiece at the end of the cutting line and draw the blade slowly toward you several times. Then, lower the angle of the saw to about 45 degrees and cut along the cutting line on the downstroke *(above)*, swiveling the frame as necessary to follow it. As you reach the end of the cutting line, grip the waste side with one hand to support it.

REPLACING SHOE MOLDING

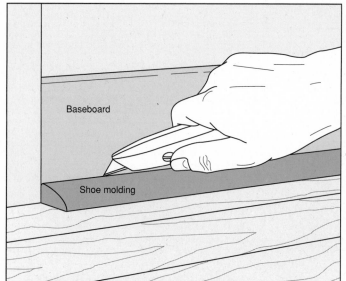

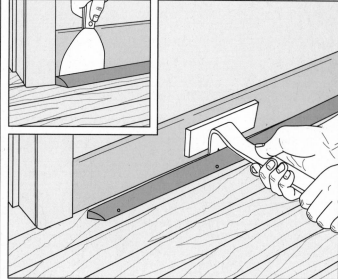

Removing shoe molding. To break any finish bond between the shoe molding and the baseboard, run a utility knife along the joint between them *(above, left)*. Remove the first piece of shoe molding at a door or an outside corner. Work the blade of a wide putty knife behind the shoe molding as far down as possible at one end of it *(inset)* and gently pry it out enough to fit in the end of a pry bar. Protecting the baseboard with a wood block or cardboard, work the pry bar along the shoe molding, pulling it out slightly from the baseboard at each nail *(above, right)*. After pulling out the shoe molding at the third nail, return to the first nail and pull out the shoe molding slightly farther. Work along the shoe molding the same way, gradually widening the gap between it and the baseboard until it is removed. Remove the other pieces of shoe molding using the same procedure, working carefully at any inside corner. If the shoe molding is not damaged, pull the nails out of it *(page 135)* and keep it for reinstallation *(step below)* at the end of your repair.

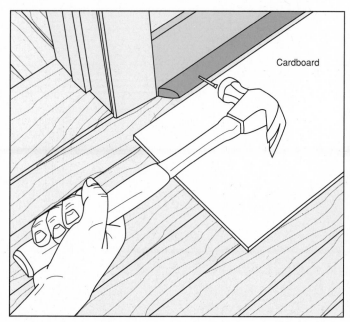

Installing shoe molding. Buy replacement shoe molding at a building supply center. To cut any shoe molding to size, use a backsaw and a miter box to cut any 45-degree angle necessary; use the old shoe molding as a template for marking any special cutting angle. Install the shoe molding in the reverse order to which you removed it, ending at a door or an outside corner; test-fit the pieces in place before nailing them. Starting 1 inch from the end of the shoe molding, drive a 1 1/2-inch finishing nail through the center of it into the baseboard every 12 inches along it *(above, left)*; use cardboard to protect the floor. Set the heads of the nails using a nail set and cover them with a wax stick; or, use a putty knife to cover them and fill any cracks or gaps in the shoe molding with a wood filler of a color that matches the wood. Sand the shoe molding and apply a finish to it, matching it with the baseboard.

USING FASTENERS

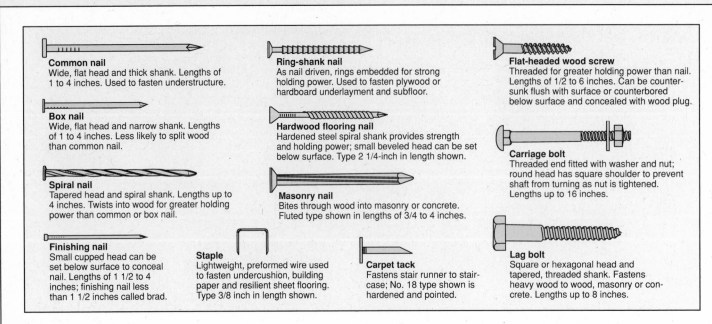

Common nail
Wide, flat head and thick shank. Lengths of 1 to 4 inches. Used to fasten understructure.

Box nail
Wide, flat head and narrow shank. Lengths of 1 to 4 inches. Less likely to split wood than common nail.

Spiral nail
Tapered head and spiral shank. Lengths up to 4 inches. Twists into wood for greater holding power than common or box nail.

Finishing nail
Small cupped head can be set below surface to conceal nail. Lengths of 1 1/2 to 4 inches; finishing nail less than 1 1/2 inches called brad.

Staple
Lightweight, preformed wire used to fasten undercushion, building paper and resilient sheet flooring. Type 3/8 inch in length shown.

Ring-shank nail
As nail driven, rings embedded for strong holding power. Used to fasten plywood or hardboard underlayment and subfloor.

Hardwood flooring nail
Hardened steel spiral shank provides strength and holding power; small beveled head can be set below surface. Type 2 1/4-inch in length shown.

Masonry nail
Bites through wood into masonry or concrete. Fluted type shown in lengths of 3/4 to 4 inches.

Carpet tack
Fastens stair runner to staircase; No. 18 type shown is hardened and pointed.

Flat-headed wood screw
Threaded for greater holding power than nail. Lengths of 1/2 to 6 inches. Can be countersunk flush with surface or counterbored below surface and concealed with wood plug.

Carriage bolt
Threaded end fitted with washer and nut; round head has square shoulder to prevent shaft from turning as nut is tightened. Lengths up to 16 inches.

Lag bolt
Square or hexagonal head and tapered, threaded shank. Fastens heavy wood to wood, masonry or concrete. Lengths up to 8 inches.

Choosing a fastener. Most building supply centers stock fasteners of many types and sizes. The chart above shows some common nails, screws, and bolts available for fastening flooring, stair and understructure components. Purchase fasteners compatible with the material and dimensions of the pieces being joined. As a rule of thumb, use a nail, screw or bolt at least 1 1/2 times as long as the thickness of the piece being fastened; use a carriage bolt at least 3/4 inch longer than the combined thicknesses of the pieces being fastened.

INSTALLING SCREWS

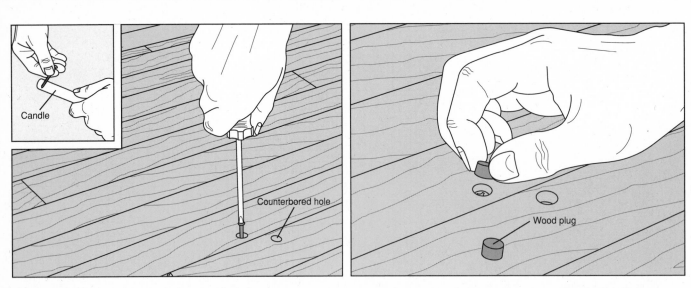

Candle

Counterbored hole

Wood plug

Driving in screws. To install a wood screw flush with or set below the surface, use an electric drill *(page 129)* fitted with a combination bit to bore a hole for it. To make the screw easy to drive, coat the threads with candle wax *(inset)*. Set the screw into the hole and turn it clockwise one or two times to start it. Using a screwdriver of the same type and size as the screw head, grip it firmly by the handle and fit the blade tip into the screw head. Turn the handle clockwise, gradually increasing your pressure as you turn *(above, left)* until the screw is set. To conceal the screw with a precut wood plug, coat the edges of the plug and the hole with wood glue, then fit the plug into the hole *(above, right)* and align its grain. Wipe up any extruded glue with a damp cloth. Allow the glue to cure, then sand the wood plug and apply a finish to it, matching it to the surrounding surface.

INSTALLING NAILS

 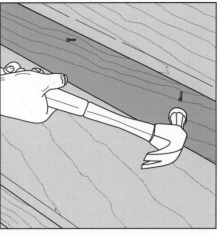 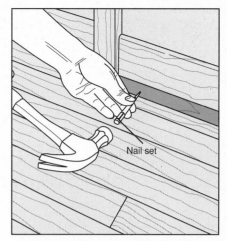

Driving in nails. Wear safety goggles when driving in nails. To fasten a joint, install at least two nails. To keep a nail from splitting the wood, use an electric drill *(page 129)* to bore a pilot hole or use an awl to punch a starter hole. To nail through one piece into a perpendicular piece, drive the nail at an angle *(above, left),* a technique called toe-nailing. To nail through one piece into a parallel piece, drive in each nail at a 90-degree angle, a technique called face-nailing; for greater holding power drive in each nail at an opposite angle, a technique called skew-nailing *(above right).* Set the head of a finishing nail *(step right).* Otherwise, drive in a nail until its head is flush with the surface.

Setting finishing nail heads. To drive a finishing nail head below the surface, use a nail set with a tip slightly smaller than the head. Wearing safety goggles, place the tip of the nail set on the center of the nail head and tap sharply on the top of the nail set using a hammer *(above),* driving the head about 1/8 inch below the surface. Cover the nail head using a wax stick.

REMOVING NAILS

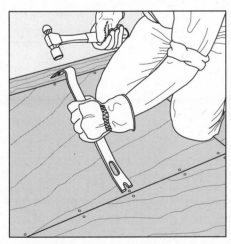 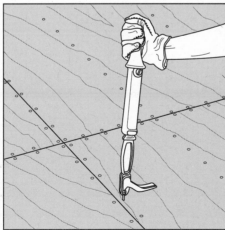 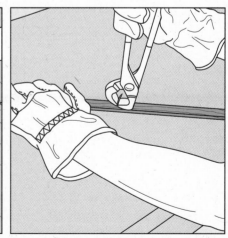

Pulling out nails. Wear safety goggles and work gloves to pull out nails. To loosen a nail, hammer on the back of the wood near the joint or use a pry bar to pull apart the joint. To pull out most nails, use a claw hammer. For a large nail or a nail in an awkward location, use a pry bar. Drive the V-shaped notch at the end of the pry bar under the nail head *(above, left),* then push down on the handle to raise the nail; for better leverage and to protect the surface, set a wood block under the end of the pry bar while you push. To pull a large number of nails out of a flat surface, use a heavy-duty nail puller. Push down on the sliding metal sleeve of the nail puller to close the jaws around a nail head, then pull the handle, using the small lever as a fulcrum to lift out the nail *(above, center).* To pull out nails with concealed heads, work from the back of the piece using a pliers-type nail puller. Grip the nail shaft between the jaws of the nail puller as close to the surface as possible, then pull back on the handle to pull out the nail *(above, right);* for better leverage and to protect the surface, set a wood shim under the jaws while you pull.

MEASURING AND MARKING

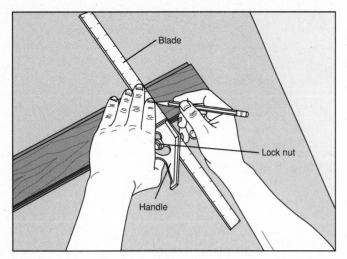

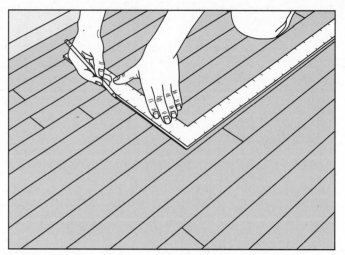

Marking a line with a combination square. Use a combination square to mark a line at 90 or 45 degrees to an edge. If necessary, use a tape measure to mark an end point for the line. To mark a line at 90 degrees, use the 90-degree face of the handle and the blade edge; loosen the lock nut of the square and adjust the blade position, then tighten the lock nut. Press the handle face flush against the edge with the blade flat on the surface, its edge aligned with any marked end point. Hold a pencil against the blade edge and draw along it *(above)*. To mark a line at 45 degrees, follow the same procedure, using the 45-degree face of the handle and the blade edge.

Marking a line with a carpenter's square. Use a carpenter's square to mark a line on a piece at 90 degrees to an edge or another line. If necessary, use a tape measure to mark an end point for the line. To mark a line at 90 degrees to another line, lay the square flat, aligning the inner edge of the long arm with the line and the outer edge of the short arm with any marked end point. Then, hold a pencil firmly against the outer edge of the short arm and draw along it *(above)*. To mark a line at 90 degrees to an edge, follow the same procedure, pressing the inner edge of the long arm flush against the edge of the piece with the short arm flat on the surface.

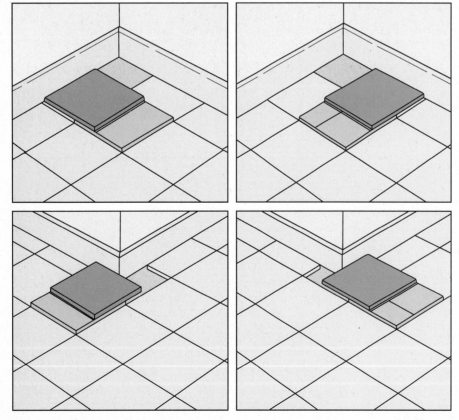

Copying lines. To mark a tile to fit at an inside corner, lay two tiles squarely on top of the last full tile between the tiles adjacent to the opening. Slide the upper tile against the wall on one side of the corner and use its edge as a guide to mark a line parallel to the wall on the lower tile *(far left, top)*. Reposition the upper tile on top of the lower tile, then slide it against the wall on the other side of the corner and use its edge as a guide to mark a line parallel to the wall on the lower tile *(near left, top)*.

To mark a tile to fit at an outside corner, lay two tiles squarely on top of the last full tile adjacent to the opening on one side of the corner; slide the upper tile against the wall on the side of the corner and use its edge as a guide to mark a line parallel to the wall on the lower tile *(far left, bottom)*. Then, keeping the tiles in the same orientation, lay them squarely on top of the last full tile adjacent to the opening on the other side of the corner; slide the upper tile against the wall on the side of the corner and use its edge as a guide to mark a line parallel to the wall on the lower tile *(near left, bottom)*.

SETTING UP A TELESCOPING JACK

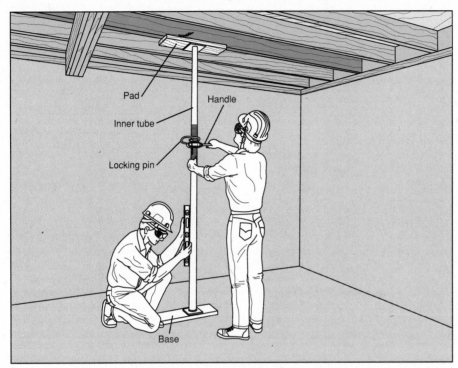

Pad

Handle

Inner tube

Locking pin

Base

Setting up a telescoping jack. To support or raise a joist or girder under a floor, rent a construction-rated telescoping jack at a tool rental agency. To set up the jack, work with a helper and wear safety goggles and a safety helmet. Assemble the jack following the manufacturer's instructions supplied with it. Measure the distance between the base on the floor and the pad fastened to the bottom of the joist or girder. Detach the locking pin from the inner tube of the jack and extend the inner tube until the length of the jack is slightly less than the measured distance; then, reattach the locking pin to lock the jack. Lift the jack to an upright position and fit it between the base and pad, centering the top plate under the pad and the bottom plate on the base. With a helper using a carpenter's level, align the jack so it is plumb *(step below)*; then, ensuring the jack is still plumb, turn the handle of the screw jack assembly counterclockwise to raise the jack until the top plate presses snugly against the pad above it *(left)*, supporting the joist or girder without raising it.

LEVELING AND PLUMBING

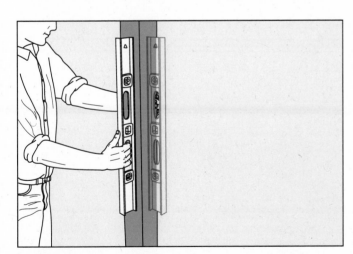

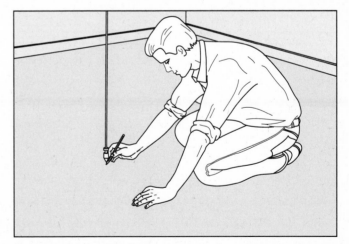

Using a carpenter's level. To check if a surface is level (perfectly horizontal), set a carpenter's level on it and examine the bubble in the horizontally-oriented vial; then, turn the level 90 degrees and stand it on the same edge across the same spot to examine the bubble again. If the bubble is centered in the vial both times, the surface is level. To check if an object is plumb (perfectly vertical), hold the level in turn against two adjacent sides of it *(above)* and examine the bubble in the horizontally-oriented vial. If the bubble is centered in the vial both times, the object is plumb.

Using a plumb bob. To mark a point on a surface that is plumb (perfectly vertical) with a point on another surface above it, use a plumb bob. To hang a plumb bob, use a ladder, if necessary. Tie the top end of the plumb bob string to a nail driven into the reference point on the surface above, the plumb bob tip about 1/8 inch from the surface to be marked below. If the plumb bob swings, steady it; when the plumb bob is still, mark an X directly under its tip *(above)*. To check the mark, lower the bob so its tip just touches the surface; if it rests at the X center, the mark is plumb.

MARKING FLOOR QUADRANTS

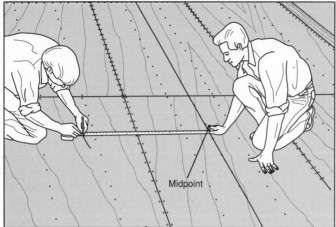

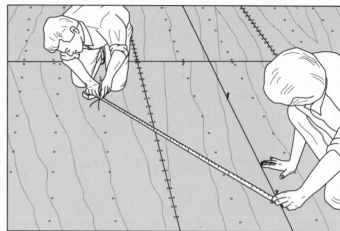

Dividing a floor into quadrants. To divide a floor into quadrants, mark two lines at a 90-degree angle to each other that intersect at the center of the floor. Work with a helper and use a tape measure and a chalk line. Use the tape measure to mark midpoints on the baseboards of the two shorter walls; then snap a chalk line on the floor between the two marked points. Use the tape measure to mark the midpoint of the chalk line and to mark a point 4 feet to one side of the midpoint on the chalk line. Drive a nail partway into each marked point. With a helper holding the end of the tape measure against the nail at the midpoint of the chalk line, extend the tape and position a pencil on the floor at the 3-foot mark; then, rotate the tape slowly partway around the nail to mark an arc on the floor *(above, left)*. Position the tape measure at the second nail and use the same procedure to mark a second arc at the 5-foot mark on the tape, intersecting the first arc *(above, right)*. Remove the nails and snap a chalk line across the floor perpendicular to the first chalk line, running it through the midpoint of the first line and the intersection point of the arcs.

USING ADHESIVE

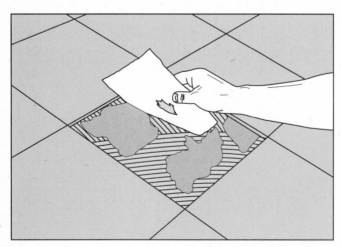

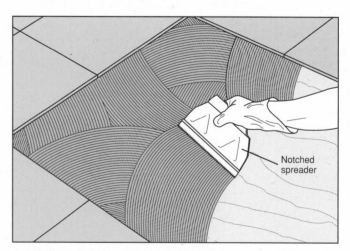

Testing for cut-back asphalt adhesive. To check if the adhesive of resilient flooring is a cut-back asphalt type, rub it with white paper, then examine the stain on the paper *(above)*; if the stain is dark brown, the adhesive is a cut-back asphalt type that may contain asbestos. **Caution:** Do not cut or sand underlayment coated with cut-back asphalt adhesive; you risk spreading asbestos dust. Instead, replace the underlayment, removing each panel of it intact. Call your local department of environmental protection or public health about proper disposal procedures for the flooring materials.

Applying adhesive. Buy adhesive recommended by the flooring manufacturer; apply it using the tool specified by its manufacturer, following any safety and use instructions on its label. Ensure that all surfaces to be coated are clean and dry. Wear rubber gloves to apply the adhesive. If you are using a notched spreader, hold it at a slight angle to the floor; pressing the notched edge firmly against the floor, use a smooth, curving stroke to spread adhesive evenly across the surface *(above)*, leaving behind uniform ridges.

FILLING HOLES IN WOOD

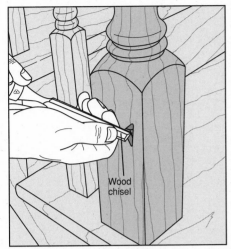

Wood filler

Wood chisel

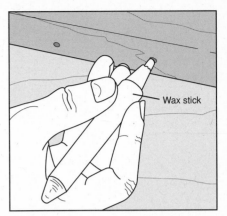

Wax stick

Patching with a wood filler. To fill a tiny crack, dent or hole, use a wax stick *(step right)*. For a large crack, gouge or hole, buy a wood filler of a color that matches the wood and use a putty knife to apply it. Clean out any damaged wood fibers using a wood chisel, working carefully along the grain *(above, left)*. Wipe the scraped spot using a soft cloth dampened with mineral spirits, then blot it dry. Using a flexible putty knife, work the wood filler into the depression, overfilling it slightly *(above, right)*; then, scrape off the excess to level it. Let the filler dry, then smooth the surface along the wood grain using fine sandpaper. Brush sanding particles off the surface and wipe it with a tack cloth, then touch up the finish.

Using a wax stick. To fill a large crack, gouge or hole, use a wood filler *(step left)*. For a tiny crack, dent or hole, use a wax stick of a color that matches the wood. For a crack or dent, rub the tip of the stick back and forth across the depression; for a hole, rotate the tip of the stick against the depression *(above)*. Smooth the wax into the depression with a finger, then scrape off any excess with a knife and touch up the finish.

WORKING WITH CHEMICALS

Using chemicals safely. Some chemicals used to repair floors, stairs and carpets can be dangerous if handled improperly; follow the safety precautions below. Always read the safety precautions on the label before opening a container, and follow the manufacturer's instructions to mix, apply and store the chemical.

• To use a chemical marked FLAMMABLE, extinguish nearby heat and ignition sources; keep a fire extinguisher rated ABC on hand.

• To use a chemical marked FLAMMABLE or marked with POISON vapor and ventilation warnings, open nearby windows and doors to the outdoors.

• To use a chemical marked with POISON vapor or ventilation warnings, wear a dual-cartridge respirator *(step right)*.

• Wear safety goggles to protect the eyes from chemical splashes. Wear rubber gloves, long sleeves and long pants to protect the skin.

• If you experience nausea, faintness, dizziness, blurred vision or a headache when using a chemical, get fresh air; seek medical help if symptoms persist.

• If you splash a chemical in your eyes or on your skin, follow the label instructions to remove it; if indicated, seek medical help.

• After using a chemical, hang any chemical-soaked rags outdoors to dry; store chemicals tightly closed, away from heat and light.

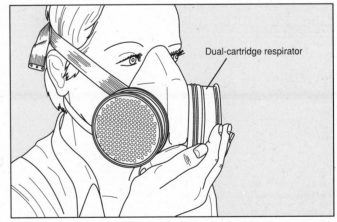

Dual-cartridge respirator

Using a respirator. Follow your owner's manual instructions to fit the respirator with filters or cartridges for the specific vapor hazard; check the date on each one to ensure it has not expired. To put on the respirator, hold it cupped under your chin with the face-piece low on your nose, then pull the headstrap over your head, adjusting it to ensure the fit is snug. Block the outlet valve with your hand *(above)* and exhale gently; if air leaks at the edges, adjust the respirator. If the respirator will not fit snugly, replace it. When using the respirator, replace the filters or cartridges if you smell or taste a contaminant, or if breathing is difficult.

IDENTIFYING A FINISH

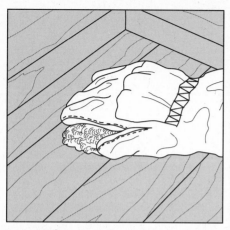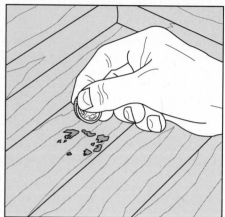

Identifying a finish. To determine if there is wax on a wood surface, scrape a low-traffic spot with a fingernail; if you can scrape off material, it is wax. Remove the wax from the surface using a solvent-based wood floor cleaner, following the manufacturer's instructions. To determine if a finish is a penetrating finish or a surface finish, scrape it with the edge of a coin. If the coin makes no mark, the finish is a penetrating finish; choose one of a color that matches the existing finish (step below). If the coin makes a powdery white mark, the finish is a surface finish and you will need to identify its type. First, test for shellac and lacquer. If the finish

dissolves when rubbed with a cloth dipped in denatured alcohol, it is shellac; if not and the finish dissolves when rubbed with a cloth dipped in lacquer thinner, it is lacquer. Otherwise, the finish is usually polyurethane or varnish; choose one of the two and do a compatibility test. Use fine steel wool to roughen the finish (above, left), then wipe off particles with a tack cloth. Brush on a thin layer of the test finish (above, center) and let it dry. Then, scrape the test finish with the edge of a coin (above, right). If the test finish flakes off, it is incompatible; otherwise, it is compatible. Once you identify the surface finish, choose the same type.

APPLYING A FINISH

FINISH	CHARACTERISTICS
Buffing wax	Produces bright shine Applied over penetrating finish to protect it Must be cleaned and buffed regularly, and reapplied periodically Available in liquid or paste
Penetrating finish	Produces soft, deep luster Good durability; will not chip or peel Low resistance to water and alcohol; must be waxed Easy to apply; dries slowly Available in liquid
Polyurethane	Produces bright, glassy shine or soft, satiny sheen Very high durability; does not darken with age or sunlight exposure Excellent resistance to water, alcohol and heat Easy to apply; fairly fast-drying Available in liquid
Varnish	Produces bright, glossy shine; may have slight yellow color High durability; does not darken with age or sunlight exposure Excellent resistance to water, alcohol and heat Difficult to apply well; dries slowly Available in liquid
Shellac	Produces glossy, clear finish; may have amber color Low durability; recommended for use only on balustrades Low resistance to water, alcohol and heat; moisture produces white marks Available in liquid
Lacquer	Produces hard, clear finish High durability; recommended for use only on balustrades Excellent resistance to water, alcohol and heat Difficult to apply well; dries quickly Available in liquid or spray; best results if sprayed

Choosing a finish. Consult the chart at left to choose a finish for a wood surface; to spot-refinish a surface, first identify the existing finish (step above), then choose a finish that matches. When buying a finish, read the label carefully, choosing one that can provide the appearance you want. Check the surface coverage of a container of the finish and buy enough for the job. Also check the clean-up information on the label; buy enough of the finish solvent to clean your tools and clean up any accidental spills. Before applying a finish, follow the manufacturer's instructions for surface preparation. Before applying the finish, apply a test patch on a matching scrap of wood to check its effect; if necessary, follow any instructions on the label to thin or tint the finish until you achieve the desired effect. To apply the finish, follow all safety precautions on the label; ensure you know how to work safely with chemicals (page 139) and how to apply the finish properly (page 141). After the job, keep the product label for reference when a touch-up or a new finish is necessary.

APPLYING A FINISH (continued)

Using a paintbrush. To apply a finish to a small surface, use a paintbrush. Choose a synthetic-bristled brush for a water-based finish; a natural-bristled brush for a solvent-based finish. Wearing rubber gloves, fill a wide-mouthed jar or can with finish and seal the original container. To load the paintbrush, dip the bristles into the finish: for a penetrating finish, coating half the bristle length; for a surface finish, coating one third the bristle length. Position the brush at the edge of the surface to be coated; on a vertical surface, at the top. Brush along the wood grain to make a light, even stroke *(above, left)*, lapping back at the end of the stroke over the surface just coated. When the paintbrush starts to apply finish spottily, lift it gently to avoid creating air bubbles and reload it. Continue the same way, overlapping parallel strokes slightly and smoothing out any unevenness immediately. For a penetrating finish, let the finish soak into the surface for the length of time specified by the manufacturer, then wipe the surface almost dry with a clean, lint-free cloth *(above, right)*; rub first perpendicular to the wood grain, if directed, then parallel to it.

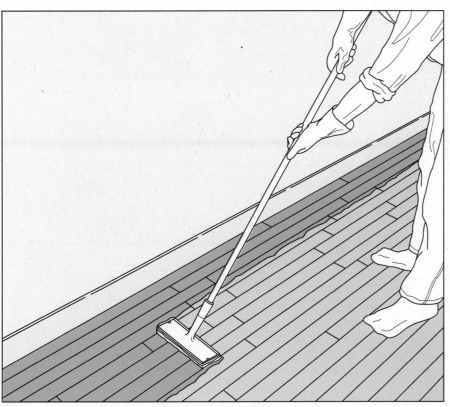

Using a paint pad. To apply a finish to a large, flat surface, use a paint pad fitted with an extension handle; coat one small section of the surface at a time. Wearing rubber gloves, fill the well of a paint pad tray halfway with finish and seal the original container. Work in stockinged feet to apply the finish. To load the paint pad, pull it over the roller of the paint pad tray: for a penetrating finish, wetting the pad liberally; for a surface finish, wetting the pad slightly. Position the pad at the edge of the section to be coated, then draw it lightly in one direction along the surface, parallel to the wood grain *(left)*. When the pad starts to apply finish spottily, lift it gently to avoid creating air bubbles and reload it. Continue the same way, overlapping parallel strokes slightly and smoothing out any unevenness immediately. For a penetrating finish, let the finish soak into the surface for the length of time specified by the manufacturer, then wipe the surface almost dry with a clean, lint-free cloth; rub first perpendicular to the wood grain, if directed, then parallel to it.

INDEX

Page references in *italics* indicate an illustration of the subject mentioned. Page references in **bold** indicate a Troubleshooting Guide for the subject mentioned.

A

B

C

D-E

F-G

H-I-J

K-L-M

N-O-P

R

ACKNOWLEDGMENTS

The editors wish to thank the following:
A-1 Rent-A-Tool Inc., Montreal, Que.; Larry Alexander, Red Devil, Inc., Union, N.J.; Jack Bostwick, Bruce Hardwood Floors, Dallas, Tex.; Scott Broney, American Olean Tile, Lansdale, Pa.; Carpet and Rug Institute, Dalton, Ga.; Hubbard Cobb, Chester, Conn.; Colonial Elegance Inc., Montreal, Que.; Ted Dean, Coplay, Pa.; James Dipelesi, Mahopac, N.Y.; Daniel Felx, P.E. Felx & Sons, St-Clet, Que.; Jack Gundlach, Beno J. Gundlach Company, Belleville, Ill.; Bernie Hamilton, Kango International Inc., Montreal, Que.; The Irwin Company, Wilmington, Ohio; Al Kaminski, Carpets Galore, Lombard, Ill.; B.W. (Pat) Keeling, Willowdale, Ont.; Michael Kronick, National Floor Coverings Association, Ottawa, Ont.; Jacques Laurin and Leon Simon, Prosol Distribution Inc., St. Laurent, Que.; Elliot Levine, Levine Bros. Plumbing, Montreal, Que.; Mapei Inc., Laval, Que.; Marble Institute of America, Farmington, Mich.; Karl Marcuse, Montreal, Que.; A. Robert Moore, Bloomingdale, Ill.; Charles Mickey Moore, National Oak Flooring Manufacturers' Association, Memphis, Tenn.; Nicholas Munro, Montreal, Que.; National Wood Flooring Association, St. Louis, Mo.; Louis D. Norton, Paper Lumber Co. Ltd., Toronto, Ont.; Ronald J. Passaro, Res-I-Tec Inc., Bethel, Conn.; Red Peloquin, 3M Company Inc., St. Paul, Minn.; Manon Ramacieri, Ramca Tiles, Montreal, Que.; Resilient Floor Covering Institute, Rockville, Md.; Scott Sherman, Mannington Resilient Floors Inc., Salem, N.J.; Jim Shimmel, Termite Damage Repair Co., Clinton, Md.; Steve Skoda, Champion Decor, Montreal, Que.; L.J. Smith Inc., New Philadelphia, Ohio; Claude Taylor, Memphis Hardwood Flooring, Memphis, Tenn.; Tile Council of America, Princeton, N.J.; Gerd Trefzger, Whitby, Ont.; Jim Walker, American Floor Covering Institute, Kansas City, Mo.; Scotty Wells, Barwood Division, James MacLaren Industries Inc., Scarborough, Ont.

The following persons also assisted in the preparation of this book:
Dominique Gagné, Robert Galarneau, Graphor Consultation, Shirley Grynspan, Julie Léger, Jennifer Meltzer, Bryan Zuraw.